RISK
ANALYTICS
From
Concept
to
Deployment

World Scientific Series on Financial Data Analytics

Print ISSN: 2737-5943
Online ISSN: 2737-5951

Series Editor: Lim Kian Guan (*Singapore Management University, Singapore*)

Published

Vol. 1   *Risk Analytics: From Concept to Deployment*
          by Edward H K Ng

World Scientific Series on
Financial Data Analytics | 01

RISK
ANALYTICS

From
Concept
to
Deployment

EDWARD H K NG
Singapore Management University, Singapore

World Scientific

NEW JERSEY · LONDON · SINGAPORE · BEIJING · SHANGHAI · HONG KONG · TAIPEI · CHENNAI · TOKYO

Published by

World Scientific Publishing Co. Pte. Ltd.

5 Toh Tuck Link, Singapore 596224

USA office: 27 Warren Street, Suite 401-402, Hackensack, NJ 07601

UK office: 57 Shelton Street, Covent Garden, London WC2H 9HE

Library of Congress Cataloging-in-Publication Data
Names: Ng, Edward H. K., author.
Title: Risk analytics : from concept to deployment / Edward H.K. Ng,
    Singapore Management University, Singapore.
Description: New Jersey : World Scientific, [2022] | Series: World Scientific series on
    financial data analytics ; vol. 1 | Includes index.
Identifiers: LCCN 2021038308 | ISBN 9789811238703 (hardcover) |
    ISBN 9789811239069 (ebook) | ISBN 9789811239076 (ebook other)
Subjects: LCSH: Financial risk management. | Risk assessment--Mathematical models. |
    Risk assessment--Data processing.
Classification: LCC HD61 .N535 2022 | DDC 658.15/5--dc23
LC record available at https://lccn.loc.gov/2021038308

British Library Cataloguing-in-Publication Data
A catalogue record for this book is available from the British Library.

For any available supplementary material, please visit
https://www.worldscientific.com/worldscibooks/10.1142/12326#t=suppl

Desk Editors: Balasubramanian Shanmugam/Lum Pui Yee

Typeset by Stallion Press
Email: enquiries@stallionpress.com

Printed in Singapore

Foreword

Risk analytics is timely risk management with insights into key factors and predictive capabilities harnessing hard data. Developing and employing advanced analytics together with the new generation of IT and digitalization will no doubt provide the winning edge in any financial firm's strategic roadmap. In banking, internal model performance and regulatory compliance are in need of systematic data warehousing and effective integration of data flows across different departments and platforms on a real-time basis. Basel III capital and other compliance requirements for banks to manage their credit, operational, and market risks, necessitate the use of complex statistical and mathematical models, especially when sophisticated financial instruments exist in the bank's trading and banking books.

Banking business, data, and models are highly intertwined, and it is timely that Dr. Edward Ng has written this book to shed light o n the subject. Edward brings both deep industry experience as well as sterling intellectual rigor to the book. He has founded and runs Dren Analytics Pte Ltd, a risk management consultancy firm, since 1999. He has also published his research in the top finance academic journals. Edward is an internationally acclaimed risk advisory expert and has consulted for Asian central banks in the Basel framework. He has also served as Berkeley-NUS Risk Management Institute Training Advisor, and has been content developer, trainer and assessor for the Financial Industry Competency Standards, a nationwide training programme for training and certification of finance professionals in Singapore.

This book is written for risk management professionals, bankers, compliance officers, as well as modelers and students who are interested in risk analytics. Readers will no doubt benefit tremendously in understanding the framework and processes involved in data warehousing and management, and the deployment of coding languages such as R, Python and SQL. Beyond just theories and concepts, readers will learn how to create solutions that can support planning and automated decision-making.

Kian-Guan Lim
OUB Chair Professor of Quantitative Finance
Former Vice-Provost
Singapore Management University

About the Author

Edward H K Ng, PhD in Finance, Edward founded and runs Dren Analytics Pte Ltd which develops risk management application solutions for and provides consulting services to banks according to the Basel II framework. Prior to this, he has been a tenured faculty of the NUS Business School for nearly 20 years, teaching and researching in banking and financial markets, which he continues to do as an adjunct finance faculty there and at the Singapore Management University.

Dren Analytics specializes in helping banks develop a comprehensive data management system as a necessary foundation to Basel II compliance plus providing customizable application solutions for credit, market, interest rate and liquidity risk management plus stress-testing. Through Dren Analytics, Edward has developed a Risk Analytics System for the Thai economy which includes bankruptcy correlations, trade credit statistics and business impacts on credit risk. He has also completed a bank inspection manual under World Bank sponsorship for an Asian central bank to implement Pillar II and trained the central bankers on this area. Besides these, Dren Analytics has developed credit, operational and liquidity risk management solutions and counts UOB Bank, OCBC Bank, Sing Investment & Finance, Thanachart Bank, ACL Bank, Government Savings Bank, State Bank of India and Bank Rakyat Indonesia among its clients.

At the personal level, Edward has conducted numerous seminars and workshops on financial management, Basel II issues and credit risk modeling and has authored a book titled *Managing Credit Data: Toward Basel II*. He has contributed his expertise to agencies, such as the United Nations, Pacific Economic Cooperation Council, and ASEAN Business Forum, and consulted for a range of clients, including Citibank, Asian Development Bank, Marketing Institute of Singapore, Singapore Computer Systems and SPSS.

As an academic, he has published in international journals, including *Journal of Finance, Global Finance Journal, Asia Pacific Journal of Management*, and *Banks and Bank Systems*. He has also sat on the editorial board of several journals and conducted executive training in both English and Chinese for bankers from Singapore, Malaysia, Thailand, Indonesia, Vietnam, Cambodia, Laos and China. Edward served as Berkeley-NUS Risk Management Institute Training Advisor, content developer, trainer and assessor for the Financial Industry Competency Standards, a nationwide training program for training and certification of finance professionals in Singapore. He is also trained as an international arbitrator and had been a Fellow of the Singapore Institute of Arbitrators. He served as Consultant Risk Specialist to Bank Negara Indonesia for the comprehensive development of risk management systems, processes and governance.

Contents

Foreword   v

About the Author   vii

Chapter 1   Introduction   1

Chapter 2   Risk Typology and Data Implications   7
2.1. Data Needed   10
2.2. Data Stewardship   12
2.3. Deployment for Use   13

Chapter 3   Risk Analytics Landscape   15
3.1. Software and Solutions   15
    3.1.1. Request for Proposal (RFP)   17
    3.1.2. Terms of Reference (TOR)   17
    3.1.3. Proof of Concept (POC)   19
    3.1.4. System Integration Test (SIT)   20
    3.1.5. User Acceptance Test (UAT)   21
3.2. Data Table and Data Type   21
3.3. Modeling   24
    3.3.1. Business understanding   26
    3.3.2. Data understanding   28
    3.3.3. Data preparation   30
    3.3.4. Modeling   31
    3.3.5. Evaluation   33
    3.3.6. Deployment   37

3.4. Data Flow   37
    3.4.1. Data quality and quantity   37
    3.4.2. External and internal data integration   38
    3.4.3. Security and access   39
    3.4.4. Analysis and decision-making   40
3.5. Deployment   41
3.6. Governance   44
3.7. Need for Integration   45

Chapter 4   Embedded R   47
4.1. ORACLE_HOME and R_HOME   48
4.2. Pluggable Database   49
4.3. RQUSER   49
4.4. R Packages and RStudio   51
4.5. Oracle R Enterprise (ORE)   53

Chapter 5   Data Audit   57
5.1. Missing   57
5.2. Invalid   59
5.3. Unreliable   61
5.4. Outdated   63
5.5. Inconsistent   64
5.6. Data Audit Report   65
5.7. Treatments for Problematic Data Values   66

Chapter 6   Data Warehousing   69
6.1. Legacy System Data   69
    6.1.1. Overwrite mode   70
    6.1.2. Record removal   70
    6.1.3. Legal priority   71
    6.1.4. Data type   71
6.2. Enterprise Data Warehouse vs Specialized Data Mart   72
    6.2.1. Data stewardship   72
    6.2.2. Access and security   73
    6.2.3. Update frequency   73
    6.2.4. Designed to fail   73
6.3. Extraction, Transfer, Load (ETL)   74
    6.3.1. Data cleansing   74
    6.3.2. Mappings   76
    6.3.3. Rejected records   77
    6.3.4. Corrections   78

Chapter 7   Analytical Data Sphere   79
7.1. Archive, Not Overwrite   81
7.2. Dropdown List, Not Free Text   82
7.3. Meaningful Categories   83
7.4. Optimal Number of Categories   84
7.5. Expandable Data Tables   85
7.6. Dated   86
7.7. Useful and New Primary Keys   86
7.8. Updatable   87
7.9. Accessible   89

Chapter 8   Risks in Financial Institutions   91
8.1. Profiling What Is Ahead   92
8.2. External Warning Indicators   95
8.3. Operational Concerns   96
8.4. Portfolio Composition   97

Chapter 9   Common Risk Models and Analytics   99
9.1. Expected and Unexpected Losses   99
9.2. Value at Risk   101
9.3. Securities Portfolio Optimization   108
9.4. Correlation   108
9.5. Concentration Index   111
9.6. Operational Loss Distribution   112
9.7. Stress Testing   113
9.8. Weight of Evidence   114

Chapter 10 Internal Rating System   119
10.1. Developing an ORR   121
10.2. Data Audit   122
10.3. Predictors and Target   127
10.4. Weight of Evidence (WoE)   129
10.5. Training a Model   132
10.6. Risk Grades/Ratings   135
10.7. Backtesting   142

Chapter 11 Deployment   151
11.1. Default and Reageing   157
11.2. Enterprise Data Warehouse or Data Mart   159

Chapter 12 Through The Cycle (TTC) Updating   161

Chapter 13 Desktop Analytics   169
13.1. Basic Excel R Toolkit (BERT)   169
13.2. Probabilities and PD   170
   13.2.1. Cumulative and marginal probabilities   171
   13.2.2. Joint, conditional and unconditional probabilities   172
   13.2.3. Binomial lattice   173
13.3. Loss Given Default (LGD)   175
13.4. Credit Valuation Adjustment (CVA), Debit Valuation
   Adjustment (DVA) and xVA   177
   13.4.1. Spot, forward and par rates   180
   13.4.2. Interest rate binomial lattice   181
   13.4.3. Counterparty default   183
13.5. R with Excel   185

Chapter 14 Resources   199
14.1. RStudio   199
14.2. Packages   200
14.3. Free Data   201

Annex A: Meeting of Minds Questionnaire   203

Annex B   211

Index   223

Chapter 1

Introduction

As evidenced by the plethora of academic and professional certification programs, Risk Management has definitely come into its own as a body of knowledge. The timing of this book could not have been better though unfortunate. The entire world is going through a Black Swan event (made popular by Nassim Nicholas Taleb) due to COVID-19. Losses to both firms and countries have reached trillion of dollars. On the well-known loss distribution, this occurrence is quite certain to be outside of the 99% confidence level or less than once in a 100 years. The event has significantly altered not only economics but also lives and society. Social distancing became a new term. What is most pertinent for the purpose of our discussion here is that it may not take another 100 years for a similar event to recur with the ever-growing global linkages. Besides, losses that are now in trillions may rise to tens or even hundreds of trillions. The Black Swan today may just be a regular White Swan in the near future. Losses of such magnitude become more frequent not unlike Category 5 hurricanes or tsunamis. All these are educated guesses but for those making investment decisions involving millions or billions of dollars, these prospects need to be analyzed and quantified rather than left to judgment.

Interestingly, this COVID-19 pandemic surfaced a largely unreported insight into the importance of risk analytics. Within three short months, erstwhile reputable and profitable airlines and department stores went bankrupt simply due to the lockdown implemented in many countries. On the other hand, no major bank has failed. This is an outcome very different from the subprime crisis of 2008–2010, where it is the banking sector, especially in the U.S., that buckled. What is different now? The answer almost certainly lies in the stress testing that banks have been required to undertake ever since that crisis. The results informed banks on the level of economic capital needed to ride out an event like COVID-19. Department stores and airlines did not have to carry out such tests. They were just like the banks before stress testing was mandatory. Although cognizant of such a possibility, there was no quantification of the level of capital needed to prevent insolvency. Risk analytics even if not voluntary has been a lifesaver for banks.

This episode has cast a favorable light on risk analytics in banks compared to other industries. However, there is still much room for development and improvement. Stress testing is a low-frequency need. Once the necessary data and models are in place, the results generated can be analyzed manually and at an unhurried pace. Even at its most intensive, the entire process needs to be executed only once a quarter. In a risk-taking business like investment or banking, quantifications of risk are required second by second. Risk-Adjusted Return on Capital (RAROC), for instance, is a transaction-level computation. The amount of risk to be taken in a prospective credit exposure must be derived before a decision on approve or reject and pricing is to be made. In a highly competitive consumer banking environment, the result is required in a second or less. The concept and formula underlying RAROC are not complex, but having a system that can automate the derivation with specific inputs is an exception rather than the norm in banking. One reason is the gap or more aptly a chasm between knowledge and deployment. Most financial institutions can easily develop risk models on a desktop computer or even laptop and use these for decision support. The models can be very sophisticated but remain as references for the decision-making process. It is common for data to be exported from a legacy system to a desktop where models are stored, processed using the model parameters and results input into another legacy system, all done manually or using agents in the database to export and import data. What is missing is the integration of model codes into the database so that data can be processed *in situ* with results being generated and stored into the same database.

At first glance, it may seem trivial to embed a model into a system that can instantly turn input data into output results. Most end-users in the risk domain are familiar with consumer-grade applications like Microsoft Excel. It takes only an entry-level course to learn how to create a formula which automatically processes any data entered. That simplicity is widely assumed of systems involving operational data like transactions. Since business processes are so automated today, it just takes a small step to pass data to a formula for results to be derived. Even senior management in large banks do not understand what the difficulty is in accomplishing that. As discussed in the chapter on analytical data, the deficiency in understanding how data are not all the same has caused much frustration in the matter of analytics automation.

The challenges faced by end-users in bridging the gap between concept and deployment is not difficult to understand. Most users do not have the requisite technical knowledge, especially about IT, to translate their wish lists into system designs. That is why there are specialists called System Analysts (SAs) trained to do that and they are usually schooled in IT or at least IS (Information System). It would then appear to be a short hop from that to turning SAs into rounded end-users for different business domains. One area where academia quickly spotted this potential is finance, especially after the popularization of derivatives that require heavy-duty number crunching and near-instantaneous decision-making. IT or IS schools started to introduce "verticals" like Finance and Logistics into their curriculum. The intent was to produce students who can hit the ground running by developing theoretically sound models, code and implement them into automated systems that support decision-making. They will be the technically competent game-changers of the analytics space. As related in the following anecdote, this aspiration has repeatedly been held back by the silo nature of academic pursuit. The pride of universities is specialists, the narrower the scope, the better. As one IT veteran commented, any leader in the field will choose to spend a spare hour in reading up about the latest technical developments instead of learning more about Finance or Logistics. In fact, doing so bounds the IT specialist to a specific vertical and adversely impacts on the career path.

The attempt to bridge the divide from the technical side has met with very limited success. Now, there is another approach. Business schools have rolled out Business Analytics as coding with Open Source languages like Python and R become cost-effective. This is to equip end-users with the technical skills to develop their own solutions. There is such a need, but it still does not address the issue of how concepts and theories can be implemented to automate decision support.

The inability of traditional academia despite pockets of well-intended initiatives to bridge the gap is likely to remain. When asked about such reluctance, a senior academic replied that it is not possible to publish

Developing "vertical" expertise in an IS school

The director of a newly established IS school in a reputable university had both academic and industry exposures and is well aware of the gap between concepts and deployment. He wanted to address this by hiring others like himself to drive "verticals" like Finance, Logistics, etc. The attempt was no smooth sailing. Senior university administrators could not understand why Finance has to be taught in an IS school. To them, students could simply read courses in the Business School, synthesize the knowledge bases and apply them in the industry. Adding to this resistance, the "publish or perish" ethos could not be overlooked. But there is no theory underlying Finance or Logistics IT. Before long, the initiative faded, and the school developed like conventional ones. Once again, the silo mentality in academia has thwarted an attempt to bridge the gap.

about such an issue and so no academic will want to jeopardize a career seeking a solution. There is also another reason why it has taken so long to embark on a resolution, and this has to do with commercial interest.

For years, modeling software like SAS, SPSS, Stata, etc. have not considered integration with databases like Oracle, IBM, SQL Server a priority. At best, products like SPSS have added tools to publish proprietary codes into languages that can be consumed by databases and turned into stored procedures. That requires additional costs. There is no direct interface between the common Transact SQL widely used in databases and software codes. That was the case till Open Source languages like R and Python came into the scene.

The possibility of integrating R into a database is game-changing. Microsoft and Oracle have understood the potential of this possibility and have embedded it into their database tools. For those who have longed for automated analytics, this is almost like a prayer answered. As R is Open Source, there is no additional cost to model development. In recent years, it has rapidly matured to be almost on par with traditional statistical software in terms of algorithms available. Finally, packages continue to be developed to integrate codes making their use increasingly easy.

At this point, nothing significant separates the Microsoft and Oracle embedded R. For the purpose of this book, the Oracle platform is chosen because most financial institutions prefer to use an Oracle database for heavy-duty processing. An added reason is that Oracle has made available a free single-user license for its database which makes development much easier. Microsoft's SQL Server is also free but valid for only six months.

Oracle has named its version of R, Oracle R Enterprise or ORE. This acronym will be used throughout this book for the sake of brevity. Installing ORE involves a number of steps that may differ depending on the Oracle database version and the operating system platform used. As this book is targeted at the masses rather than the professional programmer, the codes are based on the MS Windows operating system. According to the documents published by Oracle, these codes can be easily edited to suit LINUX or other Open Source OSs. Given all these challenges, the installation of ORE under every scenario is not detailed here, but brief instructions for installing in Windows is provided.

Some readers may remark that the ORE codes are cumbersome and unnecessary as the same can be accomplished using R scripting or an editor like RStudio. This is certainly true, but doing that is no different from coding in SAS, SPSS or similar software. The disconnect between model and analytical codes from a database which can be deployed to automate decision-making is not bridged.

The domain for analytics has widened significantly with the advent of big data. Increasing availability of artificial intelligence tools has added to the broadening of the term's definition. Data mining, machine learning, etc. have been coined to jazz up the rather drab image of analytics. Like any body of knowledge that has gained traction, qualification or specialization becomes a necessity to avoid a scattered coverage. This book is confined to risk analytics arising from my own academic training and consultancy experiences. For that reason, topics in the wider business analytics fields like Customer Relationship Management or CRM for short are deliberately unaddressed. Nevertheless, the methodology and codes proposed can be quite easily adapted to other domains.

It is the aim of this book to provide a foundation for deployable analytics for risk management professionals desiring to add value by automating their work to support decision-making. No claim is made that the R codes or packages suggested are the most efficient possible. Examples are provided to help the reader get a quick start on developing a deployable solution.

Chapter 2

Risk Typology and Data Implications

With increased complexity and understanding, not all risks are the same. The Deputy President of a large state bank asked me to help with the creation of an Early Warning System (EWS) to enhance risk management. My question to her was: What does the bank want to be warned of? Is it of dangers ahead or critical deficiencies within? A better understanding of the type of risk we wish to address is essential to designing and deploying the system needed to address it.

Risk is commonly categorized into Market, Credit, Operational, Technology, Country, Reputational, Legal, Model, etc. While these terms help define the nature of a risk, they are not so useful for analysis and management. Through years of consultancy experience, I have formulated a metaphor that may be more suitable. It is that of a ship travelling through the ocean, as depicted in Fig. 2.1.

A vessel sailing in a stormy iceberg littered sea is one easy way to explore risk typology. Any ship with some age is bound to have physical and operational deficiencies. Unless regularly detected and rectified, such problems can eventually sink the ship. These can be termed 'Inherent Risk'. They are intrinsic to the way the ship has been built.

Aside from the infrastructure issues, the cargo carried and how it is loaded are other risk factors. Among the cargo manifest may be one or two containers of explosive material. A sudden rise in ambient temperature may trigger a catastrophic event that can destroy the ship. This is parallel to a firm, especially a financial institution, having one or more large exposures that can cause insolvency. This may be known as Single Exposure Risk.

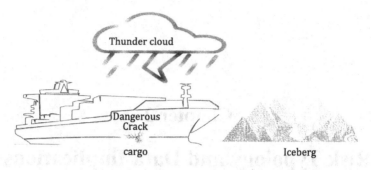

Figure 2.1.   Metaphor of a ship travelling through the ocean.

If the cargoes have been poorly loaded with unbalanced weighting, a large wave can cause the ship to capsize. In portfolio management, this is called Concentration Risk. The Single Exposure Risk is one extreme as that piece of cargo or exposure must have been large enough to cause total failure.

Regular on and offloading of containers means that there is always the chance of a bad container being taken on board. Such containers result in losses that are incremental or marginal in nature. Marginal Risk is relevant here.

All sailors know how weather affects a sailing ship's integrity. Throughout history, storms and other factors have damaged or destroyed ships. All these are part of Environmental Risk. At this time, the virus pandemic is an acute manifestation of this risk. It is one that is beyond any control and will test the adequacy of economic capital. Preparing for such a risk is the purpose of stress testing.

Finally, there is a Titanic event that is known throughout the world. Ships today have equipment to detect icebergs ahead, but such collisions still happen. This can be called Forward Risk.

With the scandalous losses from trading, compliance has emerged as a key demand in financial services. In most developed economies, large banks have to employ a Compliance Officer. Risk of non-compliance has become so prominent that automated systems for ticking every box have been developed and staff assigned to run the programs. In a strict sense, compliance risk does not fall within the ambit of analytics as there is limited scope for interpretation and discretion. It is more of testing and verification with a binary outcome of Approve or Reject.

To recap, risk can be recategorized with examples related to financial services as shown in Table 2.1.

Table 2.1   Financial services risk categories.

Risk type	Mapping to conventional categories	Example
Inherent	Operational, legal	Conflict of interest
Single exposure	Credit, market	Large state obligor
Concentration	Credit, market	Geographical distribution
Marginal	Credit, market, model	Credit applicant
Environmental	All	Macroeconomic factors
Forward	Credit, market, country, legal, model	New product or market
Compliance	Regulatory	Meeting of criteria

A valid question to ask is why create new risk types when there are existing ones. The answer lies in usable analytics more than interesting classification of the risks. Among others, there are two key considerations in analytics. One is data, where they come from and how they have to be stored, and the other is use.

Credit risk is familiar to all banks. Significant resources have been devoted to developing risk models. Due to Basel II requirements, banks have to create an Internal Rating System (IRS) for their credit exposures. In many banks, internal ratings remain on a desktop separate from the automation of credit processing. The lack of attention to managing the data flow is a key reason.

A credit applicant has to submit a range of data for assessment. Such data are usually entered into a system and later extracted to derive a credit rating. A number of issues often emerge. One, it is hard to verify if the applicant is related to an existing customer as the applicants' database is not connected to the core banking system. As will be discussed later, one wholesale entity can be assigned only one rating under Basel II. Without the ability to check if an applicant is already a customer, multiple ratings will be created, which was exactly what happened in a bank that I consulted for. Management was initially confident that manual checking will be sufficient to prevent multiple ratings but in no less than three months of implementing a credit application system, staff reported that multiple ratings for the same customer has emerged. The second issue is that there may be no place to update the entity's data after it becomes a customer. It is not uncommon for banks to treat credit application as a regulatory requirement. Only data of approved applicants who become customers matter. These are entered into the core banking or loan management system. For good reason, such systems have security measures that disallow data entry after the record is created. For those responsible for credit ratings, there is no way to update a rating as required by Basel II. Risk analytics become near impossible if application data have not been stored in a depository created for the specific purpose.

A key implication for the suggested categorization above is the focus on where data come from and if they are properly stored. That, however, is not the only consideration. Environment risk has to involve external data and these have to be integrated with internal ones to derive the magnitude of any impact. In order for stress testing to be conducted, there must be an analysis of how macroeconomic and business events impact on a bank's portfolio. Not only must the external data be captured and stored, there needs to be a means of associating them with internal ones. Such considerations are discussed in the following section.

2.1. Data Needed

For the purpose of analytics, not all data are the same. Some taxonomy can help to better manage them.

Data can easily be divided into internal and external. Internal data already reside in the organization. External data have to be acquired. In many cases, valuable external data have to be paid for, so the matter of cost needs to be considered. All indexes and prices like that for property, oil, etc. are external.

Internal data can be divided into collected or generated. Data have to be gathered from applicants before they become customers. This is usually one of the most challenging areas of analytics. Such data are seldom collected in a disciplined and well-designed manner. In days preceding digital forms, data recorded on paper are almost inevitably riddled with errors. There is no way to enforce mandatory data fields. Data types can be ignored entirely and invalid values can be entered without problems. As a consultant, I have always encouraged a switch to digital forms where mandatory fields and error-checking are enforced as much as possible. In one project that accomplished this against strenuous objections from IT-phobic staff, the client organization could analyze monthly data on the first day of the following month after migration to such forms. Before that, the staff had to spend two months to enter and clean up one month's worth of paper form data. It required a huge mindset change. Some staff insisted that it is impossible to get all clients to use a keyboard. To overcome that resistance, I had their screens replaced so that the staff can do the keying based on verbal inputs and turn the screen 180° to show the client the contents before entering the data.

Data generated by the system are much less prone to problems plaguing collected data. But they are not free from deficiencies.

Regulations require banks to track an obligor's payment performance. This is termed Days Past Due (DPD) nearly everywhere. A payment that has not been made after 17 days past the due date will get a system-generated record of 17 DPD. The accuracy of the DPD count is not in question, but the algorithm hard-coded into the system can be problematic.

Card credit is almost universal in terms of payment requirements. The cardholder must pay a minimum sum of the billed amount. For instance, that amount may be $1,000, but the minimum payment is $50. Assume that a cardholder fails to make any payment for 91 days and incurs an interest of $60 (let's ignore the penalty for this discussion). Strictly speaking, a default has occurred. In banking, an account is only "cured", i.e. returned to normal after all amounts outstanding are repaid. In this case, that will be $1,600. The $50 minimum is no longer applicable. There are banks where I have consulted for, however, the credit card system is coded such that an account is cured once the minimum sum is paid. As in the case of all legacy systems, the logic is encoded by the vendor which is usually an IT firm creating platforms for a range of business domains. Regulatory definitions for default and requirements for curing rarely factor into the logic. This is trivial for operational reasons, but for a credit risk modeler, what amounts to default and subsequent re-ageing after a cure are important metrics for the robustness of the model. Internally generated may not be operationally defective but can lead to modeling errors if used without understanding how they are produced.

External data are provided by outside parties and similar deficiencies can plague such data just like for internal ones, but there may be significant exceptions.

Stock exchange prices are widely used to proxy for environmental factors and it is commonly assumed that they cannot be wrong. This is far from reality. The stock exchange of a financial center commissioned an academic unit to cleanse their transaction data. After a couple of years, this unit simply gave up. Besides, personal experience with NYSE data suggests that reliability is not a given. Data error is the norm rather than the exception.

Data can also be categorized as enterprise or Business Unit (BU). Accounts are definitely enterprise-level data. Many BUs collect or purchase data for their own use. This divide helps with the issue of data stewardship which will be discussed shortly.

Enterprise data are also public facilities. Everyone wants to use, but nobody wants to maintain them. Unless data custodians are explicitly appointed, such data can be so corrupted that they become no better than garbage.

BU data create their own challenges. Too often, the BU that pays for them is unwilling to share with others even within the same organization. Performance, bonus and promotion are relative so there is little incentive to allow others to free ride. Here again, enlightened data stewardship can go some way to mitigate this shortcoming.

Another division of data is between primary and derived. Primary data have to be captured while derived ones are outputs or results based on them. The key consideration for primary data is how they are input as briefly discussed.

It can be easily overlooked that most legacy systems have restrictions on how data can be entered. This often is through the input screen provided. Batch input can void any warranty provided by the vendor. Similarly, editing of entered values may not be allowed. Here again, there are implications for analytics and modeling.

Consider a credit application. All data are entered through the pre-scribed input screen which is usually vendor-designed. After a review, it is found that some financial values are inconsistent, so the applicant is contacted for amendments. The corrected data cannot be re-entered into the same application system due to the security measure against tampering that has been built in. In a typical credit operation, this matter is ignored and the application is processed with manual derivation of ratios, etc. using the resubmitted data. When it comes to analytics and modeling, only what has been input and stored are available. A data audit would easily detect the validity problem of some financial values. This is an aspect that those who have some oversight on primary data should keep in view.

Derived data are very similar to generated ones and pose fewer problems except for the logic underlying the derivations themselves.

2.2. Data Stewardship

This is a topic that has almost never gotten out of academia. It is novel even to IT graduates with unfortunate consequences.

Unlike operational requirements, analytics is a good-to-have, not a must-have. If and when suitable data are not available, it can be foregone. But with big data driving analytics to the forefront of competitiveness, the scene has changed and disciplined data stewardship has now been recognized as a key factor.

A steward is one that takes care of the data much like a human guardian to a ward. Data cannot talk back or complain, so neglect is seldom detected until the state of the data becomes unbearable to those who need them. A single steward often do much better than shared stewardship, but the latter is sometimes unavoidable if more than one party need to use the same data. Customer particulars is one area where there are many users, but no one wants to be steward.

Consider banking operations. It is not uncommon for banks to have a thick invisible wall between deposit-taking and lending. If an individual new to a bank starts as a depositor, customer details will be kept by the deposit-taking systems. Should this same individual later take a loan, the credit side may not have access to the deposit-taking systems to retrieve the data and has to recreate everything. Even if access is not an issue, update can be. If the customer chooses to inform the credit side of a change in contact number, the deposit-taking side may not receive the same information. Unless there is an explicit shared stewardship, each party within the same organization may adopt a silo approach to managing its own data.

Stewardship is most challenging for enterprise data. As mentioned earlier, such data are like public goods where everyone wants to use but no one wants to take care of. It is a common mistake to assume that the IT unit should be the steward of all data. IT is rarely the user and does not have the vested interest on matters of data integrity. If users do not come together to look into this area, it is almost guaranteed that data will end up as no better than rubbish. In a large Asian bank, the data warehouse within is derisively called the garbage dump by its staff.

2.3. Deployment for Use

How data can be deployed for use is an afterthought more often than not. This is perhaps no more evident that a bank's internal rating system or IRS.

Banks can spend significant sums purchasing software, hiring modelers and even buying needed data to develop an IRS. When it is completed, everything remains on a desktop computer. Either the risk professionals overseeing the process are unaware that the output can be integrated with the legacy systems for end-to-end automation or there is insufficient budget for deployment. Careful planning would have enabled completion of this proverbial last mile. Having said that, doing so requires one who understands both the domain and technical requirements to make it possible. This is akin to needing an architect to plan a city. The best engineers (like IT professionals) and material (hardware and software) can result in roads that do not connect or structures too large or too small for use. It is for good reason that architecture is a discipline that has to cover both the building and use of landscape and facilities. There is no similar requirement for risk management despite sporadic attempts at doing so. Hopefully, this book goes some way to developing knowledge workers who can accomplish that to some extent.

Chapter 3

Risk Analytics Landscape

There are several building blocks to risk analytics. It is not uncommon that each is managed in silo. The repeated thrust of this book is that effective integration is needed to develop an automated process where analytics can support better decision-making. A brief examination of each component here is useful to understanding the gaps that may exist.

3.1. Software and Solutions

Analytics today is almost impossible without the use of software. There is software and there is solution. A solution is largely associated with a software but has its own organic database. This eliminates the need to input data directly into the software for processing. The term "solution" has, however, become more loosely used. Many vendors brand their offerings as solutions when those are no more than some packaged analysis of sample data showing nifty graphical outputs. It is safe to assume that there is no real solution that can be readily used out of the box for an organization like a bank. A deployable solution has to be customized and that requires knowledge workers who grasp both user requirements and technical specifications.

Well-known statistical software for analysis and modeling have been around for decades. Perhaps the most familiar are SAS by SAS Institute and SPSS which has since been acquired by IBM. Some software are focused more on econometrics, that is time-series analysis than statistics. E-views is one of such. The most talked about is Machine Learning (ML)

15

which can almost mimic the human brain in continually improving on problem-solving.

Statistical software have built-in algorithms for computation and model development. There are software, however, that are meant for deployment with minimal computational capabilities. It is not an uncommon mistake for organizations to acquire such software with the misunderstanding that they contain the necessary functions.

Proprietary software like SAS and SPSS come with a range of subscription fees. Over the past decade, the arrival of Open Source has significantly impacted this business model. Languages like R and Python which are free to use have increasingly been embraced as an alternative and even complete substitute of paid software. Though still requiring raw coding as in the early days of SAS and SPSS, these have been adequate for most analytical and modeling needs. It is an endorsement of R to have databases like Microsoft SQL Server and Oracle integrate the language into their SQL codes.

It has been estimated that more than a third of business software purchased are wasted because they are underused or even unused. The fraction is probably higher for analytical rather than operational software as the deliverables of the former are much less predefined than the latter. As software or solution acquisition follow a fairly well-established process summarized in Fig. 3.1, some principles underlying those for risk are worth noting.

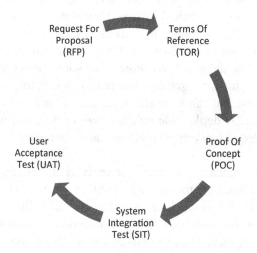

Figure 3.1.   Steps in software acquisition.

3.1.1. *Request for Proposal (RFP)*

This is a fairly open-ended request to potential vendors to describe what they can offer for a specific corporate need. Defining that need as specifically as possible is greater for analytics than operations. Consider a risk solution, for instance. What is needed for credit risk is different from that of market risk or operational risk. Even within credit risk, a solution can be for obligor rating (Probability of Default), facility rating (Loss Given Default), collection scoring, etc. Besides the purpose, there is also the issue of solution scope. Today, many vendors have latched onto the term GRC which is Governance, Risk and Compliance. These solutions go far beyond a specific risk type or area and they are vigorously promoted as comprehensive and must-have in any financial institution that is serious about risk management.

To avoid having to compare apples with oranges, it is best for the end-users of a software or solution to be acquired to be involved at this early stage. Unfortunately, this is not widely practiced. Management often consider any software purchase as an IT function and many IT units prefer it that way. Users may even be considered a nuisance as they cannot express their desires in the technical language employed in an RFP. On the other hand, many users assume that the IT professionals know what they need and gladly leave the details for them to wrestle with. The RFP is perhaps the document with the least technical jargon in the acquisition process and it is worth the effort for users to help shape it to avoid disappointments down the road.

For users to contribute meaningfully, some research is necessary. This would involve identifying products meeting the requirements and comparing them as not a single one can cover all the bases. Those who are more knowledgeable about IT would be aware of the Gartner Report which places products usually on a two-dimensional space for analysis. Whether users are willing to invest time and resources at initial stage is often the difference between an effective purchase and frustrations in time to come.

3.1.2. *Terms of Reference (TOR)*

This is usually the basis of the eventual sales contract. It covers the rights and obligations of both the buyer and the seller. For the purpose of this discussion, the most important part is the Deliverables.

I have always cautioned my client banks that what is not specified in the TOR cannot be expected to be found in the software or solution after implementation. Even more essential than for the RFP, it is necessary for the users to be scrutinizing the details of this document. In fact, users should scope the Deliverables in plain language and let the IT staff translate them into technical terms if possible. There are too many aspects of Deliverables that can be easily overlooked to cause frustration after installation. Some are mentioned here to highlight how such oversight can adversely impact on the implementation of analytics.

As advocated in this book, the possibility of using R to code is central to integrating concepts into a database for deployment. Unless the algorithms in the solution are comprehensive and can be easily customized with user-determined data values, accommodation of R codes should be considered. This is especially important if complex modeling needs to be carried out using the solution.

A second feature that is quite essential is the input of external data. It can be wrongly assumed that solutions are open to that. There are enterprise-level ones that cannot even accept the common flat files for batch data input. All inputs have to be converted to the solution's proprietary format to be read. With analytics, data sources are both varied and continually changing. Even if a solution vendor can code an automated download at implementation, that will not meet the needs of future requirements.

The third area worth considering is if the use of non-proprietary databases is possible. Here again, many vendors prefer to capture any upgrading by restricting a solution to their own databases. Practically, all such databases do not come with a data dictionary showing the tables or fields within making system migration to another platform very challenging and even impossible.

Finally, user customization in critical areas should be expected. Consider regulatory thresholds, for instance. Under Basel II, small business is defined as a credit exposure of no more than one million Euros. Across the world, this has been localized as one million local dollars either by exposure or size of the obligor. Given inflation, the threshold may be raised. As small business is classified as retail rather than wholesale, there are many implications for a bank's credit rating system. If the threshold were hardcoded, making a change in the future will require costly engagement of the vendor.

With careful attention to details, a well-drafted TOR document can serve as an effective filter to eliminate prospective solutions that do not meet with user requirements. This saves a lot of time for the rest of the acquisition process.

In my consultancies, I always advise the client to state their requirements in plain language and let IT translate them into technical jargons for the prospective vendors. The inability to do so is itself an indication that the users do not even know what they need, which is precursor to unfulfilled expectations after the purchase.

3.1.3. *Proof of Concept (POC)*

This is when vendors demonstrate their wares to validate their claims. With hardware and even operational software, the POC can make or break a prospective sale. The deliverables are more tangible and precisely defined. For a note counting machine, for instance, failure to correctly count a sample will likely disqualify the product. Similarly, for a piece of operational software like instalment computation of residential mortgages, incorrect answers will result in the same. With analytical software or solution like for risk, the POC can be a wasted opportunity to select the right product.

A key reason why POC may be less rigorous than desired is the laxity in scoping the TOR. A vendor can only be expected to demonstrate what is specified as required. Even then, it is common that software vendors go through the POC with canned presentations, most of which have little or no relevance to the subject matter of interest. For buyers who have invested little in deciding on what they want, such presentations can be entertaining as they are likely to include all the bells and whistles like drag and drop, slice and dice, drilldown, etc. To sweeten the offer, some vendors even arrange for site visits which are essentially junket trips for analytical software unless there is a working deployment to show.

Like for the TOC, a few principles can be adopted to make it far more effective as personal experience has proven. First, do not let a POC session to be free play. Create a standard scenario or set of tasks that every vendor has to perform. These tasks will be the same as what the risk management staff will want to carry out in their actual work. Second, insist on a live demonstration rather than screen shots. Far too often, vendors talk about what their software can do but cannot show how it is done. It is near guaranteed that what cannot be demonstrated does not exist. The usual response to that is that any specific requirement can be coded, but that is essentially useless as doing so involves time, cost and uncertainty.

The third principle is a challenge to apply and needs some knowledge and understanding about analytics. An IT veteran once said that his industry is perhaps the most unscrupulous in the world as they often patch third-party products to demonstrate a capability not found in their own. This sleight of hand is possible as most audiences are not sufficiently competent to see through it. With analytical software, the likelihood of this happening is much higher as not all have the breadth and depth of algorithms built in. In fact, multimillion-dollar enterprise-level software may rely on Microsoft Excel to carry out the calculations. The purchaser may not even discover the reality until months or even years after installation and possibly by staff who were not involved in the POC. By then, it is too late for recourse from the vendor and a new acquisition has to be made to cover the deficiency.

A cleverly camouflaged third-party patch will be hard to detect, but vendors seldom bother to do that. One way to detect any piece of a presentation that is not organic to the product being assessed is to pay attention to the screen design. All reputable software have their proprietary looks like color, font size, menus, etc. That is usually consistent throughout. A significant change is almost certain to be caused by the insertion of a third-party piece presented as part of the software. Personally, I feel that doing so is borderline fraud and have reprimanded vendors who try to deceive my client banks that the capability is organic to their software. Unfortunately, this practice has been accepted in the IT industry. As a sales representative of a reputable software once said, no sale will be made if a presentation does not resort to this trick.

One way to make a POC effective is to score every vendor by a set of criteria. Here, only the users can do so. It is worthwhile to assign larger weights to "must-haves" and smaller ones to "good-to-have". Scoring goes a long way to make an objective and defendable decision on the final selection.

3.1.4. *System Integration Test (SIT)*

This is largely a technical concern but even here, the absence of user involvement can pose problems in future.

In a large bank, data from different legacy systems have to be integrated to compute results for regulatory submission. One of this is the level of capital. For a bank with international operations, it means data feeds from sources overseas and different time zones. How the datasets have to be integrated is a question that the IT unit is unlikely able to answer though they can program the requirements. Unless users provide the needed guidance, the SIT step can take a much longer time than necessary to complete. For an analytical solution, whether data can be directly batch entered in flat file format is a critical issue to be validated through testing.

3.1.5. *User Acceptance Test (UAT)*

For most purchases, this will be the final test before signing off the contract. While the term suggests that it is when users get to road-test the software or solution to their satisfaction, getting them involved only at this stage is almost certainly too late. If anything, the UAT will be a formality if the earlier stages have been rigorously overseen by users.

For analytical software, the UAT should focus largely on the accuracy of computations and reliability of code execution. A wide range of scenarios is needed to validate the organic algorithms. If R can be embedded, as many routines as possible should be tried with results independently confirmed using another tool. It cannot be assumed that the customization of R in the software is bug-free.

It is advisable that users carry out the UAT rather than hand the business cases to IT for their testing. Only one or more risk professionals able to integrate programming codes into business domain requirements can make that happen.

3.2. Data Table and Data Type

Databases are converging in design and capabilities, but data table and data type design are quite another matter. Analytics have been hindered by the lack of attention to these areas as they cannot be easily rectified when deficiencies show up.

One area that is often neglected is the choice of columns or fields in a table. These are determined usually by the vendor or at most the IT unit of the organization. Rarely are the end-users consulted. The problem arises when external data have to be integrated to internal data for analysis. An example is the use of an external indicator to update internal values like loan collateral. Mortgaged properties need to be revalued regularly to determine the net credit exposure of the lender. In different countries, properties can be classified differently. What is common though is that a single property index cannot be suitable for all property types, especially if there are clear geographical distinctions. No one index can reflect price changes within the city and out in the countryside or an apartment together with a house on a piece of land. If a data table has not been designed with a column that can suitably capture such categories, it will be an immense challenge when an update is needed. Much time and effort have to be spent assigning each record to a property category.

Data type or format is another area that could do with more attention at the database design stage. Unsurprisingly, legacy systems of old place a far higher priority on legal than analytical requirements. Columns of tables often are usually designed with the alphanumeric data type VARCHAR for convenience unless numeric values are required. If a collateral is pledged for a loan, it is the legal title that is recorded. In some cases, just the bitmap image is scanned and stored. This makes it almost impossible to perform any analysis on the market value using some indicator as benchmark.

As it is at the heart of analytics, how data are stored plays a critical role. It is not easy to change a column or the data type in a database. Any deficiency can last for years if not decades like in the case of a large bank required to develop its Loss Given Default (LGD) metrics. LGD requires at least seven years of default data. Though the bank has such history, all collateral data were stored in bitmap format in the past. There was no way to categorize the collateral type to derive recovery rates. A new system has to be created to address the deficiency, but it will take years for the collateral data to be sufficient for the risk quantification needed.

A few principles followed can go a long way to ensure that data tables and data types are fit for analytics use. First, create tables according to the requirements of the risk to be analyzed rather than the nature of business operations. As an illustration, consider loan application in a bank. As an operation, it makes no difference if the application is for wholesale or retail credit. From the IT perspective, a single credit application table is enough to store all data. Wholesale credit risk, however, is very different from those of retail, especially under Basel II requirements that every wholesale obligor must be assigned its own credit rating. As this is not required of retail obligors, the scope of data to be collected for each category is different. Besides, wholesale credit applicants submit details like corporate accounts while retail applicants provide demographics. A single table for all applicants will be cluttered by fields unused for one type of applicant or the other. When it comes to analytics, the data have to be segregated as wholesale or retail, especially for credit risk modeling.

Second, anticipate what kinds of analytics will be needed in future. One of my client banks was in the early stages of migrating its core banking system. The data tables designed were operationally sound except that the applicant name and title were hard coded into a single field. This means that analysis of outcomes like default rates by gender, for example, will be challenging in time to come.

Third, anticipate the need for Foreign Keys in a data table. This technicality goes over the heads of most risk professionals and some elaboration is necessary.

A Primary Key in a data table serves as the unique identifier of a record. For a table of bank collaterals, the Collateral ID is a common choice. The value of this field or column must be unique for each record. Database integrity screens will disallow replicates.

A Foreign Key is designed to combine columns of different tables to facilitate analytics. This is accomplished by matching the data value in a Foreign Key in one table to the value in of the Primary Key in the other. To illustrate, consider the need to update real estate collateral values as part of a bank's regulatory capital adequacy ratio requirement. With thousands or hundreds of thousands of properties, it is not economical to have every single piece of collateral professionally revalued annually. A practical approach would be to use a suitable index to adjust their values and such index data have to come from external sources. Property values do not change by identical or even similar magnitudes. Prices of high-end condominiums may have risen steeply when those of houses have fallen. It is, of course, possible to identify the property type of each collateral and apply the appropriate index change, but that would be labor-intensive and likely open to errors. A much more efficient way is to enter the property type into the Foreign Key of the collateral table. Matching the data values in this column to that of an external index which has property type as its Primary Key will enable automated updating. If a Foreign Key has not been created when the table was designed, it can be a costly oversight when the need occurs.

Fourth, use numbers instead of text where possible except when a number does not have its own intrinsic interpretation. In one bank, gender was captured as 0 and 1, presumably 0 for Male and 1 for Female. Later, the data entry staff decided to use 1 and 2. Over the course of three decades, the Gender field was populated by 0, 1, 2, 3 and 4. When it came to using gender as an input for analysis, there was no way to know what the values represent. Aside from binary values where the exact text should be used, numbers allow for greater flexibility in analytics and modeling. The numeric value of a firm's size by asset or equity will be preferred to Small, Medium, Large, etc. as the threshold for categories will change over time.

Fifth, use categories instead of freeform text. This is true even for sensitive numeric data like personal income, for example. After becoming CEO of a large bank, the analytics savvy banker removed all freeform text fields for online credit application. Even the field for personal income was replaced by a drop list of ranges. It was later leaked that this CEO stopped all software purchase unless it is proven that those existing in the bank could not be used to produce the needed analysis. In using categories, however, it is preferable not to include an "Others" option for any data field. It is near guaranteed that once available, this value becomes the mode for the data column as it too easy for data entry staff to not bother with choosing a more appropriate category.

Sixth, do not allow for NULL values. This, however, can only be enforced when a form is completed. Today, nearly all digital forms have incorporated this feature by refusing submission if any mandatory field is left empty.

Seventh, include any error-checking algorithm possible. This is quite easy with online forms, but it takes the involvement of end-users at the design stage. For example, most banks will have a policy on the minimum and maximum age for a credit applicant or guarantor. Checking for non-compliance with policies not only reduces data errors but also improves operational efficiency as that will reduce the need for rectification or remedial action later.

The principles above are gleaned from years of consultancy experience and certainly not comprehensive. Applying them, however, is a significant challenge as it requires a mindset change which even top management cannot demand from those responsible for implementation. Besides, these principles have to be followed at the design stage. Once the cement of coding has dried, it will take costly man-days for changes to be made.

3.3. Modeling

Modeling is a large part of analytics. In many organizations, this task is performed by mathematicians, statisticians or outsourced to academic consultants. Even in large financial institutions, models are developed on desktop computers and remain there. Often, modeling is a responsibility of the enterprise risk management division with data manually collected from business units. These business units may not even be aware of the existence of such models or have no use for them in their decision-making. This is one glaring deficiency in most risk analytics implementation. Despite significant investments made in trying to derive a good understanding of the risks ahead, the knowledge is often not put to effective use.

As a value-add, many software vendors have included built-in models. One of the most popular is credit scoring. A credit applicant is immediately given a score associated with the level of credit risk using data input to the software. For many banks, that sounds like a good extra that saves the need for developing internal models. As the saying goes, if it is too good to be true, it probably is.

There is no one-size-fits-all model for social sciences. Motivations for specific actions are different across cultures and regulatory environments. In some countries, a corporate default is just a rational decision. Directors acting on behalf of the entity do not bear any consequences. There is the well-known Chapter 11 in the USA where a firm can continue to operate under court supervision even after declaring bankruptcy. That is untrue of other countries where a director who has sat on the board of two defaulted companies will be barred from directorship for life. Default in the latter country or countries then goes far beyond financial implications on the corporation and is likely to be a final resort. The drivers of a credit risk model using default as the dependent variable can be significantly different between countries with different regulatory regimes. The personal cost involved in one but not the other can produce significantly different models to predict corporate default. For this reason alone, any model prepackaged by a software vendor is not only of little value but may lead to wrong risk quantifications resulting in bad decisions.

There are varying schools of thought on how models should be developed. The most widely accepted is the empirical approach using available data to identify effective predictors of a target outcome. Use of financial ratios to model corporate default is a popular example. The other approach is to eschew data altogether and formulate likely scenarios and predict outcomes. This is based on the philosophy that the future cannot be a projection of the past. While true to some extent, there is fallacy in not needing historical data to forecast the likelihood of a future event. A statement like "it is likely to snow in the Sahara Desert next year" will be immediately dismissed as incredulous regardless of how sophisticated the scenario derivation is. The reason for doing so is that it has never snowed as far back as any living person can remember. Any forecast without a basis is quite useless and basis must come from history. Even stock market speculators need a basis for their speculations. A model can still be unsubstantiated by historical data and it is termed a Random or Naïve Model and that is commonly used as the worst that any properly developed model can be in predictive performance.

There is a well-received methodology for business modeling. It is termed CRISP-DM which stands for cross-industry process for data mining. It is commonly depicted as in Fig. 3.2.

3.3.1. *Business understanding*

A modeler must first understand the business needs for the model to be developed. Even in the risk domain, there are different requirements.

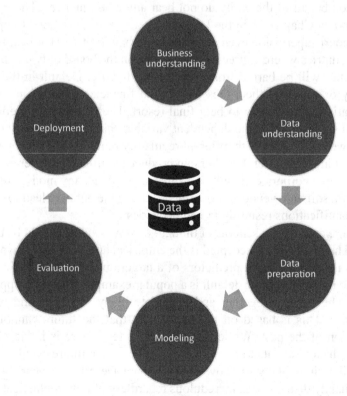

Figure 3.2.   CRISP-DM process.

A credit risk model is aimed at reducing losses from credit exposures while a market risk model may be meant to determine the level of economic capital needed to support a securities portfolio. There are many areas that have to be considered and some of the more important ones are discussed here.

At the high level, there is the business environment. This itself covers a wide scope, but cultural and regulatory factors are probably most pertinent. Among some people, risk-taking is welcome and exciting. Failure or bankruptcy is of no shame. Besides, a bankrupt can be entitled to keep what are regarded as essentials for normal living and such can include a yacht if that has been supportive of the individual's quality of life. Defaulting on a bank loan is no worse than getting a parking ticket. In other cultures, that may be a great shame leading even to suicide. The motivation for default then can be very different and that has significant implications on the modeling of credit risk.

There are modeling approaches based on the concept of rational default. These largely build on the option-pricing theory that equity is like a call option. When a firm's assets are worth less than the value of its debt, equity holders should rationally default by not exercising the call to buy them back by paying off the loan. In a regulatory regime where there are no personal consequences to a corporate default, this premise is reasonable. There are countries, however, that tie personal welfare to the firm being run and bankruptcy which must result from default can seriously impair a director's ability to conduct business in future. In such places, the decision to default cannot simply be based on option pricing models.

The effect of local conditions means that there is no global or universal model for any kind of risk and can be applied out of the box. A highly accurate model in one regime may be a complete failure in another.

Even the same piece of global standard translated into local regulations can be enforced very differently. Basel II and III are supposed to interpreted with sufficient uniformity to level the playing field across the world. In reality, regulators in different countries can apply the principles as differently as night and day. Basel II attempts to provide as much precision as possible to the definition of default. One of these is 90 Days Past Due (DPD) and on the surface it is definitive. In one country where I consulted for, the regulators take a very lenient approach to its application. A credit card holder may be more than 90 DPD but can have delinquencies reset to zero just be paying the minimum amount required. Under Basel II, a default is cured only after all amounts outstanding have been repaid. Without an understanding of such a business environment, a modeler following a textbook template may obtain results that are unreliable.

3.3.2. *Data understanding*

All types of data are available for risk modeling, but often what is usable is precious little, especially when it comes to internal bank data. Knowing how the possibilities and limitations of the different types with respect to the methodology goes a long way to develop reliable models. Data types can be broadly divided into Nominal, Categorical, Ordinal and Cardinal.

Nominal data are simply labels for identification. A good example is postal code which can take on an unlimited range of values theoretically. The postal code can be just numeric in one country and alphanumeric in another. There is no intrinsic property to such data with respect to risk, but that does not mean they are of no use. Experienced data preparation can extract information even from postal codes. Location may be a factor in operational risk, for instance, and postal codes can be aggregated to produce that variable.

Academia by large has no interest in nominal data as it is hard to formulate theories for prediction using them. It can be very different for business modeling. Even the most information-less nominal data values can be useful for decision support. This is especially true of the Weight of Evidence (WoE) methodology which is discussed in detail in later chapters. Consider color which has little or no intrinsic information value. It is almost impossible to develop a theory that individuals who prefer to wear specific colors are of higher credit risk. A business model with such a result can, however, be used for credit application (whether to approve or reject) even in the absence of a theory. If modeling shows that those who wear red are more likely to default than the rest, it does not matter if there is no theory or explanation for such a result. A bank can still apply the model at the time of credit application to assign a higher risk to applicants in red clothing. That is one value of the WoE approach, but it is also a bridge too far for academics which explains why nominal data is often overlooked in textbooks.

Categorical data are more structured than nominal ones. Industry for firms and gender for individual persons are the most common in banks. In conventional Classical Statistics methods, categorical data offer little value unless they can be converted to digits. They are commonly used to create dummy variables for nested modeling. Disregarding them, however, can be a mistake. As will be discussed in the WoE approach, such data are best suited for deriving the probability of a binary outcome like Default/Non-default. In fact, the nominal data discussed earlier can be turned into categorical ones with WoE, as will be shown.

Ordinal data have relative values. "Large" is bigger than "Small". For the purpose of risk modeling, one of the objectives is to determine if there is any monotonous relationship between a factor and an outcome. Ordinal data provide a ready rank order to do that. For the purpose of theory formulation, this and cardinal data are regarded as best suited for modeling.

Cardinal data are the most refined. Age, income, etc. belong to such. They can be further divided into discrete and continuous. Year, for example, is discrete as 2019 goes to 2020 without any values in between. Distance, on the other hand, is continuous. Discrete cardinal data is similar to ordinal data as far as modeling properties are concerned though the latter is likely to be defined for a more limited range.

Aside from data types, there is a need to examine the level of missing data and how they may be treated in modeling. In classroom analysis, missing data are simply ignored since nothing can be done about them. For business modeling, what is missing may have implications on the data collection design.

There are suggested techniques to deal with missing ordinal or cardinal data. Interpolation is one possibility. If Sales for 19X2 is missing and that for 19X1 and 19X3 are available, a reasonable estimate can be made using average or trend with the known values. It is more challenging with categorical data unless there is a good basis to make inferences.

In one modeling consultancy engagement, I found that there were very few "Divorced" values for the Marital Status field relative to "Single", "Married" and "Widowed". There was also a high percentage of missing data. In this country, one in two marriages end in divorce, but there is still a social stigma in being a divorcee. It is unsurprising then that those who are divorced would rather leave the field empty when completing a loan application form. It would not be a concern if the missing values have no predictive power. In this case, they do as a statistically significant predictor of default for females using a Classification and Regression Tree method. Given knowledge of social conditions, it is not unreasonable to assume that most of the missing values belong to the "Divorced" category and hence marital status may be a useful indicator of credit quality at least for females.

3.3.3. *Data preparation*

Raw data are seldom ready for modeling. If Classical Statistics which assumes a known distribution were employed, practically no collected data can be used without some preparation.

The biggest challenge is often the distribution for cardinal values. Whether it is income or financial ratios, the data are severely skewed. Textbooks suggest several ways to transform and make them usable for statistical method. The most common is using natural logarithm or log transformation for short. A value of 1,000,000 may lie far out if the rest are around 100, but log(1,000,000) equals 13.82 which is not that much greater than log(100) equaling 4.61. Log transformation, however, is very limited as it cannot be applied to non-positive numbers. That immediately rules out many financial ratios. Even for those variables where this technique can be used, the distribution often remains very skewed.

Another way is termed Winsorization which is to remove the extreme values. What is considered extreme is subject to the modeler's judgment. Doing so creates its own problem which is the loss of power. Outliers can alter the sign of a coefficient in some cases and removing them may produce results contrary to correct ones.

Binning and bucketing have become more popular because of automation that has made them easier to perform. The terms have been used interchangeably although one refers to using fixed intervals and the other using fixed number of data points or observations per segment. A major advantage of using this approach is that extreme values or outliers need not be sacrificed but have their impact significantly reduced as they get assigned to the smallest or largest bin.

Another need for data preparation may be after the first round of modeling. To increase the predictive power of a factor, two or more values may be grouped. For instance, the default rate of age bands 20–25, 35–40 and 55–60 may be very similar. Instead of having the three bands as different inputs, a grouped band X may be created as replacement. The power of age will be enhanced as X predicts differently from other bands whereas three different bands have the same predictions earlier.

Data preparation is unlikely to be a one-time process. In fact, it can be central to create effective models when the association or causality between factor and result is far from monotonic. The sophisticated Vector Machine method is essentially an algorithm-based approach to preparing data through grouping to derive better models.

Besides the relatively mechanical preparations, there is often the need to apply transformations based on judgement to achieve consistency. This is particularly so for financial ratios.

Consider Return on Equity which is computed as Net Income/Equity. All financial ratio analysis discussions equate a higher value with better financial health hence lower credit risk. What is overlooked in academic discussions is the industry reality that both Net Income and Equity can be negative for many firms. Since the ratio of two negatives produce a positive, a firm with a huge loss over a small negative equity may produce a large positive ROE. If ROE is used without any conversion, it can confound the model. Detection of the existence of a double negative has to be carried out in a data audit which is described in a later chapter. For data preparation, there is a need to decide how such values can be converted to preserve both the direction and magnitude of causation.

One possible replacement is to assign a negative to the ROE for such occurrences. That will at least remove the confounding effect. However, the case of a double negative is not the only one that has to be dealt with. A positive Net Income over a negative Equity will result in a negative ROE identical to a negative Net Income over a positive Equity of same magnitudes. From a practical credit risk perspective, a firm that is earning profits even when it has negative equity is likely on the way to better financial health than another making losses on positive equity. Here again, a judgment call has to be made on how to achieve consistency in associating ROE with credit risk. Replacing the negative ROE with a positive value for the case of positive divided by negative values is one option.

The ROE illustration is just one of the many issues that have to be addressed in data preparation when it comes to financial ratios. The existence of zero Current Liabilities resulting in incomputable Current Ratios, the comingling of Net Total Assets (which can be negative in value) but not explicitly stated as such with Total Assets, the use of both positive and negative signs for Debt are common and have to be dealt with for a model to be consistent.

3.3.4. *Modeling*

Modeling techniques continue to expand and there is no single taxonomy that can cover them all. Many excellent textbooks and articles provide highly qualified discussions on this topic, so it is not the aim here to accomplish that. Only issues pertinent to risk analytics are covered in depth.

The most common way to categorize modeling approaches is Nonparametric vs Classical Statistics. As the term suggests, Classical Statistics has a longer history. It centers on the use of a theoretical distribution as the basis to test a hypothesis. Using data, the modeler attempts to find enough evidence to reject a Null Hypothesis. This was termed British empiricism which promoted data-based or empirical approach to deriving theories about cause and effect. It serves as the conceptual framework for analytics today.

Classical Statistics is popular because of the clarity provided in the modeling process. Data of the population which are all the possible observations are assumed to be spread along a known distribution. The most commonly used is the Normal Distribution as it has been found to best fit natural outcomes like the amount of daily rainfall, for instance. This distribution is bell-shaped with equal portions below and above the mean value which is intuitively appealing to the concept of unbiasedness.

As it is reasonably assumed that any random observation comes from the Null Distribution, it is the Null Hypothesis that a value observed is one of such. Modeling involves the assessment of whether the observed value belongs to the Null Distribution. If it can be shown that the value lies at the extreme of the Null Distribution, the Null Hypothesis can be rejected with a low probability of error, which implies a high level of confidence. Figure 3.3 is commonly used to illustrate this process known as hypothesis testing.

The use of the Normal Distribution has gone beyond hypothesis testing as it is found to most closely represent the spread of securities returns. As will be discussed in later chapters, the estimation of Value at Risk or VaR is based on the same principle underlying confidence levels.

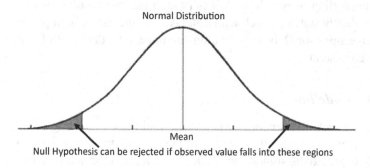

Figure 3.3.   Hypothesis testing.

Most social data values do not conform to any known distribution. This simple fact can result in the rejecting of the Null Hypothesis even if that conclusion is incorrect. Nonparametric approaches mitigate that deficiency by not relying on theoretical distributions. Instead, counts of specific outcomes are used to detect the power of prediction. In credit risk modeling, the Classification And Regression Tree (CART) and the WoE approaches have gained increasing acceptance as being reliable techniques. A key advantage of Nonparametrics over Classical Statistics is the ability to employ categorical data directly without converting them into numerical values.

Modeling for analytics is both an art and a science. It is rare for a first cut model to meet the backtesting requirements under Basel II even under development conditions. Employing different approaches from the start can help reduce the need to redo data preparation which is often the most time-consuming part of the CRISP-DM process. Comparing models developed using both Classical Statistics and Nonparametrics can provide insights on how some variables or values may be dominating the results obtained.

3.3.5. *Evaluation*

In a conventional modeling process, a sample of data is divided into two or three parts. If it is two parts, one will be used for training which is the jargon for developing the model and the other used for testing or evaluation. A third part is for validation but that adds little to the quality of the model. Using a testing sample is known as out-of-sample testing.

The purpose of evaluation is to assess the predictive power of a model. Many techniques have been developed, but only one will be discussed here as it has implications on the return of a good risk model. That is the Misclassification or Confusion Matrix shown in Table 3.1 for a credit approval model.

Table 3.1.   Misclassification matrix.

Actual	Predicted		
	Non-default	**Default**	**Total**
Non-default	0.78	0.04	0.82
Default	0.01	0.17	0.18
Total	0.79	0.21	1.00

A sample of bank customers comprising those who have defaulted (Default) and those who have not (Non-default) is divided into two: one for training and the other for testing. The model developed from the training sample is then applied to the testing sample to predict whether a customer is a defaulter or not. The Misclassification Matrix evaluates the level of accuracy of predictions.

The testing sample consists of 82% who have not defaulted and 18% who have. In the cell with 0.78, 78% of all customers in the testing sample were correctly predicted as Non-defaults. Conversely, 4% have been given the incorrect prediction. The results suggest that the model has a 95% accuracy which seems impressive. This percentage has, however, to be viewed against the typical default rate of a credit portfolio. Globally, average corporate default rate is around 2% under normal conditions. A model that assigns Non-default to all the customers in the testing sample will achieve a 98% accuracy level. Although this is too high a threshold for any empirical model to exceed, it serves as a reference for assessing the accuracy rate of any model.

The Matrix also provides information about modeling errors. These are termed Type I and Type II errors in Statistics. Type I error is when the Null is true but the model incorrectly rejects it and Type II error is when the Null is false but the model fails to reject it. It is a common mistake to describe Type II error as accepting the Null when it is false. The sole aim of hypothesis testing is to reject the Null if possible. There is no need to accept the Null as it would be the default conclusion if there were no model.

Models are compared using the probability of making a Type I error. A model that has no more than 1% of doing so is considered superior to another with no more than 5%. This principle informs the modeling of credit risk approval. If all loan applicants can be broadly divided into Good (will not default) and Bad (will default) credit risk, a bank will want a model that approves as many Good and rejects as many Bad as possible. Since errors are always possible, there is a need to decide if wrongly approving a Bad risk or rejecting a Good risk is more costly to the bank. Some simple assumptions can help in the analysis. If the recovery rate from a default is 60%, a $100 loan can result in a loss of $40 if made to a Bad customer. If this customer was not rejected at the loan application, the bank would have saved $40 credit loss. A loan could earn a 2% net interest spread. If a Good customer is wrongly rejected at loan application, the bank would lose the potential $2 interest income on the $100 loan. It is evident that not rejecting a Bad credit costs more than not approving a Good one. The better model will be the one that is more effective in doing so.

From the above discussion, a credit approval model should be based on the Null Hypothesis that a loan applicant is a Bad risk. The model should provide the basis for rejecting this Null which essentially leads to the conclusion that the applicant is Good. The Type I error will be not rejecting the Null leading to a Bad risk being approved as customer. A bank will certainly want to minimize this error compared to the mutually exclusive alternative of wrongly rejecting a Good risk.

The Misclassification Matrix provides valuable information on the return of a good risk model that is probably not discussed outside of this book. The analysis arose from a good question on the value of modeling. Risk management has largely been viewed as a cost center and an obstruction to business development. Is there any value in a credit approval model and can the return be computed? With some reasonable assumptions, there is a means to doing so.

As concluded earlier, the correct Null Distribution for credit applicants is Bad. It is reasonable to assume that there are proportionately many more Bad than Good risk. For the sake of this analysis, let us assume that 70% are Bad and 30% are Good.

In practical credit risk quantification, there is no absolute Bad or Good risk. A customer is neither certain to default or not default. Under Basel II, every credit customer or obligor must be assigned a Probability of Default or PD (at least for those categorized as wholesale). No obligor can be given a 0% PD and only those who have already defaulted are assigned 100% PD. There is always a positive PD and so the Bad can be those with a higher value.

With commercial credit ratings, a 20% PD is usually the highest for those who have yet to default. For this discussion, a 20% PD will be assigned to Bad and 1% assigned to Good. To complete the inputs required, the net interest income of a loan is 2% and the recovery rate from a defaulted one is 60%. With these data, a payoff from a credit risk model can be derived.

If there are 100,000 credit applicants, 70,000 will be Bad and 30,000 Good. Without a credit approval model, a bank will employ a random approach to approving or rejecting any applicant. The easiest is the toss of a coin. A head means approval and a tail results in rejection. Employing this method, 50,000 applicants will be approved of which 35,000 will be

Bad and 15,000 Good. If \$100 were loaned to each, the expected payoffs from these applicants who become customers and the return on the loan portfolio will be as follows:

Expected payoff for each Good and Bad customer

Good: $(0.99)(\$102) + (0.01)(0.6)(\$100) = \$101.58$

Bad: $(0.8)(\$102) + (0.2)(0.6)(\$100) = \$93.60$

Return on loan portfolio

Amount loaned = \$5,000,000

Total expected payoffs = $(15,000)(\$101.58) + (35,000)(\$93.60) = \$4,799,700$

$$\text{Return} = \frac{\$4,799,700 - \$5,000,000}{\$5,000,000} = -4.00\%$$

Unsurprisingly, the bank will make a loss on the credit portfolio if it randomly approves applications given the preponderance of Bad risks. This result alone should motivate risk modeling, but it can be shown that a good model makes a significant difference.

Assume that a credit risk model is developed with the Misclassification Matrix shown in Table 3.1. As discussed earlier, the accuracy rate is not spectacular, so such models are not difficult to create.

Instead of the random 50/50 chance of approval, applicants are assessed using the model. According to the Misclassification Matrix, 78/82 or 95.12% of the Good (Non-default) applicants will be rated Good and hence approved. Only 7/18 or 38.89% of Bad applicants will be rated Good and approved. Out of the 100,000 applicants, $(0.9512)(30,000)$ or 28,537 Good and $(0.1111)(70,000)$ or 3,889 Bad get approved to become customers. The total number of customers will be 32,426 and the total loans \$3,242,600. The payoffs and return on the credits can be recomputed as follows:

Expected payoff for each Good and Bad customer

Good: $(0.99)(\$102) + (0.01)(0.6)(\$100) = \$101.58$

Bad: $(0.8)(\$102) + (0.2)(0.6)(\$100) = \$93.60$

Return on loan portfolio

Amount loaned = $3,242,600

Total expected payoffs = (28,537)($101.58) + (3,889)($93.60) = $3,262,799

$$\text{Return} = \frac{3,262,799 - \$3,242,600}{\$3,242,600} = 0.623\%$$

The return may appear small but relative to the one for the that without a model, it's 4.6% difference which is sufficiently material. There is definite value in risk models and this result is likely true of any form of risk analytics.

3.3.6. *Deployment*

This is discussed in greater detail in a later section.

3.4. Data Flow

Data flow is not only a critical but also another weak link in the risk analytics process. It is near myth that data flow seamlessly across an organization. The reality is that many legacy systems used for operations and transactions have been developed by vendors who want to differentiate rather than integrate. A simple check on the CustomerID used in different product systems will easily attest to that. Almost no two systems use the same data type. Some can run into tens of digits and characters while others do not allow for non-numeric values. The concept of Single Customer View has been proposed ever since computers were affordable to private entities, but till this day it remains largely an unachieved ideal.

There are several challenges that need to be addressed in this area. Data quality and quantity, external and internal data integration, security and access, analytics for decision-making are discussed in the following sections.

3.4.1. *Data quality and quantity*

Garbage In Garbage Out (GIGO) needs no explanation. Sadly, the phenomenon is more pervasive that most organizations and even academics would like to acknowledge. In fact, rotten data are almost accepted as inevitable in practically all financial institutions. Incorrect data produce incorrect results leading to incorrect decisions.

There are two areas of data quality that needs examining. The first is reliability. Reliable data are most desired but not easy to ascertain. The feasible approach is to determine what is obviously unreliable.

In a particular country, most financial institutions have relied on corporate financial returns collected by the government. Firms submit audited accounts, but these are almost never checked for reliability. A simple financial ratio analysis, however, immediately throws up questions. The Current Ratio is widely used as an indicator of liquidity. When the derivation was run on the data, a number showed the error "Divided by zero". On closer examination, it was found that these were associated with zero Current Liabilities. These are financial data of going concerns, not dormant companies. In very exceptional cases, it is theoretically possible that a firm has paid off all its outstanding liabilities before the end of the financial year, but the number of cases suggest that what has been reported is unlikely to be reliable.

The second important aspect of data is currency or whether they are updated. This is a serious challenge for internal data in financial institutions but can also be a problem with regulatory submissions. In the same country mentioned above, many financial ratios remain unchanged year after year. A simple audit reveals that some active firms simply resubmit the same set of audited financial statements for a few years before updating them.

It is clear that any analytics or models with unreliable and outdated data produce incorrect and even misleading results. As will be elaborated on later, data audit must be made a part of the risk analytics process if outcomes are used to support major decisions.

3.4.2. *External and internal data integration*

Very little attention is paid to the need to integrate external data with internal ones. Even regulators may not be informed of the criticality of this aspect in updating market values.

A key development in risk analytics is the move to use economic instead of accounting values. The market value of a collateral matters far more than the book value. For a bank with thousands of property mortgages, updating the market value of property collaterals is a challenge if not a costly exercise. In reality, most banks do not look into market values till there is a need for liquidation to recover a defaulted loan. This is inconsistent with the concept of credit risk exposure where net exposure is the gross amount less risk mitigation which is the value of the collateral here.

As discussed earlier, the lack of consideration in the design for Primary and Foreign Keys to map external data to internal ones is a common reason why market values are not regularly updated. If and when required by the regulator, a financial institution would perform offline processing by extracting the needed data to a spreadsheet and incorporate the external indicator. Not only is such an approach inefficient, but the results are also usually not stored into a database which can be readily accessed in future. Besides, any documentation on the exercise is likely to be piecemeal and not preserved for future guidance and improvement.

As will be discussed in greater detail in a later chapter, data integration is perhaps more important for operational than credit or market risks. Being relatively more recently quantified, operational loss data is scarce or even unavailable in most banks. Even with those collected, reliability is in question. It is almost a given that operational losses are downplayed to the minimum possible for reputation reasons which impacts on the regulatory capital required. External data especially from insurance companies can not only supplement deficient internal ones but also serve as benchmarks for insurable losses. But here again, the need to integrate internal and external data is dependent on the availability of Primary and Foreign Keys to match fields like events.

3.4.3. *Security and access*

Access to data for analytics is much less straightforward than classroom exercises assume. In many large organizations, legacy system data cannot be read without proper authorization. Analysis and modeling are rarely good enough reasons to warrant access.

Any attempt to develop analytics and modeling can be stalled at the gate if data cannot be first extracted. And even if access is allowed, writing back results or outputs is almost impossible. Legacy systems are usually designed by vendors with prohibition on means of data entry other than the interfaces provided.

The matter of security leads inevitably to the need for data warehousing. This is by now understood, but developing a usable data warehouse or even just a data mart is the subject of another chapter.

3.4.4. *Analysis and decision-making*

Analytics serve different purposes. The most common is to provide insights that can be deliberated on for future decisions. For this purpose, offline analysis with data extracted into a spreadsheet is usually good enough. With computerization now a norm rather than an exception, many organizations are looking to analytics for real-time decision support. Terms like Online Analytical Programming (OLAP), slice and dice, drill-down, etc. have been created to describe what is desired. In essence, the desire is to be able to tap into live data to enable perspectives from different angles for a more comprehensive understanding of the subject at hand. In this respect, movies are far ahead of reality.

OLAP is much more challenging than it sounds. In a large organization, data warehousing is a critical requirement as legacy systems do not allow for direct access. Database vendors have promoted multidimensional designs for easy slice and dice, but not many organizations have successfully customized the concept to their internal requirements. Data cannot be drilled down to the month if the month value is not first captured in the DATE column. The Business Information System manager of a large organization complained of the immense pressure when decision-makers demanded actionable analysis despite 400 reports being generated and distributed daily. She was at her wits end trying to understand what exactly these colleagues of hers want. Unfortunately, such a situation is very pervasive.

For analytics professionals, it is worthwhile to invest time and resources to determine what outputs are desired. Learning from costly consulting missteps, I have designed a Meeting of Minds questionnaire for this purpose. Over time, I have educated most clients on what they may want to look for and that approach is often well received. A sample of this questionnaire is found in Annex A.

Analytics for real-time decision support is heavily dependent on data flow. Unless data can be made available on an open-ended basis, this purpose cannot be fulfilled. However, beyond the data themselves, the issue of technology has to be considered, especially in a large organization with widely distributed operations. Data from a source in another time zone and legacy system may not be easily integrated into the main database. Here again, time and effort have to be devoted to examine this aspect and resolve all impeding issues.

3.5. Deployment

Analytics for decision support has moved from the more glacial strategic long-term decision-making to instantaneous ones. This is perhaps no better demonstrated by retail credit approval which can take less than five seconds from the time data are entered into the system. Such a process requires forward deployment of models developed and translated into simple business rules for more efficient processing.

Vendors who understand the dynamics have delivered standalone solutions covering data capture to modeling, output generation and even reports. While this meets most or all of the deployed system objective, it creates the problem of integration with the core database. The standalones become silos not unlike self-sufficient credit card systems that banks have been using. It is a quick answer to a need, but it generates a long-term problem.

For an organization preferring to have a deployed instantaneous decision-support system, the location of the model or business rules has to be considered. Besides, there is also the need to design how data will be integrated to the core system for further analytics like Single Customer View, for instance. The three lines of defense risk governance framework proposed by the International Financial Corporation (IFC) as shown in Fig. 3.4 provides the landscape to guide where and how risk solutions should be deployed.

The first line of defense is at the business operations. This means that business unit staff must be able to perform risk quantifications on site which in turn means that risk models have to be deployed there. For credit application, the applicant must be assigned a risk rating. With trading in the Treasury, VaR values must be computed in near real time to ensure that limits are not breached. For such to happen, risk models need to be on location. It is possible, of course, to have them stored in a desktop computer and transaction data manually entered to derive the needed results. That will suffice for a small bank or branch with low transaction volumes. A reasonably large bank will encounter delays detrimental to its ability to compete. In a large Asian bank with a decades-old system, for instance, manually processed results were outdated by the time the traders receive them, resulting in incorrect pricing of securities. If possible, a tested credit rating model should be part of the loan application system, as shown in Fig. 3.5.

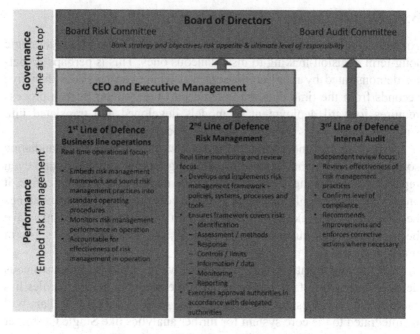

Figure 3.4.   Risk governance framework.

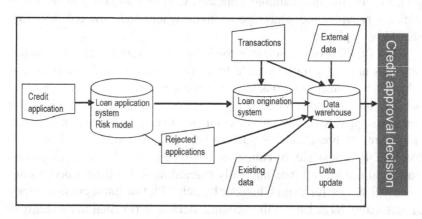

Figure 3.5.   Embedding of credit rating model into loan application system.

As will be expanded in later chapters, reaching that level of automation requires a lot more architecting and coordinating than often anticipated.

The second line of defense lies with the risk management unit or Enterprise Risk Management (ERM) as termed in many banks. This is equivalent to the central kitchen of risk management and it is easily assumed (incorrectly) that automation is the default. All the heavy-duty risk analytics are performed here, but more often than not, the processes remain manual. Take Asset Liability Management (ALM), for instance. It is a standard regulatory requirement that the Asset Liability Committee (ALCO) must evaluate the bank's liquidity and banking book interest rate risks daily by reviewing the relevant gaps in the balance sheet. While Repricing or Funding Gap is commonly found in ALM applications, Duration Gap derivation has to be customized to the credit products. Banks that do not have the needed expertise leave this Gap out of analysis altogether. For those that do, duration computation is likely to be done using a spreadsheet with data extracted from the core banking system. Automated data feeds are rare.

Deployment of risk solutions has to start at the ERM. As a consultant, I have strongly advocated that my client banks embed at IT specialist in the ERM to make that happen, but that is usually met with resistance. Unless there is passion, an IT staff does not want to be confined to risk management on the career path. The IT unit is also unwilling to transfer or second a staff who may be available to perform other tasks. And there is the difficulty in finding someone who is competent in both IT and risk areas. Nevertheless, the benefits of being able to have that embedding goes a long way to automating deployment. In some developed economies, there is recognition of the value of training professionals who can synthesize knowledge bases. Business Analytics programs at both the undergraduate and graduate levels have been introduced.

The third line of defense is the Internal Audit. Even here, there is a need for automated deployment which has almost never been considered. Take the case of Operational Risk, for instance. Vendor solutions will likely include the Risk Control and Self-Assessment (RCSA) module which requires every operational unit to estimate the frequency and severity of risk events likely to occur for the coming year. The RCSA forms the basis for monitoring and control measures as the high severity ones warrant greater attention. Over the course of time, such estimates should improve in accuracy and it is for the Internal Audit to test the actual outcomes against estimates for independent validation. As an Operational Risk system is likely to be centrally managed at the ERM, the Internal Audit will have no access to the RCSA unless there is a conscious effort to deploy that for the purpose of verification. The term "risk audit" has gained traction, but professionals dedicated to this task are rare if they exist. Without a good understanding of risk, Internal Auditors serving as the third line of defense are likely to review documentation which they may not comprehend.

3.6. Governance

Risk governance has received much greater attention since the string of crises that have hit financial institutions. The three lines of defense advocated by the IFC was popularized and its implications on the deployment of risk solutions were discussed above. It may not appear obvious, but governance principles can be applied to risk analytics. These cover production of analytics and models, creation and access to one or more knowledge bases and validation of analyses. All these aspects involve responsibility and accountability which are at the heart of governance. For transparency and sustainability, policies should be formulated by the Risk or Risk Management Committee of the Board of Directors.

Responsibility for analytics and modeling may not be straightforward. Overlaps or gaps are not uncommon. Unclear responsibility leads to unclear accountability. In large organizations, several units may even be developing the same models resulting in competition and confusion. It is part of good risk governance to have clear lines of responsibilities for model development. As expertise in this area is usually limited, it may be worth designating a single business unit to be responsible for model development. In most banks, that unit is the ERM. This consideration can be extended to model validation. Since validation should be independent of development, the Internal Audit may be a suitable unit for that to be carried out. However, there will be a need to have the necessary expertise within for that to be achieved. One possible solution is to second risk modelers to Internal Audit for a period to create a temporary separation between validation and development. With global banks, external expertise may be engaged to achieve true independence.

The need to do the same is less pressing for analytics as different areas of an organization have different informational needs.

It is increasingly recognized that the investments made in analytics should be preserved. One way in which this is done is the creation of one or more knowledge bases. Such creation, however, requires thoughtful design especially in the connections between different modules. After creation, controlled access is another aspect that has to be considered.

In large organizations, a Risk Committee is usually ultimately responsible for all risk matters which include models and analytics. In the USA, regulators of financial institutions have mandated that at least one member of the Board must be conversant with risk to ensure proper governance.

3.7. Need for Integration

It is the repeated emphasis of this book that all the components of the risk analytics landscape have to be integrated to attain effective use. Data warehousing is central, which is the reason a whole chapter on creating a risk data mart is devoted to its discussion. The larger the organization, the more challenging it is to integrate. Just getting the different stakeholders to come together to discuss and plan is not even feasible in some places.

A common misperception about risk analytics is that it is under the purview of IT or ERM. The former commands the necessary resources like hardware and software. The latter has the name "Risk" which means that it should be responsible for anything associated with the matter. While IT and ERM must be part of the conversation, implementation and upkeeping of the system, it is not necessary that either or both should be made in charge. As discussed earlier, risk analytics cuts across an entire organization in terms of inputs needed and outputs generated. This is seldom understood though mentally assented to. In reality, many information consuming business units or BUs resort to the quick fix of acquiring silo systems that meet their specific needs. Adding to this pragmatism is the matter of budgets leading to an unwillingness to share. The Wholesale Banking unit of a large bank purchases legal notices on bankruptcies being pursued. This unit refuses to share the data with any other including Retail Banking or allow them to be input into any database. The acquisition is out of their budget and they are not going to let others free ride on the investment. The market information division of a central bank guards foreign exchange rate that it collected during the pre-internet days as jewels. Such information is power and they are not going to let it dissipate.

The turf mentality is probably the hardest to overcome. Top management often encounter silent resistance even after the heads of BUs sign on to an integration initiative. Analytics remain a good-to-have, not a must-have. Besides, it is hard to develop Key Performance Indicators (KPI) for this area. Preventing a $100m loss is hard to validate whereas generating another $100m of revenues is obvious. Practically all attention to risk analytics have to follow publicized events involving huge losses.

Chapter 4

Embedded R

As mentioned earlier, an essential aspect of developing automated deployable risk solutions is to be able to integrate models and analysis into the database. This chapter shows can that can be accomplished.

With Open Source, R has become popular. It is used even by investment funds for multimillion-dollar decisions which is an endorsement of the reliability of the built-in algorithms.

R is certainly good enough for standalone analytics and modeling. RStudio is a widely used interface for coding. Vendors like Microsoft and Oracle have, however, grasped the value of embedding the language into their databases to facilitate deployment. This is a boon to automating analytics and modeling for decision-making. Before the arrival of R, large organizations usually rely on software like SAS, SPSS, Stata, etc. to perform analysis and develop models. Data have to be extracted, processed using these software and results returned to the database for reports or online analysis. The software or outputs cannot be easily integrated with the Structured Query Language (SQL) of databases to allow for seamless execution. Some attempts have been made to translate the proprietary codes into stored procedures that can be called, but compatibility often remains a challenge. Besides, such commercial software incurs recurring costs.

This chapter is devoted to describing R in a database. A separate one will focus on using R in Microsoft Excel which is best suited for Online Analytical Programming (OLAP) supporting the slicing and dicing of data for real-time planning and strategizing. For very small banks where

47

Excel is used even as the database, that will be sufficient for the automation of risk analytics.

Embedding R directly into SQL is a big step even if the execution of the codes can be better designed. For automated risk quantification in the first line of defense as depicted in the IFC diagram, the integration of model codes into the database for processing is necessary. Even in other areas where risk analytics and modeling are undertaken, the embedding of codes makes updating much easier and documentation that goes toward the creation of a knowledge base more convenient.

Though not very different, Microsoft and Oracle SQL codes are not identical and the same goes for the embedded R. For the sake of brevity, only the Oracle version is discussed here, but it only takes a little variation for the same to work in Microsoft SQL Server. To recap, the rest of the chapter is based on installing Oracle in Microsoft Windows and using SQL Developer as the interface. Those familiar with UNIX and SQL Plus will not have a problem using scripts for the same purposes.

Oracle has named its embedded version as Oracle R Enterprise (ORE). An overview of this component can be found in https://www.oracle.com/technetwork/database/database-technologies/r/r-enterprise/overview/index.html. The integration has matured to the point that R is now organic to an Oracle database. After installation, a subfolder R is automatically created in Oracle home like \\…\dbhome_1\R. ORE, however, still requires an independent R installation to function.

The latest version of ORE available at the time of this edition of the book is 1.5.1. The Open Source R associated with this is the 3.3.0 version although 3.5.1 may be tweaked to work with ORE 1.5.1.

Getting ORE to work with R is not automatic. A variety of settings is required and these are described in sufficient detail.

4.1. ORACLE_HOME and R_HOME

After installation, the Environment Variables have to be edited to create an ORACLE_HOME, as shown in Fig. 4.1.

If the Path has not already detected the R installation, it has to be edited to include the path to the \bin folder of the Oracle installation. The same has to be done for the installation.

In Oracle documentation, the username used is RQUSER, so it will be used throughout this book.

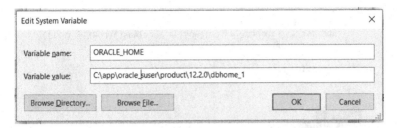

Figure 4.1. Editing ORACLE_HOME directory value.

4.2. Pluggable Database

ORE has to be run from a pluggable database (PDB) and not the root database. In a typical Oracle installation, a PDB is created by default. Depending on the version, a PDB named ORCLPDB or PDBORCL is the name assigned. If the default option is not chosen, a PDB can still be created after installation, but this is not covered here.

The Oracle Listener has to be edited to include the PDB. This is done by adding the highlighted section to the file tnsnames.ora which is usually located in \\...\dbhome_1\network\admin, as shown in Fig. 4.2.

A separate connection has to be created for access to the PDB. The default connection selects Basic for the Connection Type. While this can work, it throws up execution problems when the R script gets lengthy. A more robust configuration is to select TNS, as shown in Fig. 4.3.

RQUSER has to be first created and this is described in the following section.

4.3. RQUSER

This account cannot be created like other accounts. RQUSER requires two roles to be granted. One is RQADMIN and the other is RQUSER. These privileges are not generated unless the RQUSER account is created appropriately.

There are many sources of instructions to set up the RQUSER. One with better clarity can be found in the following link: https://explore bigdataanalytics.wordpress.com/2014/12/16/setting-up-ore-1-4-1-with-oracle-12c-12-1-0-1-r-3-1-2-on-windows-machine/. Though the versions mentioned are outdated, the steps are still largely relevant to the

```
ORCL =
  (DESCRIPTION =
    (ADDRESS = (PROTOCOL = TCP)(HOST = localhost)(PORT = 1521))
    (CONNECT_DATA =
      (SERVER = DEDICATED)
      (SERVICE_NAME = ORCL)
    )
  )

ORCLPDB =
  (DESCRIPTION =
    (ADDRESS = (PROTOCOL = TCP)(HOST = localhost)(PORT = 1521))
    (CONNECT_DATA =
      (SERVER = DEDICATED)
      (SERVICE_NAME = ORCLPDB)
    )
  )
```

Figure 4.2. Inclusion of the PDB in the file tnsnames.ora.

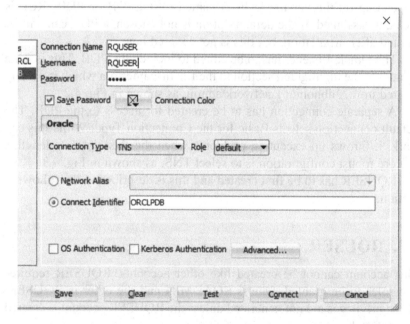

Figure 4.3. Selection of TNS.

latest ones. To compensate for the possibility of web links being taken down, some of the more important steps are described here.

ORE is installed with the command \\...\dbhome_1\R>server.bat--install using Run as Administrator. If the PDB has been installed by default, it will be automatically detected. Otherwise, a PDB has to be created before this step.

It is recommended that SYSAUX instead of USERS be entered for the option PERMANENT tablespace.

When Choosing ORE user is reached, enter RQUSER. If the account has not been created beforehand, it will be created in the Oracle database. If all the steps return a PASS, the RQUSER account has been successfully created. In the SYS connection, expand the Other Users folder and edit the user RQUSER. Verify that the RQADMIN and RQUSER roles have been granted as indicated by the checked box under Granted. If these two roles cannot be found in the Granted Roles tab, it means that the RQUSER has not be properly created and the process has to be repeated.

As the RQUSER runs on the PDB, that database has to be opened and made current. This can be done by running the following two SQL statements:

```
Alter pluggable database ORCLPDB open;
Alter session set container = ORCLPDB;
```

4.4. R Packages and RStudio

Organic ORE packages are likely installed in the library subfolder of R. These include OREbase, OREcommon, ROracle, etc. For more sophisticated analytics, these packages are insufficient. Additional packages can be downloaded from https://cran.r-project.org/. These packages come in both UNIX and Windows versions, so it is essential to select the appropriate one.

One package may be dependent on one or more of others. In ORE, the necessity for a package and its dependencies is usually not clearly explained in Oracle error messages. One way to extract more information from errors is to use RStudio to replicate the ORE script.

RStudio is a tool independent of R. Due to ease of use, it is popular even for scripting. Like most well-designed workspaces, RStudio incorporates useful panels. One of these is the list of packages that are downloaded and whether they have been installed for the session. In RStudio, the lack of a package for a specific function is explicitly made known. Installing any new package is made easy by simply selecting the Tools table, as shown in Fig. 4.4.

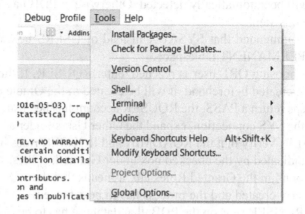

Figure 4.4.   Tools dropdown menu.

When a package is downloaded using RStudio, all its dependencies are automatically downloaded as well.

More about RStudio is discussed in a later chapter, but it is worth noting here that it would be helpful to synchronize the library used by RStudio with that of ORE, else scripts that are tested in one may not work in the other due to version difference in R. To change the library path, check the current one in RStudio. After launching the application, type the following:

```
>.libPaths()
[1] "C:/Users/[username]/Documents/R/win-library/3.6"
[2] "C:/Program Files/R-3.6.0/library"
```

If the R version installed is 3.6.0, a library would automatically have been created in the folders, as shown above. Packages downloaded will be stored in this library which is different from the one for ORE.

To redirect all package installations and use to the ORE library, first add the path to that library as follows:

```
>myPaths <- .libPaths()
>myPaths<-c(myPaths, 'C:/app/[username]/product/12.2.0/dbhome_1/R/library')
>.libPaths(myPaths)
```

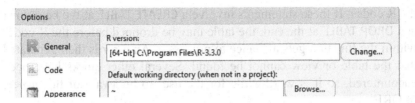

Figure 4.5. Changing the version in R version box.

The ORE version has to replace the RStudio one if they are not the same. This can be done using the RStudio menu by selecting Tools, then Global Options and changing the version in the R version box, as shown in Fig. 4.5.

The synching of R versions and library is important if RStudio is used to troubleshoot an ORE script which is known as an rqScript. The rqScript is created as a procedure in Oracle and run in entirety. When an error is encountered, it is not evident which line may be causing it. RStudio allows for every line of the R script to be processed separately. The error-causing line can be easily identified and fixed. It is one effective trouble-shooting approach. More discussion about RStudio is found in a later chapter.

4.5. Oracle R Enterprise (ORE)

Unlike standalone R, ORE cannot be executed by itself. It works as a function akin to a stored procedure within the Oracle database. This function has to be embedded between a BEGIN and an END. The function is known as an rqScript which has to be created. Once created, a script's name is stored in the database and cannot be reused unless overwritten or dropped and created anew. It is then called by a transact SQL statement like the following:

```
select * from table(rqEval(NULL, 'select 1 result from dual', 'function'));
```

The specifics of this SQL statement can be found in Oracle's documentation and are not discussed here. It is worth noting, however, that this adds a layer of complexity to the coding of R that may not be well understood. For instance, SQL statements are executed before the R codes. If these statements involve a CREATE TABLE at the beginning and DROP TABLE at the end, the table may be dropped before the R codes within the function gets a chance to process it. An error is then generated that the table or view cannot be found. Several other quirks have been encountered, so it is worthwhile for the user to be aware of this aspect of ORE.

There are several limitations in ORE. One that is quickly obvious is the lagged version of R that is compatible. At the writing of this book, ORE is only able to work with R 3.3.0 when 3.6.0 is already launched. Packages developed using R later than 3.3.0 cannot be run from ORE. Typically, an error message will appear stating this as the reason.

Another limitation is the use of proprietary ORE versions of packages. For standalone R, the package dplyr is widely used. ORE has a customized version OREdplyr, so the package dplyr will not be accommodated.

Installing a package for standalone R using RStudio is straightforward. Entering part of the package name will automatically lead to a drop list of relevant packages. It is just a matter of selecting the correct one and it together with dependent packages will be downloaded from the CRAN website. For ORE, installation can be carried out in two ways. One is to download the compressed file from CRAN and decompress it in the library subfolder of the R folder in the Oracle installation. The R folder is usually found in C:\app\[user]\product\[version]\dbhome_1\R. This approach, however, does not allow for verification of compatibility. The other way is to first open a command prompt preferably with administrator rights. Typing R like C:\windows\system32>R will launch the ORE applet Rterm. To install a package Q, enter install.packages("https://cran.r-project.org/web/packages/Q/index.html"). This leads to a prompt to select the CRAN repository to download the package. Despite a site's appearance on the list, many packages are not available in many repositories. An error message will show up if a package is not compatible with ORE. Even when a package is successfully downloaded and installed, there may be a host of dependencies that have to be installed before ORE can complete the task. The package VARS, for instance, requires a number of other packages to function. Each only appears as missing in the error message when an rqScript is run.

To recap, the purpose of setting up ORE is to enable R script to run off data in an Oracle database directly and return the outputs there. If accomplished, this allows for fresh data inserted to be processed by the same script and results made available for querying. All these bypass the traditional need to manually extract data to an independent piece of software for analysis and modeling and insert outputs into a database manually again. Concept to deployment is completed within the same environment at almost not additional material cost.

Chapter 5

Data Audit

Data are at the heart of analytics and models. The most advanced software cannot compensate for data deficient in critical aspects. The implications of data issues may not be apparent. For academic research purposes, they can be overlooked with little cost, but if million or even billion-dollar decisions are made based on the results generated, the gravity is of a different order. These deficiencies discussed here are based on actual work on real data. Before any risk analytics or modeling is carried out, data audit is a necessity to ensure that any results obtained are reliable.

5.1. Missing

Data completeness is almost never possible in a real-world situation. Even system-generated data can be missing for unknown reasons. Given its pervasiveness, data inadequacy is taken for granted and seldom regarded as a serious issue. A convenient treatment is to drop the variable or factor from analysis or modeling. This is, however, a luxury when there are few variables in the dataset to begin with.

While inadequacy itself is unlikely to produce misleading results, one popular treatment may. Some statistical softwares offer automatic value substitution for missing values. The substitute can be a choice of the mode, mean, median or any chosen value. On the surface, this appears a reasonable way of dealing with the matter. For some variables, it can produce misleading inferences.

For a variable with binary values, the mode is the value with more observations. Gender is either Male or Female. If the dataset has 30% of values missing and a distribution of 51% Male and 49% Female, it means that it contains 35.7% Males and 34.3% Females. The Male to Female ratio remains unchanged at 1.04:1.00. If value substitution is applied, Male is the mode and whatever is missing will be assigned that value. This distorts the distribution severely to 65.7% Male and 34.3% Female or a ratio of 1.92:1.00.

The ORE script to determine completeness of the entire dataset is as follows:

```
begin
-- sys.rqScriptDrop('Analytics') May need this line to drop script if it is
not automatically overwritten;
sys.rqScriptCreate('Analytics',
'function() {
library(ROracle)
drv <- dbDriver("Oracle")
con <- dbConnect(drv, username="rquser", password="password",
dbname="ORCLPDB", prefetch=FALSE, external_credentials=FALSE)
df <- dbReadTable(con, "DT", schema="RQUSER")

# Percentage of completeness for dataset derived using complete.cases
function
complete_df <- data.frame(nrow(df [complete.cases(df), ]) / nrow(df))
}',
v_overwrite => TRUE);
end;
/
select * from table(rqEval(NULL, 'select 1 complete_df from dual',
'Analytics'));
```

where DT is the database data table which is read into the R data frame df. The script divides the number of rows where data is complete by the total number of rows in the dataset. The result will be a figure from 0 to 1 inclusive.

The script can be modified to compute the completeness for a specific column or variable. The ORE script is as follows:

```
begin
sys.rqScriptCreate('Analytics',
```

```
'function() {
library(ROracle)
drv <- dbDriver("Oracle")
con <- dbConnect(drv, username="rquser", password="password",
dbname="ORCLPDB", prefetch=FALSE, external_credentials=FALSE)
df <- dbReadTable(con, "DT", schema="RQUSER")
v <- data.frame(df[, c(3, 3)])

# Completeness derived for specific column/variable v
complete_v <- data.frame(nrow(v[complete.cases(v), ]) / nrow(v))
}',
v_overwrite => TRUE);
end;
/
select * from table(rqEval(NULL, 'select 1 complete_v from dual',
'Analytics'));
```

The column or variable v is in the third column of DT so df now contains only this column of data.

There are different techniques to impute values for what are missing and most of these are based on fairly strong assumptions. They can help make modeling viable, but the results may turn out misleading even without the users being aware of the cause.

There is no theoretical threshold for the minimum level of data adequacy required. Intuitively, a less than 50% availability naturally invites the question of reliability. More than half of the sample being unknown means that the missing value(s) can dominate the results. This is the case with nonparametric methods like Decision Tree where the NULL can be a significant predictor. The problem is not knowing what this NULL stands for.

5.2. Invalid

Outright invalid data values can corrupt an analysis or model.

In one piece of empirical research on how the daily returns on the NYSE interact with returns on the NASDAQ, the initial correlation results were significantly negative. This is counterintuitive and nearly impossible. The thousands of observations were scrutinized and eventually, one was found to have a negative value greater than 10,000. This is clearly invalid. After this datum was removed, the correlation was significantly positive. One invalid value in thousands can reverse a correlation.

While obvious in most cases, invalid values may need domain knowledge and understanding to detect. In a specific Asian country, several firms reported zero Current Liabilities in their audited financial statements. These are medium-sized going concerns with active transactions. Having all transactions in cash is highly unlikely. Zero Current Liabilities by itself is not a major concern, but the Current Ratio which is Current Assets divided by Current Liabilities becomes infeasible. According to accounting standards, any debt due within the year should be treated as a current liability. It is nearly impossible for a going concern not to have some of such on the books on the financial year closing date. Wages, trade credit, etc. are unlikely to be all settled at once if the firm has been operating for years and continues to do so. In all likelihood, the zero Current Liabilities is almost certainly a failure to keep proper accounts.

Invalid values are numerical, so the ORE script to derive the fraction of invalid values is as follows:

```
begin
sys.rqScriptCreate('Analytics',
'function() {
library(ROracle)
drv <- dbDriver("Oracle")
con <- dbConnect(drv, username="rquser", password="password",
dbname="ORCLPDB", prefetch=FALSE, external_credentials=FALSE)
df <- dbReadTable(con, "DT", schema="RQUSER")

# Invalid defined as value of column v equal or less than K
invalid <- data.frame(NROW(subset(df, v <= K)) / nrow(df))
}',
v_overwrite => TRUE);
end;
/
select * from table(rqEval(NULL, 'select 1 invalid from dual', 'Analytics'));
```

where K is the threshold value for being invalid. It is essential to note that R comprises nrow, ncol, NROW and NCOL functions. The uppercase ones are necessary for vectors (single row or column), while the lowercase functions are used for arrays.

The range of invalid values is impossible to predetermine. Following are some common ones for both corporate and personal entities that can be useful references.

Possible corporate (going concern) invalid data values

Zero current assets
Zero current liabilities
Negative gross assets
Negative gross cash

Possible personal invalid data values

Age greater than reported highest
Negative age

5.3. Unreliable

Detecting unreliable data values is challenging but remains a necessity. Unlike invalid values that are obviously impossible, unreliable ones are plausible but highly improbable. There are broadly two types of unreliability: one is cross-sectional and the other time-series.

According to the Income Tax authority in a specific country, there are around Q individuals reporting earned income of one million dollars or more, Q being less than 100. In one of the local bank's credit card database, there were almost five times as many unique individuals with more than one million dollars of income. It is certainly possible that individuals have unreported earned income to the tax authority, but a 400% difference is highly questionable. A credit model with personal income as a predictor would probably have misled the bank in the credit approval process. Dogged investigation eventually found that the error was caused by a mixing of currencies in the database. That does not pose a legal or operational problem to the IT unit but can be catastrophic for modeling. With the cause eliminated, the number of million-dollar income cases became considerably smaller than the national statistic. The incomes were not obviously invalid and a mechanical modeling process would not have spotted the issue. Detecting such unreliable values requires an understanding of the business concerned just as the first step of the CRISP-DM process advocated.

Corporate financial data and ratios are prone to manipulation and hence unreliable values. It is said of a particular Asian country that none of the public financial reports are reliable. One way to detect cross-sectional reliability is to identify outliers. Any firm reporting a 1,000% equity growth over a year is suspect unless that is from a base close to zero. In conventional Statistics, values outside of three standard deviations are safely considered outliers. This may not be suitable for financial ratios as most of them are severely skewed. This poses a challenge, especially for Classical Statistic methods like Ordinary Least Squares where outliers can dominate the model.

The number of standard deviations to use as threshold to detect outliers is dependent on the financial ratio and even the industry analyzed. Return on Equity is much more skewed than Return on Asset holding other variables constant. If K is the chosen threshold of absolute number of standard deviations the ORE script to identify outliers is as follows:

```
begin
sys.rqScriptCreate('Analytics',
'function() {
library(ROracle)
drv <- dbDriver("Oracle")
con <- dbConnect(drv, username="rquser", password="password",
dbname="ORCLPDB", prefetch=FALSE, external_credentials=FALSE)
df <- dbReadTable(con, "DT", schema="RQUSER")
unreliable <- data.frame(NROW(subset(df, v >= K*abs(sd(df$v)))) /
nrow(df))
}',
v_overwrite => TRUE);
end;
/
select * from table(rqEval(NULL, 'select 1 unreliable from dual',
'Analytics'));
```

Identifying outliers across time employs the same script except that the values for v must be based on dates. This is elaborated on under the section of inconsistent values.

5.4. Outdated

Whether a value is outdated depends on the data collection interval. If financial ratios are derived annually, data that are nine months old may still be the most current available. On the other hand, the same vintage will be extremely outdated for daily transacted prices. Outdatedness, however, is obvious if the data are dated. In case of time-series analysis, historical values are needed, so they are not outdated in the sense of not being current. There is then a need to check if a historical value itself is outdated.

One easy way to detect an outdated value is to compare it with the previous one. In one country, it is not uncommon for small firms to submit the same set of financial statements for several years before updating them and all these are audited by qualified professionals.

In ORE, the creation of lagged values requires more coding than the earlier tests. Packages created have simplified the process. These include data.table, plyr, plm and dplyr. Note that ORE has its customized version of dplyr named OREdplyr.

First, a lag function must be defined as follows:

```
lg <- function(x)c(NA, x[1:(length(x)-1)])
```

For instance, financial statement data are grouped by firm names or IDs for consistent lagged value creation. The ORE script to derive the percentage of outdated values is as follows:

```
begin
sys.rqScriptCreate('Analytics',
'function() {
library(ROracle)
library(OREdplyr)
drv <- dbDriver("Oracle")
con <- dbConnect(drv, username="rquser", password="password",
dbname="ORCLPDB", prefetch=FALSE, external_credentials=FALSE)

# Create a lag function lg
lg <- function(x)c(NA, x[1:(length(x)-1)])
df <- dbReadTable(con, "DT", schema="RQUSER")

# Sort by chronology column v2 and grouping column v1
df <- arrange(df, v1, v2)
```

```
# Define lag lv3 as lag of v3
df[, lv3 := lg(v3)]

# Define outdated as identical current and lag values
outdated <- data.frame(NROW(subset(df, v3 == lv3)) / nrow(df))
}',
v_overwrite => TRUE);
end;
/
select * from table(rqEval(NULL, 'select 1 outdated from dual', 'Analytics'));
```

where v1 may be the firm name or ID, v2 the year of a financial statement and v3 the variable of analysis such as total assets. It is likely that outdatedness has to be evidenced by unchanged values for many variables, such as total assets, sales, and current liabilities, so a joint test of v4, v5, etc. is necessary. An alternative routine is to create an explicit loop where each row value is compared to the previous one to see if they are identical.

5.5. Inconsistent

This is perhaps the most challenging deficiency. Some data values invite suspicion even if each is valid. When analyzed over a window period, a pattern emerges that makes the time series questionable. For instance, the turnover in a firm may be fairly stable over a decade. In one year, the figure is 10,000 times as much and then falls to the long-term trend thereafter. It is highly likely that the turnover spike is an error.

Identifying inconsistencies is possible only with an understanding of domain where the data are produced from. Even among corporate financial statements, what is inconsistent in one industry may be normal in another. In a feast or famine business, highly volatile turnover may be the norm rather than the exception. Usually, it is an extreme outlier that can drastically alter a Classical Statistic estimate. An inconsistent value does not create serious problems for modeling and analytics.

What is considered inconsistent can be identified using any of the preceding R scripts adjusted for the criterion chosen.

5.6. Data Audit Report

Using R to generate results is insufficient for industry use regardless of its academic value. Most decision-makers do not read codes and want insights that can be easily digested. A data audit report that is simple meets such a need. Such a report can be manually generated by piecing the different diagnostics explained above. Doing so could be quick and easy but misses the value of creating a knowledge base that future analysts can build on and learn from.

It is advocated here that any results generated should be stored in a database for analytics. To do that, the outputs in R have to be written back to Oracle. Assume that we want to write the preceding results into an Oracle table named DATA-AUDIT which is separately created using SQL if it is not already existing. The R script to accomplish that is as follows:

```
begin
sys.rqScriptCreate('Analytics',
'function() {
library(ROracle)
library(data.table)
drv <- dbDriver("Oracle")
con <- dbConnect(drv, username="rquser", password="password",
dbname="ORCLPDB", prefetch=FALSE, external_credentials=FALSE)
lg <- function(x)c(NA, x[1:(length(x)-1)])
df <- dbReadTable(con, "DT", schema="RQUSER")

# Creating all problem data tables
complete <- data.frame(nrow(df[complete.cases(df), ]) / nrow(df))
invalid <- data.frame(NROW(subset(df, v1 <= 0)) / nrow(df))
unreliable <- data.frame(NROW(subset(df, v1 >= 4*abs(sd(df$v1)))) /
nrow(df))
dt <- data.table(df)
dt[, lv1 := lg(v1), by = c("v2")]
outdated <- data.frame(NROW(subset(dt, v1 == lv1)) / nrow(dt))

# Merged the data frames using cbind function
dataaudit <- cbind(complete, invalid, unreliable, outdated)
}',
```

```
v_overwrite => TRUE);
end;
/
```

```
* Create DATAAUDIT table in Oracle and insert results derived
create table dataaudit (complete number, invalid number, unreliable
number, outdated number)
insert into dataaudit (complete, invalid, unreliable, outdated)
select * from table(rqEval(NULL, 'select complete, invalid, unreliable,
outdated from dual', 'Analytics'));
```

The function cbind merges the four data frames by column.

5.7. Treatments for Problematic Data Values

The easiest way to deal with problematic data is to remove them. For risk analytics and modeling, that approach can be costly as such values combined can account for more than 50% of all available. As internal data are precious little, to begin with, discarding should be the last resort. There are several ways to treat data as part of the data preparation step. Though none is ideal, each is worth exploring. One way to evaluate the reasonableness of a treatment is to rerun a model to assess for any significant change.

The first and simplest is correction. Since a negative gross total asset value is invalid, changing the sign is easy. This way is especially pertinent to debt which may be recorded as a negative value in a financial statement. The second is substitution with derivation. As discussed earlier, a zero current liabilities value for a going concern cannot be valid unless it is an exceptional case. Simply imputing a replacement amounts to guesswork. A more reasonable approach is to estimate current liabilities from the rest of the balance sheet items. Since liabilities are assets less equity, what is not of long-term nature can be assumed to be current.

A third way is substitution by interpolation. This is especially useful for time-series data which is erroneous due to entry error. If equity for a particular year is unreasonably large, it can be replaced by an interpolation of the year before and the year after.

The fourth uses inference. If the gender value is invalid, other demographics may provide insights to the correct value.

As part of good governance, it is important to document all the treatment approaches used. Risk models have to be updated regularly and results can vary significantly simply due to a change in this aspect.

Chapter 6

Data Warehousing

It is almost impossible to support analytics directly from operational or legacy systems. Organizations that have tried quickly face issues too challenging even for professional IT service providers. There is increasing recognition of this matter, but data warehousing remains a hit and miss undertaking in most places.

The criticality of data warehousing has been recognized by the creation of cloud-based data warehouses. That is a boon to many types of industries, but for banks, it may not make a material difference. In most regulatory regimes, banks are required to keep data within their own premises. Even data centers are disallowed except for archived data. Creating a fully owned and controlled data warehouse is not an option.

In one bank, around $30m was spent on developing a data warehouse by the IT associate company over 5 years. When the project was completed, not a single piece of datum could be extracted and used for analysis. The bank CEO ordered that this blunder be kept a secret to avoid embarrassment. In reality, such outcomes are fairly common. Knowing the difference between operational and analytical data can help reduce the frustrations often encountered.

6.1. Legacy System Data

Operational systems also known as legacy systems are created for transactions. For that reason, the data captured and stored are usually not catered to analysis. That is perfectly acceptable to users of these data such as business or operational unit staff. For a salesperson, a wrong postal code is

69

immaterial as long as the sale goes through. Experience shows that there are preferences that make legacy system data challenging for analytics.

6.1.1. *Overwrite mode*

To save storage space, nearly all legacy data are kept in overwrite mode. If a bank exposure has been cured after a default, the past status of being a defaulter would be overwritten. For legal and operational reasons, the default is history and no longer relevant and that has absolutely no impact on credit operations. If one credit risk modeler extracts the legacy system data, there will be no indication that the obligor once defaulted. The credit risk model is likely to be deficient since parameters predicting a default have been associated with the opposite outcome (since default is not instantaneous, parameter values would lead and not be contemporaneous with the state of default).

One of the most important aspects of data warehousing is the retention of historical values. In many types of analytics, examining a time series provides insights that are not available with cross-sectional data. This is especially in the area of risk and return. Many models look at unexpected variations or shocks rather than absolute changes or levels to understand what moves a target metric. An unexpected change is a significant deviation from the expected one. The expected change itself requires historical data to model movements over time. Analytics is essentially detecting meaningful patterns and modeling the development of profiles for insights. Both are dependent on a trail of evidence cumulated over time. Overwriting destroys the trail.

Since all operational data have to originate from legacy systems, they have to be captured and stored at regular intervals to create the time series needed. This is where data warehousing requires knowledge and inputs by consumers of analytics as only they know the more suitable intervals for each type of data.

6.1.2. *Record removal*

Records that are no longer of use are deadweights in a legacy system. Where the average useful duration of a record is several years at most, disciplined housekeeping to remove outdated records is needed. Though the storage cost per terabyte has been declining over the years, legacy systems designed decades ago continue to be used as system migration can be risky. Automated record removal remains. In one bank, the address of former credit card customers were deleted to prevent mail from being erroneously sent to them.

Historical data is essential for analytics regardless of operational usefulness. In fact, some models cannot be developed without those very data that are no longer in use. If one is modeling bankruptcies, data of bankrupt firms are needed. An insurance firm wanting to predict mortality must have data on deceased clients. Only data warehousing designed to retain operationally defunct data can meet the needs of many types of analytics.

6.1.3. *Legal priority*

Compliance with legal and regulatory requirements is a top priority in operations. All other concerns are at a distant second. Capturing data in a way that is analyzable is rarely considered.

Banks, for instance, often grant credit with collateral. Worldwide, the largest segment of credit is residential real estate. With few exceptions, a loan to a homebuyer or investor requires the title deed to the property be held by the bank. From a legal perspective, the key concern is the correct recording of the title. In whatever language, a title deed does not offer any analytical value other than the worth of the property itself. There is almost no way to tell if a house is terraced, semi-detached or standalone. Similarly, an apartment can be a high-rise, a walk-up, a flat or a condominium. If the bank wishes to use a suitable property index to mark the collaterals to market, it is either impossible or takes a great deal of manual labor to categorize the properties into appropriate types. However, that is of no concern to the residential mortgage unit as marking to market adds zero value to the operations.

Most legal data are in free text form. To turn them into analyzable data in the mart, a mapping process has to be created. It is not uncommon that those responsible for analytics to simply give up trying as that takes too much time and effort.

6.1.4. *Data type*

Even where the data value is numeric and should be easily processible, data type differs across legacy systems. This is perhaps no more evident than in CustomerID or UID. Every legacy system has been designed for the operational requirements of a specific product or service. Even where there is a concerted effort to assign a single value to the UID, the data type in a system can alter the format. In one bank, for instance, the UID in one product system is 1234567 while it is stored as 00001234567 in another system. It is easy to see that they both should represent the same UID, but when processed in analytics, the two values may be treated as different.

Like for legal data, there is a need for a mapping process to ensure that analyzable data in a data mart are consistent.

6.2. Enterprise Data Warehouse vs Specialized Data Mart

By now, it is recognized that data warehousing is not an option for analytics. Many organizations have, however, attempted it with limited success. A common failure lies in trying to create an enterprise data warehouse from scratch instead of developing specialized data marts one at a time. From a technical perspective, creating an enterprise-level data warehouse is akin to building an entire city on an empty piece of land as a single project. The challenges to do that are not hard to imagine. For the sake of producing usable analytics, it is worthwhile to understand the issues that confront enterprise data warehousing.

6.2.1. *Data stewardship*

This topic has been discussed earlier. In a large reputable Asian bank, the new CEO who had training as a programmer decided to stop all IT purchases until he can be shown what information needed cannot be generated from the data and software existent in the bank. Unsurprisingly, that instruction was never carried out except on paper.

Outdated data is not a concern for operations. They are for analytics. No decision-maker would accept outdated values for risk measurement. Without data stewardship, nobody looks into updating.

Stewardship is far more viable when the users of data have control over them. A data warehouse suffers the same problem as an enterprise operational database. Everyone wants to use the data, but no one wants to maintain them.

6.2.2. *Access and security*

Even where stewardship has been carefully established, implementing it on a data warehouse is not easy. There is the matter of security. A data warehouse is likely to be under central administration and IT would probably be made the gatekeeper. User departments need proper authorization for access. Managing that aspect is usually not an IT unit's priority. Besides, IT is far more concerned about data corruption than outdatedness. It is a widespread experience that users can only get data extracted by IT and do not have the right to push data into storage.

Access is much more possible if a data mart is under the control of the user department. Technical advice can be provided by IT, but only the users really know what the value of data is. When access is cumbersome, users are likely to start creating their own repositories which well-planned data marts could have become.

6.2.3. *Update frequency*

For efficiency, data update is likely to be carried out at the same interval. However, data do not get outdated at the same rate. Profile data like company ownership structure do not change often. An annual update would suffice unless there is an exception. Others like Accounts Payable do not remain the same every month. What is three months old can be very misleading.

If a data warehouse were overseen by the IT unit, update will probably be at a fixed interval for all data types if that is even carried out. Users are in the best position to know how frequently each kind of data should be updated. In any case, a failure to update will impact them more than anyone else, so there is vested interest in this mundane task.

6.2.4. *Designed to fail*

An enterprise-level data warehouse success story probably does not exist, at least not for financial institutions. A global bank was the pioneer and poster child of data warehousing when the concept was first embraced. Data warehouse vendors often cite the significant insights that this bank attained due to the ability to analyze, drill down plus slice and dice data for strategic decisions. Decades later, the Chief Information Officer who oversaw the implementation unofficially admitted that the project was a complete failure and the warehouse scrapped not long after the initial buzz. With another large Asian bank, the data warehouse was so despised that it was named the rubbish dump by the staff. And the story is the same for a second large Asian bank where the new Chief Risk Officer bypassed the data warehouse and IT unit altogether and created his own data mart using his ERM budget.

It is essential to distinguish between data warehousing and data warehouse. The former is a process that is necessary for analytics and modeling. The latter is the use of a single enterprise-level repository to store data, a design quite certain to fail. Data marts tailored to the needs of specific users is the only approach that can achieve the goal of data warehousing.

6.3. Extraction, Transfer, Load (ETL)

Extraction, Transfer, Load (ETL) is an integral part of data warehousing. Legacy system data have to be extracted, cleansed and transferred to the data warehouse or mart. In many organizations, this is deemed an IT concern. Like all aspects of generating analytical data, the failure to engage users in designing is almost certain to result in fatal failure. The outcome is a warehouse that is a data dump that no one touches. In a large bank made reference site for a multimillion-dollar data warehousing software, the warehouse was full of garbage with the bank's staff being totally unaware. In fact, users were repeatedly assured by IT that all data have been cleansed over a two-year period. After being unused for a while, this warehouse was replaced by another branded software. The outcome, however, remains unchanged. A simple post-mortem reveals that nobody took ownership of the ETL design. The software was acquired with the IT department's budget with no user involvement in the installation. The IT staff responsible for error filtering admitted that the function was never activated as users were not asked and did not volunteer any rules. The following are some lessons that can be applied.

6.3.1. *Data cleansing*

Operational data are usually full of errors. This is not of concern to those using them as relevance of most data is only for the transaction period of a day or more. To be of use for analytics, they must be cleansed and this is only done during the ETL process. The challenge here is setting the right cleansing rules. An individual of more than 200 years old is obviously erroneous, but what is the threshold age to determine if a person is too old or too young to be a customer of the organization? Setting such rules require the collaboration of many different types of actual and potential users. With rare exceptions, forming a working group to carry out the task is near impossible in many places. If all data could be cleansed before being warehoused, there is no need for data audit except for missing and outdated values.

Even where cleansing rules have been set, coding them in the ETL tool can be fraught with problems. Users, if involved, only know what they want and are seldom able to express those in technical terms. For instance, independent customer age cannot be less than 16 if that is the minimum age allowed by the authorities. However, it is not uncommon for programmers to have no interest in the logic and meaning of the rules. Whether greater or less than a threshold means error is of no concern to them and a "<" instead of ">" in the code makes no difference as long as the routine executes. The filtering rule should rightly have been "age ≥ 16" for the value to be accepted, but the opposite "age < 16" makes no difference technically to a programmer. Unless those who set the rules know how to read codes, cleansing process can turn into a garbage collection exercise.

As error filtering is usually coded with SQL, it is useful for analytics professionals to have some basic understanding of this language. They need not be programming the ETL process but can verify the SQL codes against the logic of the rules to ensure that they are consistent. A simple example is shown in Table 6.1.

Table 6.1   Examples of error-filtering rule.

Rules to filter out data values with errors	
Logic	SQL code
Personal age must be no less than 16 years old	SELECT age from database where age ≥ 16
Personal income cannot be negative	SELECT PersonalIncome from database PersonalIncome ≥ 0
Current assets must be greater than zero	SELECT CurrentAssets from database where CurrentAssets > 0

6.3.2. *Mappings*

Many types of operational data are not in readily analyzable format. Occupation, for instance, is often in free text form. Even with those in structured numeric format, that may not be consistent with what has been designed in the data mart. The CustomerID, for example, has been formatted as a seven-digit field but is captured as 0001234567 in one legacy system. The leading zeros have to be stripped before the CustomerID for this system to be warehoused.

The need for user involvement here is perhaps most significant. Nobody else in an organization will be more knowledgeable about the values best suited for analysis. Mappings are not static and can change due to external conditions. Take the variable Industry, for instance. In the past, a specific industry, say Quarrying may be a significant part of the economy. As remaining resources become uneconomical to extract, the industry may be reduced to a heritage status with only several small firms operating till they have no reason to. For the purpose of risk analytics, merging Quarrying with the closest industry possible like Mining, for example, may increase the power of prediction as it reduces the unnecessary fragmentation of observations across industries. Users of the warehoused data should monitor this aspect to maintain relevance.

A helpful consideration for mappings is likely integration of external data, especially indices. The first reason for that is the possible need for marking to market values. As mentioned before, collaterals must be updated at least annually to recalibrate the net exposure that a credit position is exposed to. Professional valuations are too costly for assets like property. A reasonable approach is to update using appropriate indices. If mappings have been designed with the specifications of external indices in mind, integrating external data into internal ones using the Primary Key (PK) and Foreign Key (FK) method which has been described significantly, reduces time and effort. As it is an annual exercise, efforts made in this consideration is definitely a worthwhile investment.

Another reason for taking account of external data is empirical research. Operational loss analytics is pertinent here. To facilitate comparisons consistently, Basel II has carefully formulated a structure for capturing operational loss events and data. An event should be recorded according to a three-level definition. The top two are prespecified and common across all Basel II compliant regimes. The lowest level is left to a bank's discretion. As known in the banking industry, operational loss data are sparse. It is recommended that external data be used as reference. One such source is insurance compensations. For this to be possible, there must be a mapping of internal loss events to external definitions. Only then can a bank's own losses for a specific event be compared with those from the insurance industry.

6.3.3. *Rejected records*

Cleansing will result in records being tagged as erroneous. A critical issue is what should be done with these records though it is obvious that they should be fixed and returned to the ETL process, at least in theory.

The practical considerations for dealing with rejected data are far greater than most will realize. First is where to store such records. This is relatively easy to resolve with one or more tables set aside in the data mart for such data. Second is who will be responsible for making corrections. This aspect is so challenging that a separate section is devoted to its discussion. Third is how will cleansed data be reintroduced into the data mart. Do they have to go through the ETL process just like the first pass or can they be inserted directly? If the former, have the ETL codes been appropriately customized to pick up such data together with the regular operational ones? If the latter, who is to ensure that the data have been properly corrected?

The above are practical issues that seldom attract any attention and effort from stakeholders. As usual, IT has little interest in the matter. Users, other the other hand, have vested interest to see this done correctly but are often not technically competent to know what needs to be done.

There is no one theoretically or conceptually correct approach to dealing with this issue. A disciplined process helps, however. One way is to set aside a designated time to reinsert rejected records that have been corrected. If the time interval is short like a day or a week, a problem with the timestamp is unlikely. If it is longer, thought should be given to this value.

In most databases, a timestamp is automatically created when a record is captured. This value is often also regarded as when an event or transaction occurred. For much of banking business, time precision is unimportant, but for payment delinquency, it can have material implications. Once delinquency or commonly termed Days Past Due (DPD) reaches 90, an obligor is considered to be in default. DPD of less than 90 but more than

60 is not uncommon. Consider the possibility that a 70 DPD payment was made but the record was rejected due to some data-entry error. It was corrected and then inserted into the data mart after 30 days. Using the computer-generated timestamp, the payment would have occurred 100 DPD which requires the obligor to be categorized as a defaulter. This result impacts on the modeling of credit risk in time to come. In the light of this possibility, it may be necessary to create a separate DateTime field to correctly capture when an event or transaction occurred.

6.3.4. *Corrections*

If erroneous data are valuable enough to be salvaged, they have to be corrected and re-inserted into the data mart. This is easier said than done.

For a start, who should make the correction is an immediate challenge. It is a rather mundane task and almost inevitably left to clerical staff. Some filtering rules may be established for automated corrections, but even these cannot be applied indiscriminately. If the date of birth has been wrongly entered as 28 May 1800, what should the correct value be? A senior staff does not necessarily know the answer, but a junior one will probably have little interest to get it right.

Many errors cannot be predicted and so corrections have to be based on a good understanding of the domain and experience. For instance, a tuition agency hiring tutors may require a minimum level of educational qualification. An entry like HS (probably High School) or Sec (for Secondary) is likely to be incorrect, but that needs someone knowledgeable about the tuition business to know.

Aside from the competency of the one making corrections, there is the matter of what the "right" data value should be. Even if the educational qualification entered is clearly inadequate for tuition work, there is a whole range of values that are valid. The saying "the cure may be worse than the disease" can apply here.

When corrections must be made is another issue. Ideally, errors should be fixed within the same day, but here again, creating analytical data is not mission critical. Without a policy, it is near certain that the errors will never be corrected and those data ignored. Timing of corrections goes beyond whether the task is carried out. In some records, there is a DateTime stamp that records when the data are captured. This issue has been discussed in some detail earlier.

Chapter 7

Analytical Data Sphere

From years of consulting for and developing analytical solutions, I have come to realize that one of the biggest challenges in this area is the inability to distinguish analytical data from operational ones. From a metaphysical perspective, data are just data. There is no reason why analysis cannot be made of data that are available. It is unsurprising then that many decision-makers are frustrated in not having good insights to guide them and blame all responsible for data for their incompetence. At this juncture of the book, it is clear that not all data are alike. With every organization attempting to leverage on their data assets, I have always advised the need to create an analytical data sphere. What follows are some features that can help guide this attempt.

The ideal analytical sphere would be one that is designed with the purpose to serve as the knowledge, research and analysis hub for the organization. This is tall order but given the increasingly competitive edge provided by good analytics, it is no longer a luxury. A simple conceptual design that I have proposed to clients is shown as follows.

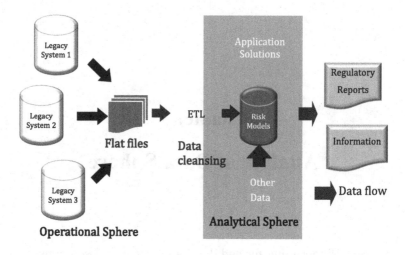

There must be a clear divide between the operational and analytical spheres. Attempting to layer analysis directly on top of legacy systems by adding data tables, etc. is almost futile. Those who have worked with IT units of any structured organization would know how jealously the systems are guarded from interference. Even a simple request for data can mean seeking proper authorization and filling in of forms specifying which field and for what period. The most practical way is what data warehousing has been about, i.e. extracting data as flat files, transferring them to a staging area and loading them into a cleansing process before storage.

Analytics would be a dream if data warehousing is properly implemented. Sadly, this is an ideal that is unlikely to have ever been achieved. The former CIO of a global bank that was a data warehousing pioneer told me personally that after several decades, the entire warehouse was scrapped. While the creation of a single data warehouse is almost met with failure, the assembly of focused data marts has seen much better success.

The analytical sphere is where models can be developed and stored. It is also where other data like external indicators can be integrated with those that have undergone the ETL process. Results from analytics can remain here and if combined with policies, user guides, research findings, etc., this virtual space can serve as the knowledge base of the organization. It will be the go-to location for answers and data that can be sliced, diced and input into models for decision-support.

The creation of an analytical sphere remains an aspiration in most organizations. While some of the requirements are understood in theory, the nuances are often lost to those responsible for the design. Misses are much more pervasive than hits. What follows are some of the considerations gleaned from decades of consultancy and also direct involvement in helping clients with the endeavor. They may not be comprehensive but are sufficient to guide efforts in the same direction.

7.1. Archive, Not Overwrite

Legacy systems can live with data overwrites and actually prefer that to save storage space. A customer's address is immediately replaced by the most current one with nearly zero tracking implications. Historical values are almost irrelevant and a deadweight. Once a piece of datum is overwritten, it is lost unless a costly forensic recovery is attempted. Operational staff are largely unconcerned.

Many data warehouses or marts are simply near facsimiles of the legacy systems. Whatever is overwritten is also lost. Addresses are not of great value, but data like historical credit ratings are. Banks have to derive a credit migration matrix as part of the Basel II regulatory requirements. This matrix tracks the change in ratings usually over one year as part of broader credit risk management. If past ratings are overwritten, there is no way to compute such statistics.

Time-series analysis is essential for projections. Without archived historical values, it is almost impossible for an organization to try to predict where it is heading to. Modifying legacy systems to accommodate that is near infeasible as vendors would not tolerate any corruption of what they have installed. The only way to retain historical data is in the analytical sphere created to allow for that. To have time-series data, however, a Date or DateTime column has to be created. This seems a trivial requirement except to those who understand database and data tables. In the legacy system, a CustomerID can be the Primary Key which has to be unique for a Customer data table. When warehoused and cumulated over time with a DateTime column to capture the chronology, CustomerID can no longer be unique as it will recur. That means it can no longer be the Primary Key and has to be replaced by another that remains unique over time. This is just one of the many considerations in designing the analytical sphere. It is also the reason why efforts toward that end often fail because users who desire the data seldom understand the technical constraints while IT does not have the business understanding to anticipate the issues.

Archiving also means an exponential increase in storage space over that used for the legacy system feeding the data. Although cost per gigabyte continues to drop, there is still a need to plan for sufficient space. Since analytical data are not mission-critical or constrained by the same level of regulatory restrictions on off-site storage for operational data, the cloud may be a suitable option.

7.2. Dropdown List, Not Free Text

With the move to digital forms, it is now possible to enforce the input data type. One major bank seized the opportunity to use dropdown list selections for the Income field of personal credit applicants. Interestingly, this was done during the leadership of an analytics-savvy CEO who was demanding analyzable data to be captured. After his regime, this bank reverted to free text for convenience. This is a good case study of how difficult it is for the analytics mindset to take root in an organization. One generation of staff may have bought in to the value of carefully designed data type, but the next cannot be bothered as they are not the immediate beneficiaries.

Numeric data values like Income can still be processed, but text values like Occupation or Industry are almost useless for Classical Statistics methods. In one bank that I consulted for, there were thousands of free text occupations stored in the data warehouse which is simply populated with legacy system data. Many were gibberish.

Dropdown lists ensure that only valid values are captured without errors. The downside is the restriction in the range, so an entirely new category has to be forced into existing ones unless the list is updated. A disciplined process of regular review goes a long way to ensure that the list is always relevant.

Even where the data type from the legacy system is not a dropdown list, it is helpful to make that the default option in warehoused data.

As mentioned before, it is worthwhile to design the dropdown list categories with external references in mind for easier mapping. Industry is one field where the benefit of doing so is almost immediate. Credit portfolio diversification requires analyzing the default correlations between industries and such data have to be obtained from external sources like the country's commerce ministry. If a bank's own industry categories are aligned with those already used, the correlations can be easily applied. Otherwise, much effort has to be made adjusting internal categories to external ones. This consideration is relevant to practically all categorical values where there are external references.

7.3. Meaningful Categories

A dropdown list alone is not sufficient to support effective analytics. Two common deficiencies occur. One is the inclusion of the category "Others". It is near guaranteed that if Others is available on the dropdown list, it will become the mode, i.e. with the most entries. In fact, "Others" can even have more counts than all the other categories combined.

The problem with Others is that it has no intrinsic meaning. What does Others for Occupation or Industry mean? If this value turns out to be a strong predictor in nonparametric models like Decision Tree, how does one use the results to predict? When helping a client bank create, a dropdown list to replace its free text Industry field, I forbid the staff from including "Others". Unsurprisingly, this met with vocal objections as it makes data entry much more demanding when meaningful choices have to be made.

The other deficiency with dropdown list is a reliance on external prescriptions. This may sound contradictory to the earlier suggestion that categories should be designed with external references in mind. Here, it is about employing such references without consideration for their practical use.

In most countries, firms must be registered with a Securities Industry Code (SIC). The SIC can run into a thousand numbers to accommodate all kinds of businesses. Since the SIC is closely tied to industries, it can be easily used as a substitute when inputting applicant data.

The SIC itself is not an issue and has been used extensively for finance research, especially in the USA. It is how firms in a specific country choose to register that can pose a challenge.

In one specific country, 70% of firms choose the SIC for Wholesale and Trading regardless of the nature of business. For that country's Department of Commerce, the SIC selected is inconsequential unless analytics is carried out within. When attempting to develop a corporate credit risk model, I found it near impossible to include Industry using the SIC as a factor since what has been captured do not have any meaningful economic implications. A supermarket is registered as Wholesale and Trading and so is a data center or acupuncture service.

Anyone designing a dropdown list has to take into consideration the business culture. The best list may be rendered useless by choices already made in another domain just as in the case of the SIC. No single list is ideal for all environments but a simple principle helps in choosing the categories and that is no category should have too few or too many observations. If there are 10 categories, the average for each one is 10%. Using a 50% variation margin, the minimum is 5% and the maximum 15% of all data. A check against the values in the legacy system will be useful to determine the final categories in the dropdown list.

7.4. Optimal Number of Categories

Dropdown lists should be designed with modeling in mind. In Statistics, there is the matter of power of a predictor. Power resides in the ability to discriminate. If Gender is a good predictor, there would be a statistically significant difference in outcomes for Male and Female.

Power is very much dependent on the distribution of predictor values. Too few or too many values dilute power. Industry is a good factor for discussion. If all firms are categorized into either Manufacturing or Services, developing a good model is a challenge. Many firms in Services have to manufacture specialized components needed. A dental implant specialist, for instance, may have to custom build the parts. It is then not an entirely Services firm. If the model is meant to predict workplace safety, the results may not be as significant as expected since there are too few categories to capture the intrinsic drivers of the target outcome.

Too many predictor values create a similar problem. If there are a thousand values for Industry, many within the same business sector may share the same predictive properties. If Manufacturing were divided into Light Manufacturing, Clean Manufacturing, Heavy Equipment Manufacturing, etc., there may be little separating Light and Clean Manufacturing as far as workplace safety is concerned.

There is no magic number of categories. The aim is not to underfit (too few) or overfit (too many). If the sample size for modeling is large, more categories can be accommodated, but dropdown lists are not frequently revised, so it may be better to lean on conservatism. In my consultancies, I propose 9–15 categories for most data fields.

7.5. Expandable Data Tables

Legacy systems cannot be altered easily. Modifying any existing table or adding a new one is almost never allowed. It is in the analytical sphere where this can be done. Any mistake made here does not impact on business operations despite possible adverse impacts on analysis outcomes.

Modifying or adding a data table is certainly not a technical hurdle. The issue that needs addressing is permission. Here again, an understanding of what an analytical sphere is meant for can be a challenge.

It is near universal that any type of enterprise-level database is under the control of the IT unit. With its priority on security and integrity, an IT unit often regards the data warehouse as another legacy system. Once installed, it cannot be modified in any way and access to data is by approved requests. In many banks, business units attempting their own analytics and modeling have given up on the enterprise data warehouse. In one bank that I consulted for, the Chief Risk Officer decided to use his own department's budget to build the risk data mart despite the bank having a multimillion-dollar enterprise data warehouse that has been cited as reference site by the vendor. Requesting for data from the warehouse was as bad as having a root canal with the IT unit located in another postal code.

Only end users know what analytical data are used for and they must have the right to modify, update and add as their needs change. How this can be done has to be addressed through policies and planned data stewardship. Freedom of access, however, must always be balanced with proper control. Letting one and all make changes as they see fit is a recipe for data corruption and eventually dereliction. In one of my consultancies, the risk management staff were given unfettered access to change the Occupation categories. An interesting addition was Airline Steward/ Stewardess. When asked why the specific occupation, the explanation given was that such professionals are always flying around and therefore bad credit risk. And then there was the category, Teacher. The explanation this time is that teachers are always looking at the stock market screen at their free time and also bad credit risk. This was amusing except to the senior staff who designed the original list. She was livid that her careful choices were mangled by others with their personal beliefs.

New tables created should be meaningfully linked to existing ones with the use of Primary and Foreign keys. This is discussed shortly. Orphaned tables create clutter quickly and contribute to the warehouse or even mart becoming a data dump.

Once a new table replaces on old one, mapping at the ETL process must be updated, else new columns will be unpopulated. The same challenges in dealing with the IT unit arises again.

7.6. Dated

Since legacy system data are usually the most current, the DateTime stamp is not important. In many systems, the default date of 1 Jan 1500 is imputed if no explicit date is assigned.

Dating is essential for time-series analysis. If the impact of an external factor on an internal event is to be measured, the timing of both has to be properly aligned even if they need not be synchronous. Timestamp will be useful if one wants to analyze if business volume tend to be higher during specific periods of the day.

The challenge of DateTime stamp is that what is not captured in the legacy system cannot be available in the analytical sphere. A possible mitigation is to ensure that dating is enforced during the ETL process. At the minimum, there will be a chronological sequence in the data even if they are not precise. This, however, leads to the issue of corrected data being re-entered after undue delay resulting in a wrong DateTime, as discussed earlier.

7.7. Useful and New Primary Keys

It is conventional for IT to set a Primary Key for each data table. Though a good discipline, it may pose a problem in data warehousing and use for analytics.

A Primary Key is meant to match a Foreign Key so that records from two tables can be merged. A property index, for instance, can be used to adjust property collateral values to update loan to asset ratios. It is quite impossible and too costly for each mortgaged property to be professionally valued every year. On the other hand, using a single real estate price index to adjust them all would be too crude as value change may differ significantly across property types and regions even within the same country. To make a reasonable update, property type field needs to be designed to match a ready external index for different types and possibly different locations. Unfortunately, Primary Keys in legacy systems are rarely set for such a purpose.

The importance of a properly designed Primary Key will usually become evident when external data have to be integrated with internal ones. Marking of asset values to market is one of the common requirements in this respect. Another is the need for impairment accounting. In all these cases, there must be a way to identify what internal records are impacted by external factors. For a small dataset, it can be done manually, but in a large organization, a more systematic approach will significantly improve efficiency.

A Primary Key in a legacy system data table may not be usable for data warehousing due to the cumulative nature of analytical data, as was briefly discussed before. Here, we consider a possible mitigating strategy.

The column UID, ID or CustomerID may be unique in a customer table in a loan system. This column serves the useful purpose of extracting all facilities associated with a specific customer. When warehoused, the same value is repeated every time the ETL is run and will no longer be unique. It cannot remain the Primary Key then. One possible solution to this challenge is to create a column that concatenates the ID with the DateTime stamp. Since the latter value changes all the time, this new column will be unique and can serve as the Primary Key. When used for analytics, substrings can be employed to separate the ID from the DateTime. Users have to make this requirement known during the data warehousing project design though for it to happen.

7.8. Updatable

As the value of analytics get recognized, more non-operational data will be sought and input into the database. Together with those warehoused, these have to be regularly updated. How the updating is carried out must be planned.

First, there must be a screen for manual inputs. It may come as a surprise to some that no consideration is given to this requirement. In one of my consultancies on operational losses, I asked the staff responsible where they will be inputting the data for loss events. They were stumped, but this was not the only case of such unawareness. In another case, the risk management staff wanted to use external data to recalibrate internal asset values. Once again, no thought was given to how such data is to be entered and updated. There may be many reasons for such oversight, but one possibility is the lack of understanding of the difference between operational and analytical systems. With the former, the vendor has designed the data entry screens and demonstrated to the client their reliability. Desktops have to be provided for what is termed as User Acceptance Test (UAT). By the time the system has been accepted, data input is a non-issue. It is a very different matter in the analytical sphere. By design, data warehouses or marts are no more than receiving depositories to those responsible for the technical process of warehousing. If additional data entry or update is needed but not made known, data would be just stored in a warehouse with no doors and windows. It may sound trivial, but it is paramount that users of analytical data make known the need for updating when the analytical sphere is conceptualized.

Second, some updates may be too massive in volume for manual data entry even if this were possible. An investment fund may need to regularly input thousands of securities prices. Automated batch updating would be the only meaningful option. Flat files can be downloaded from sources and then inserted into the warehouse. Whatever the method, there has to be a plan on how often this is done and at what time of the day it is done. Once again, the need for a Primary and Foreign Keys match has to be considered in advance.

Third, the source of data for updating has to be clearly identified. It is often assumed that some types of public data are out there and all that is needed is to download them. Take the risk-free rate, for instance. Textbooks explain how they can be estimated from the yield curve which is constructed using government debt securities transacted. The yield curve for developed economies may be purchased from vendors like Bloomberg or Thomson Reuters, but for many emerging economies, such are not available. Even asset transaction prices are not captured by the government itself. In such a case, a simple term structure of interest rates has to be constructed using data from different sources and some informed integration. Automated feeds are quite out of the question, so temporary storage has to be planned before updating to the data mart.

There are different approaches to updating. New data values can be appended to existing ones on the same tables or a new table can be created for each new batch. With appending, the issue of Primary Key has to be addressed and planned as discussed earlier. If a new table is created every time, the static variables to be reused have to be determined. Here again, only users of the analytical data can make meaningful decisions.

7.9. Accessible

Analytical data have to be far more easily accessible than operational ones. In the heydays of data warehousing movement, there was much talk of drilldowns, slice and dice, etc. The dream then was to have data available real-time to support strategic and tactical business decisions. But those were also the days before there is a clear understanding of where analytical data can be found. Having analytical data, however, does not mean they are accessible. Here again, the conventional association of data with IT and reports is a major stumbling block.

Despite reams of reports being produced, many heads of information department continue to be pressed for actionable analysis. There is an almost universal disconnect between what IT staff perceive as information vs what the business users look for. The data and canned analysis are certainly there in the reports, but they cannot be employed for a business unit's specific requirements. It may sound trite, but the report generation mindset is far more entrenched than often realized. Even at the writing of this book, I am working with the national agency of a country to enhance their risk analytics. My inclination is to produce derived data like credit risk correlations, for instance, that a bank can acquire and use for their own modeling and decision support. The agency, however, has different ideas. What they want are static reports beyond what they are already offering the banks. That is the understanding they have of what analytical data are and it is pervasive. Sadly, this is reinforced by software vendors out to impress by their wide range of ready reports, especially targeted at regulatory compliance. The truth is that *ad hoc* analysis imposes a far greater demand on the data model design than most users realize. If location is not made a column in the table, risk levels by geographic distribution is simply not possible.

In a large organization, accessibility cannot be a one-size-fits-all arrangement. Depending on needs, a tiered approach is likely to be more manageable. Access to enterprise-level data will be granted to those who support senior management. BUs can also access data relevant to their own requirements. The issue of data stewardship needs to be considered here.

A word of caution expressed by the CRO of a global bank is pertinent here. She became concerned that her ERM subunits have developed a silo mentality. Credit Risk staff cares only about credit risk and Market Risk staff only about market risk. This culture will be reinforced if access is limited to risk type users, so even within the ERM, there must be accommodation for occasional access.

Chapter 8

Risks in Financial Institutions

Stripped to its essence, financial service is about risk-taking. There is no tangible product or hedonic service provided to the client. In taking deposits, a bank is assuming the credit risk on behalf of the depositor. Insurance is about taking on an event risk. Perhaps the only type of financial service which requires nearly no risk-taking is passive fund management. Here, the financial institution offers diversification which is beyond the means of most individual customers. Risk analytics then is not an option in a financial institution.

There are many ways to approach what needs to be analyzed and modeled. One metaphor that I have offered earlier is that of a ship sailing in rough waters. I will apply that here to financial institutions.

First is where the ship is heading toward. Even with modern technology, icebergs remain a hazard. The equivalent for a financial institution is strategic direction. Heading into a new country or entering another line of business is fraught with potential dangers that are not immediately obvious. In the recent years, several global banks and insurance companies have divested themselves of entire countries or regions as they are unable to gain traction even after decades of presence.

Second is the existing external environment. A monster storm can capsize the largest ships. For a financial institution, political and regulatory volatility can do the same. A new government may overturn one policy in favor of another. How life insurance can and cannot be sold may mean feast or famine for a specific company.

Third is wear and tear on the vessel which is inevitable. Minor cracks may be ignored without much harm in the short term. It is a matter of time before they become critical and even fatal. Technology in financial services accelerates rapidly. Today, securities transactions are made in nanoseconds known as high-frequency trading. An outdated system may quote stale prices that can lead to massive losses.

Finally, there is the possibility of dangerous cargo carried on the ship. Explosive or toxic material needs transporting across the world. Risky businesses need credit and insurance. Unlike the first three areas, this type of risk-taking is largely a matter of choice and can be calibrated to suit the financial institution's appetite.

The key reason for employing this metaphor is to identify the types of data required and analytics and modeling that are relevant. The following chapter covers the technical aspects involving R codes. Here, a discussion may be helpful to provide a helicopter view.

8.1. Profiling What Is Ahead

Any financial institution would like to grow and that means entering into new domains or expanding the existing clientele. Either means taking on risk of the unknown. An insurer signing up a new customer has little or no in-house information about the entity. A bank evaluating a potential obligor faces the same challenge.

The need here is to develop a profile of the prospective customer or market. That requires collection of new or primary data. The acronym KYC or Know Your Customer has become mandatory because of crimes like money laundering. A bank can no longer claim ignorance when questionable transactions take place. The conventional legal principle of innocent till proven guilty is turned on its head. Any financial institution caught servicing a confirmed crime has to prove its innocence through a rigorous KYC process and global banks have been levied multibillion-dollar fines for negligence in this area. The challenges of collecting the necessary data for compliance starts here.

In all likelihood, data entry forms come with the legacy system purchased for a product or service. A wholesale credit application form will have fields for financial data. A retail credit application form will have demographics. Acquisition of the system will probably be a joint decision between BU and IT. Rarely is anyone from risk management, analytics or modeling consulted on what types of data should be captured.

In a large Asian bank, data for new retail credit applicants were missing some residential address details. Though not legally critical, that limited the ability to create a profile of the geographic distribution of applicants and customers. The column in a data table was empty. This lasted for several decades till a systematic data audit was carried out. Initially, nobody could explain this peculiar occurrence. It took a long time for IT staff to eventually provide the explanation. Decades ago when computers were still using the Disk Operating System (DOS), screen resolution was 640×480 pixels. There was not enough space on the screen for the missing field to be included, so IT decided to drop it. Not even the retail credit BU was consulted. Despite the rapid rise in screen resolution, this decision was never revisited and so the bank continued to miss out on one of the address values.

Profiling is akin to taking a snapshot of the target. In the language of modeling, it will be a Point In Time (PIT) image. Deriving a credit risk rating of a loan applicant and estimating the mortality score of a new insured are examples of such modeling. It is termed PIT because the profile developed is technically good only at that point in time. It is like a photograph capturing only that moment when it is taken. Everything can change thereafter.

The reliability of the model is dependent on how well the relevant factors or predictors measure the target subject. If it is an iceberg, the size, shape, movement and other attributes are compared against benchmarks to derive a profile of this specific one in terms of the danger posed. In a bank credit application by a new potential obligor, data like financial ratios or demographics are used.

Both the completeness and quality of data need attention here. Non-mandatory data are often neglected by those collecting them. For the analyst or modeler who needs to derive a profile like a credit rating, for example, the deficiency can be frustrating. And then there is the quality matter. Even when data are collected, they are not necessarily reliable. A firm reporting a sudden spike of 1,000% growth over the last year using unaudited financial statements may be manipulating its financials. Here again, the issue is irrelevant if business development is priority.

Whatever data are not captured or properly captured will not be available for profiling. It is worthwhile, therefore, for analytics professionals to give their inputs on how primary data should be collected. One cardinal rule that applies to any kind of economic activity is to use dropdown values instead of free alphanumeric format for a field that will be used for modeling. Telephone companies or telcos have understood this principle and redesigned its online application forms with dropdown lists wherever possible.

As explained earlier, a PIT profile is only good for the moment the snapshot is taken. A stock investor may undertake an exhaustive analysis of the security's fundamentals before buying but will certainly not assume that the issuing firm's financial health remains unchanged over years or even months. That is why there will always be securities analysts gathering the latest information to update the attractiveness of stocks resulting in recommendations like Buy, Sell or Hold. Similarly, credit rating agencies or CRAs like Standard & Poors continually upgrade or downgrade ratings with new information. If a bank extends a 10-year loan to a firm, the financial health of the obligor 3, 5 or more years from credit approval is likely to be different from when the initial profile was derived. Banks are expected to update using financial data of the firm, but unless it is a listed entity, there is no legal obligation for these to be provided by the customer. The reality is that practically all banks are not able to keep track of the credit worthiness of their debtors. One way to mitigate this problem is to use behavioral data.

With few exceptions, core banking systems automatically generate a payment delinquency record termed Days Past Due (DPD). Once payment is not received on due date, the clock starts. Under Basel II guidelines, 90 DPD triggers a default. Since most defaults are of this nature, 90 DPD can only be reached after 89 DPD. By tracking such data, it is possible to monitor the creditworthiness of an obligor without resorting to an update of the PIT profile. In fact, studies have shown that such behavioral modeling often termed behavioral scoring is a better predictor of default than a PIT model. For convenience, this approach can be termed Through The Cycle (TTC) as it is done through the credit cycle until the loan is fully repaid or written off. Of course, this TTC is not the same as that used by CRAs which means a rating good for an economic or business cycle.

DPD data is generated by the core banking system and direct access for analytics is often infeasible. Besides, records of matured loans may not be kept to free up storage space for increasing transaction volume. Only by systematically warehousing such data can they be available for modeling when the time comes.

8.2. External Warning Indicators

Any business would welcome early warnings of impending risk events but none more so than financial services. Unlike those selling products and services for revenues, financial institutions make commitments that can last for years which is why the term "exposure" is often used. Such exposures cannot be terminated unilaterally. A bank is not permitted to stop a loan for no valid reason. An insurer cannot renege on a coverage when the outlook has deteriorated. Investment funds are the exception as they can liquidate a position no longer favorable.

Most are exposed to risks that cannot be precisely quantified when the transaction is first made. What is optimal at the point of commitment can be risky when the external environment has changed. Regulations, for instance, have overturned many once good decisions. Any early warning that negative developments are forthcoming would be welcome by all responsible for an entity's welfare.

To assess the impact of an external factor, there must be a mapping of this factor to the relevant internal data of analysis. If the concern is real estate collateral values in a bank, there must be a way to match an external indicator to calibrate these values. A land price index may not be as well suited for condominium values as a condominium index. Mapping can be easily done on a standalone utility like an Excel spreadsheet. The property collateral data can be extracted from the database and the indicator value simply merged by date or other criteria. Doing so on a regular automated way would, however, require some forethought on the data table design.

The need to design appropriate Primary and Foreign keys has been discussed. Not only would most analytics users be unfamiliar with this technical matter, the mapping process may not be straightforward even if well understood. In a data table of real estate collaterals, the Primary Key may be the loan ID rather than the property type. Even the availability of a condominium index cannot be easily mapped to all condominium values. As with nearly all analytical database issues, the input of the end user goes a long way to making the design more friendly.

A helpful consideration in this aspect is to list all the economic and business variables that may impact on losses. Property price, interest rate, exchange rate, inflation rate, etc. are some of the common ones. There are vendors of such data and a subscription can be made to those relevant.

Separate tables can be created with a concatenation of the variable and the DateTime column as Primary Key. This can only be done in the analytical data sphere and by users.

8.3. Operational Concerns

Any going concern experiences wear and tear. This is usually categorized as operational risk. Left unattended, small defects can turn into large ones, eventually sinking even a supertanker. Though nobody is likely to dispute this prognosis, analyzing and managing it is an entirely different proposition.

A practiced approach in financial institutions for operational risk management is to start with a Risk Control and Self-Assessment (RCSA) exercise. Operational units will review business processes to identify what has gone wrong in the past and may go wrong in the future. Risk events are assigned terms like "Wrong data entry", for example. For each event, an assessment is made of the frequency of occurrence and the severity of loss each time it happens. Many challenges arise from this point on.

Few operational units like to disclose their shortcomings, particularly potential ones. Experience suggests that if forced to, unit heads would opt for trivial events like losing some stationery. Unless there is an irrefutable accounts trail where assets have to be written off, events are best left unexposed to avoid attracting scrutiny and need for explanation on remedial actions and control. So, for an IT unit, a system being hacked and fixed need not show up on the radar if there was no monetary loss even if many man days were expended to deal with the matter. It is highly likely that the number of events is severely unreported with any analytics made unreliable.

Even when an event is included in the RCSA, the loss severity is almost certainly underestimated. Consider the case of a fire at a branch office. What is burned and lost may not amount to much, especially if insurance coverage has been secured. The excess over the compensation will be reflected in the Income Statement. What is not trivial though is the opportunity cost of business lost over the days when the branch has to be closed for renovation. Besides, there are the manhours expended to return the place to a usable state. All these are not captured by payments made to product or service providers of the financial institution. The British Banker's Association term the opportunity costs Indirect Loss that need to be estimated for every risk event.

While operational risk events can occur endogenously, some are caused by external triggers. An earthquake can lead to absenteeism which in turn cause transaction failures and losses. This dependency is an area that risk analytics can add much value to if only the RCSA data are reliable.

To better capture operational losses due to an event, there is the need to include Direct Invoiceable Loss, Direct Non-invoiceable Loss and Indirect Loss. The first type is automatically reflected in the accounts. An invoice is issued by a product or service provider and has to be paid for, so an expense is recorded. It is the second type that is almost always overlooked. They do not show up in the accounts but are no less tangible. If the IT unit has to expend manhours fixing a hack, there is a real loss despite no payment being made to an external party. The loss has to be estimated and one way to do that is to regard the remedial work as being outsourced. The cost of outsourcing serves as a good estimate of this loss. Not accounting for it can lead to long-term consequences. One or two hacks a year may not seriously impact on the productivity of the IT unit, but a higher frequency may lead to the need for more staff and higher operating cost. Indirect Loss can be the opportunity cost of loss of productivity and that can exceed the Direct Loss. The CEO's laptop being misplaced may not cost much tangibly, but the disruption may be to work that is worth much more.

8.4. Portfolio Composition

A ship carrying dangerous goods is comparable to a financial institution having risky exposures or deals. In the recent years, large banks have been brought down by derivative trades that have turned sour. This is sometimes detected by measuring concentration risk.

Reviewing the portfolio is a regulatory requirement for nearly all types of financial institutions. There is, however, no instruction of what to look for although measuring concentration is one area recommended. Even here, no metric or threshold has been suggested. Besides, how concentration is to be defined is left open. A high level of exposure to a single customer like a transaction counterparty will certainly fit the bill. That cannot be said of exposures to related or associated customers. That will need a judgment call. Even more challenging is the ability to detect associations. In some regions, private efforts have been invested into quantifying the depth of association between one entity and another. Two distinct firms owned by the same entrepreneur and having intensive business deals with each other will be regarded as having a deep association. Such data are welcome by analysts but likely to come at a cost.

Concentration or its opposite diversification can be evaluated along many dimensions. It can be based on geography, product, customer type, distribution channel, etc. Once again, whatever has not been captured in the data cannot be analyzed. If the channel through which an application is received is not part of the data entered or automatically generated, it will be quite impossible to assess concentration by channel. As for external data that need to be acquired, room must have been made in the data warehousing design for these to be accommodated.

Chapter 9

Common Risk Models and Analytics

There are many kinds of risk models and analytics, and the range is expanding. Excellent books have covered them in detail, so it is not the intent here to reinvent the wheel. Only the most common metrics are discussed first with a synopsis of the concern or theory followed more extensively by the ORE codes that can be used to obtain the results and store them in the Oracle database for decision support. Another chapter is devoted to using R in Microsoft Excel for the less time-critical analyses like those for strategic planning.

9.1. Expected and Unexpected Losses

With risk analytics, losses are not all the same. Ever since Basel II, Expected and Unexpected Losses have very much become part of the risk lexicon.

Expected Loss (EL) is a loss that can be expected or unavoidable with the nature of risk taken. Defaults in credits have to be expected unless exposures are entirely risk-free, which does not exist. For credit institutions like banks, this concept of EL is important. Since it is expected, a bank must set aside part of its capital to absorb the loss to ensure that key fund providers like depositors are not made to bear it. Under Basel II, a loss reserve must be created to cover EL at the minimum. Since this reserve is expected to be "lost", it will not count as part of a bank's regulatory capital.

99

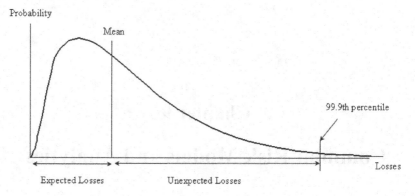

Figure 9.1.   Credit loss distribution, EL and UL.

If the EL is an unbiased estimate, there is a near equal chance of the actual loss being realized below or above that level. It is immaterial if the loss is lower but can lead to insolvency if it is higher and the bank has no funds other than the loss reserve to absorb it. This is where regulatory capital enters the picture.

A loss greater than EL is termed Unexpected Loss (UL). This designation is rather unfortunate and confusing as unexpected connotes an occurrence outside of expectations. As discussed above, such a loss occurs with a 50% chance so it cannot be regarded as beyond expectations. Figure 9.1 explains the relationship between EL and UL.

A credit loss distribution is typically skewed to the right, reflecting lower probabilities of larger losses. The area under the curve is 100% of the probabilities. If losses all come from normal conditions, the mean is near identical to the median which is at the 50th percentile of the area. This is also the EL as there is an equal chance of the next loss being realized above or below this mark.

Any loss greater than EL is the UL. Since the curve is theoretically endless, a meaningful cap needs to be placed to translate the UL to economic or regulatory capital for banks. Basel II established that losses up to 99.9% of the distribution should be this cap.

In regulatory terms, a bank must set aside a loss reserve to cover the EL which is up the 50th percentile of the loss distribution and regulatory capital from that mark to 99.9th percentile. The 99.9th percentile level is also termed Worst Case Loss (WCL) at 99.9% confidence level in some literature. To illustrate, assume that EL is $300m and WCL is $800m.

This means that a loss reserve of $300m and regulatory capital of $500m must be set aside.

9.2. Value at Risk

Value at Risk (VaR) is perhaps the most widely used metric for measuring risk. The acronym VaR is used to avoid confusion with VAR which is the R expression for Vector Autoregression.

At its most basic, VaR is the maximum amount of loss that will occur at a specified level of confidence. It is most commonly applied to a portfolio of security returns with a diagram (see Fig. 9.2).

Security returns distribution is usually bell-shaped with near equal part gains and losses. VaR is only concerned with losses, so the gains half is not a consideration. Decision makers will first have to decide on a confidence level. Figure 9.2 depicts 99% which means that the VaR value is reached where the area under the distribution to the right of the dotted line is 99%. That leaves 1% to the left. If the value is $146,000,000, it means that there is a 99% chance that a loss for the next period will not exceed that amount.

The purpose of VaR is to determine a level of economic capital needed to prevent insolvency. An easy way to understand this concept is to assume that all investments are made using debt. The classic case for this is a bank making loans and investments with deposits that have to be returned on demand. If there are defaults, these deposits will be lost and the bank has to make good using its own capital. Failure to cover the losses leads to the bank's insolvency.

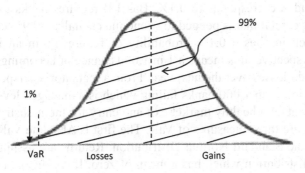

Figure 9.2. Security returns distribution and VaR.

It is worth noting that VaR is equivalent to the UL explained in the above section. For a securities portfolio, there is no EL as investors do not expect a loss when the investment is made.

Another way for the modern generation to comprehend the value of VaR is to consider computer games. In an even game where it is equally easy to score a point as to lose one, the player always has the chance to recover as long as the Game Over sign does not pop up. A minor difference between this and financial risk is that the game will only be over following a series of losses. With investments, a single loss can be equal to the accumulated losses of a computer game. The thrust of the matter remains, however, that recovery is always possible as long as it is not Game Over. VaR provides the threshold with a probability that this will happen.

To illustrate, assume that a bank has a $1bn loan portfolio funded entirely with deposits. Based on empirical analysis, there is a no more than 1% chance that a loss from defaults will be $100m or more. If the bank has capital of at least $100m, there is a 99% chance that it can remain solvent. Should the loss exceed $100m and no additional equity is available, it will be Game Over for the bank. The amount of $100m is what is needed for the bank to stay in the game with a 99% confidence level. This sum is now termed Economic Capital.

VaR is commonly expressed in shorthand form. VaR99 or VaR990 means VaR at 99.0% confidence level. VaR999 then is 99.9% confidence.

Economic capital is also the basis for commercial credit ratings and bank capital adequacy ratio under the Basel II framework. Letter grades like AAA, B+, etc. assigned by credit rating agencies like Standard & Poor's correspond to fairly specific probabilities of Game Over. AAA, for instance, reflect an approximately 0.03% or 3 in 10,000 chance for that to happen and A corresponds to 0.1%. Basel II requires banks to maintain regulatory capital that is pegged to economic capital at 99.9% confidence level which implies a 0.1% probability of failure. From an individual bank's perspective, this means a 1 in 1,000 chance of becoming insolvent due to credit losses over the next year. From a regulator's perspective, this translates into 1 in 1,000 banks failing which is a managed level of attrition to maintain a healthy market exit and entry for the industry.

There are three measures of VaR. The first is Absolute VaR which is based on the Standard Normal Distribution. Returns are assumed to follow this distribution which has a mean of zero. If so, the area under the tail end beyond −2.33 standard deviations is 1%. In the case where the standard deviation of returns for a $1bn securities portfolio is $15m, there will be a 1% probability that the loss will be $34.95m or more. There is a corresponding 99% chance that losses will not exceed that amount, so having economic capital of $34.95m provides a 99% confidence level of staying in the game.

Both theory and evidence show that expected security returns are positive even for the shortest holding period of one day. A more realistic measure then is Relative VaR which differs from Absolute VaR by applying a mean return from historical data. Since even daily returns are positive on average, Relative VaR is also known as Daily Earnings at Risk (DEAR). Not only can there be a capital loss on the portfolio value, there is also the loss of earnings for the day.

Assuming that the mean expected daily return on the $1bn portfolio is 0.03%, which translates into $300,000. If the standard deviation is $15m, the Relative VaR will be $34.95m less $300,000 which is equal to $34,650,000. Since average expected return is always positive, Relative VaR will always be smaller than Absolute VaR.

A minor digression is worth discussing here due to difference between evidence and concept. In estimating Relative VaR, a risk professional may use historical data that produce a negative average return which is certainly possible. Using the mean statistic obtained, a Relative VaR larger than Absolute VaR is derived which contradicts the normative relationship between them. It is neither the data nor the method that is wrong. It is VaR that has been misunderstood.

VaR is a risk quantification and control metric. Risk is always about future outcomes. Although historical data are often used to forecast what those outcomes may be, any metric is still meant to be applied to the future. So, historical security returns are used to predict the distribution of future returns. A negative average historical return, however, does and should not imply that the future mean return will be negative. There will be no new investments if the expected return is negative. Even short sales cannot be completed as there is the need for the long side to effect the transaction and buyers cannot be expecting a negative return. The implication is that Relative VaR should not be larger than Absolute VaR regardless of the historical data employed for estimation.

The third measure is Empirical VaR. Actual security returns are used to plot the distribution. The 1% or one percentile is then used to determine VaR990. From an operational use perspective, this is the most accurate measure of VaR. This is especially so since the Normal Distribution assumed using Absolute and Relative VaR can severely underestimate the tail end of the returns distribution. Actual security returns are fat-tailed or kurtotic.

Using historical data, there are three broad approaches to estimate VaR. These are known as the Delta-Normal, Historical Simulation and Monte Carlo Simulation methods. Many papers and articles have been devoted to explaining these three approaches, so they are not discussed here. It will suffice to describe the R codes to accomplish one of them.

The Historical Simulation approach uses a random number generator to randomly select a sample from historical returns. The ORE code to select a random sample of 500 returns from an Oracle data table of S & P 500 index levels over the years using the **data.table** package can be as follows:

```
begin
sys.rqScriptCreate('Analytics',
'function() {
library(ROracle)
library(data.table)
drv <- dbDriver("Oracle")
con <- dbConnect(drv, username="rquser", password="password",
dbname="ORCLPDB", prefetch=FALSE, external_credentials=FALSE)

#Create lag function
lg <- function(x)c(NA, x[1:(length(x)-1)])
df <- dbReadTable(con, "SNP500", schema="RQUSER")
dt <- data.table(df)
dt[, lINDEXLEVEL := lg(INDEXLEVEL)]

#Derive return as the first difference in logarithm of the levels
dt$RETURN <- dt$INDEXLEVEL / dt$lINDEXLEVEL-1
df <-data.frame(dt)

#Select sample of 500 returns
sample <- df[sample(nrow(df), 500), ]

#Find 1% quantile
VaR990 <- quantile(sample$RETURN, c(0.01))
}',
```

```
v_overwrite => TRUE);
end;
/
Insert into var (VaR990)
select * from table(rqEval(NULL, 'select 1 VaR990 from dual', 'Analytics'));
```

One evident deficiency of the Historical Simulation approach is the limitation of returns to that of the past. This essentially constrains stressed returns since the bulk of history is normal. The VaR obtained may significantly underestimate the extent of losses possible under severely adverse scenarios. Since VaR is a metric for surviving through a crisis, the Historical Simulation approach has to be applied with caution.

The Monte Carlo Simulation approach tries to remedy the weakness of relying purely on history. There are many variations to this approach so it is not unusual that 10 risk modelers can produce 10 different VaR990 values using the same dataset. A common thread running through all Monte Carlo simulations is the use of random values generated by a known distribution. For VaR, a model is usually first chosen for asset price movement. Since modeling allows for any parameter to be introduced to capture extreme conditions, stressed returns can be incorporated. Most asset pricing models rely on the Normal Distribution to account for the random diffusion of returns, so this distribution is widely used for VaR estimation.

VaR is regarded as the gold standard for risk quantification by global agencies like the International Monetary Fund (IMF) and Group of 20 (G20) nations. It has increasingly been employed for risk-based decisions, especially in risk budgeting.

In the early 1980s, Banker's Trust used a measure that is similar though not explicitly termed VaR to make Approve/Reject decisions on credit applications. Using the measure of duration, the amount of risk capital needed to support a credit exposure is derived. This amount is the product of the exposure amount, modified duration and change in interest rate. Since a loan is conceptually similar to a bond, an interest rate rise will cause a fall in its market value. This is the risk that Banker's Trust wanted to quantify and provide risk capital for up to a specified level of confidence much like in VaR. Using a historical distribution of interest rate volatility and the confidence level, the corresponding amount of rate change is determined. Dividing the first-year interest income by the risk capital, a return termed Risk-Adjusted

Return on Capital (RAROC) was obtained. Only returns above an internal threshold are approved. This model is generally viewed as one of the earliest adoptions of tail-end loss as the measure of risk as compared to earlier use of standard deviation in securities pricing. Before the use of Probability of Default (PD), Loss Given Default (LGD) and Exposure at Default (EAD) were made widespread by Basel II, this approach was highly regarded for risk-based decision-making and even pricing.

One of the significant uses of VaR is for risk budgeting and this is largely due to the growth of professional fund management. Capital budgeting is the allocation of financial resources to fund projects or investments. Risk budgeting is similar in spirit but focuses on the determination of capital needed to avoid an insolvency-causing loss up to a set level of confidence. A property of VaR that appeals to risk budgeting is that it is not linearly additive and diversification helps reduce the level of risk capital needed. Like RAROC, it can be used to support risk-based decisions.

Consider a $500m fund W invested with returns standard deviation of 10%. If returns are normally distributed with a mean of zero, there is a 99% confidence that a loss will not exceed $116,500,000, which is equal to 2.33 standard deviations multiplied by $50m. This $116,500,000 is the basis of risk capital for the fund. If the investment is financed entirely with debt, this amount is the capital needed to avoid insolvency with a 99% confidence level as a loss beyond that results in an inability to fully repay creditors. Management is evaluating whether to add another $500m fund X or Y to W while staying within a risk budget of $200m. The returns standard deviation for X is 9% and that for Y is 12%. As standalone investments, X appears less risky than Y, but the considerations of a portfolio are different. Returns of X are 70% correlated with those of W while Y returns are uncorrelated or correlated at 0%. Applying the formula for correlated returns of a portfolio $\sigma_p = \sqrt{w_w^2\sigma_w^2 + w_x^2\sigma_x^2 + 2w_w w_x \rho_{wx}\sigma_w\sigma_x}$, where w_i is the weight of asset i in the portfolio, σ_i is the standard deviation of i returns and ρ_{ij} is the correlation between returns of i and j; the standard deviation of a W and X combination is 8.76% and that for W and Y is 7.81%. Using the 2.33 standard deviations for 99% confidence level, the loss for W and X portfolio is $2.04m and that for W and Y is $1.82m. Y then should be the preferred addition to W to stay within the risk budget of $2m. This is a simple illustration of the benefit of diversification and is now a key consideration not only in fund management but all forms of businesses.

VaR is also the metric approved in Basel II for a bank to use its own model to determine the level of Market Risk regulatory capital. The amount required is to cover a loss at the 99% confidence level scaled up to a 10-day holding period. The level of internally determined capital must pass backtesting before it is accepted as regulatory capital. This test is based on the assumption that the VaR estimated is exactly for a 1% chance that a loss on any day exceeds that value. Backtesting requires the use of actual returns after the model has been implemented. Conventional validation of statistical models uses a control or holdout sample to test the accuracy of a model and it is termed out-of-sample testing. Backtesting is also known as out-of-time testing as the test data employed must be after those of the training sample. If returns on the market portfolio are not serially correlated, the probability of a loss exceeding the VaR level follows a binomial distribution. The R function dbinom(k, size=n, prob=p) computes the probability of k occurrences over n outcomes each with a probability p. So, dbinom(0, size=250, prob=0.01) gives a 8.1% probability that there will not be a single day where the loss exceeds VaR level (termed exception) over a typical 250 trading day year. Basel II requires that no more than four exceptions be observed in the backtesting period for the model to pass. Cumulative binomial probabilities can be derived in the function pbinom (4, size=250, prob=0.01) which gives a 89.2% probability. If the VaR value is based on a 99% confidence level, there is a near 90% chance that it will pass backtesting.

Risk analytics can go beyond simply quantifying potential losses to estimating additional costs. A bank may want to pass backtesting with a higher chance. To do so, it can set a more conservative level of VaR at a 99.5% confidence level. Assuming that the amount of capital required at 99.0% confidence is $x. The probability of achieving four or less exceptions will be pbinom(4, size=250, prob=0.005) which is 99.1%. A 99.5% confidence is equivalent to 2.58 standard deviations. Compared to the 2.33 standard deviations for 99.0%, there will be an increase of 10.73% capital required. If the cost of capital is 15%, the cost of improving the chance of passing the test is 1.6%. Here is another example of how risk management is not exclusively cost-centered but may be employed for profitability. The higher cost needed to ensure a better chance of passing the backtesting can be compared to the opportunity costs of compliance failure. This can be a significant input into the consideration of whether to expand the trading desk for more revenues.

9.3. Securities Portfolio Optimization

One of the most common goals of analytics is optimization. Among such, optimizing the selection of a securities portfolio is perhaps done more than others.

There are many routes to optimizing a portfolio. Each depends on the key assumptions of what is return and what is risk. There is near consensus of what return means despite variations in the actual measurement. The percentage change to the initial price or level at the end of the holding period is usually good enough. Risk measurement is quite another matter.

The broadest definition of risk is loss due to unfavorable price change. The challenge is to establish a parameter that captures the likelihood and magnitude of such an event. Price variability or volatility is the most commonly accepted parameter, but that stops at the exact statistic to be used. Variance and its square root form standard deviation are accepted without question, but there are other statistics that have emerged as important considerations given the vast improvements in computing power. Skewness or the third moment has taken on more importance when a loss counts more than a gain of the same percentage. VaR and Conditional VaR also known as Expected Shortfall have been increasingly used for the risk measure. Books and articles have been written on the conceptual and theoretical issues on this subject.

A widely used approach is quadratic optimization which is either to minimize the volatility constrained by a minimum rate of return or maximize the return constrained by a maximum level of volatility. There is now a package developed for portfolio optimization known as Portfolio Analytics. This package has some dependencies that require R higher than version 3.3.3, so it cannot be run on ORE. It will be discussed in greater detail in the chapter on Basic Excel R Tool (BERT) which is the free add-in for Microsoft Excel. It is also more suited for that environment as the analysis is not time-critical for decision support.

9.4. Correlation

When default correlations go up, the tail end of the loss distribution sometimes termed WCL also goes up. Similarly, VaR is larger where security returns correlation is larger. With these insights, correlation analysis has been given increased attention.

There are two broad types of correlation measures. One is the Pearson Correlation which is more widely used. This is the covariance of two variables divided by the product of their individual standard deviations. The formula is $\rho_{xy} = \text{cov}(x, y)/\rho_x\rho_y$. The other is the Spearman Correlation which is non-parametric. This determines if there is a monotonic relationship between two variables.

While correlations themselves are not direct indicators of risks, a change in correlations can serve as predictors of the overall level of risk. Since correlations are bivariate in nature, a matrix is necessary to capture the statistic for more than two variables. With three stock indices, the ORE script to derive a correlation matrix can be as follows:

```
begin
sys.rqScriptCreate('Analytics',
'function() {
library(ROracle)
drv <- dbDriver("Oracle")
con <- dbConnect(drv, username="rquser", password="password",
dbname="ORCLPDB", prefetch=FALSE, external_credentials=FALSE)

# Read STOCKINDICES table into data frame
df <- dbReadTable(con, "STOCKINDICES", schema="RQUSER")

#Compute correlation for columns 2 to 4 with Column 1 not processed
as it is datetime
corr <- cor(df[, 2:4])
corr <- data.frame(corr)
}',
v_overwrite => TRUE);
end;
/
Insert into corr (corr)
select * from table(rqEval(NULL, 'select 1 corr from dual', 'Analytics'));
```

Though the above is a correlation between index levels, it takes a small step to compute returns before the correlations.

Correlation impacts on the credit loss distribution in a way that is not immediately obvious. An example is needed to illustrate this.

Table 9.1.   Loss distribution for credit portfolio of *X* and *Y*.

Outcome	Prob	Loss ($)	EL ($)	Cum prob
No default	0.8797	0	0.0000	0.8797
X default	0.0003	100	0.0305	0.8800
Y default	0.1194	200	23.8810	0.9994
Both default	0.0006	300	0.1786	1.0000
	1.0000		24.0900	

Assume a credit portfolio of $300 comprises two exposures: *X* for $100 and *Y* for $200. The PD for *X* is 0.09% or 0.0009 and for *Y* is 12.00% or 0.1200. The technical definition and meaning of PD is elaborated on in a later chapter for it is akin to the likelihood of defaulting. The correlation between *X* and *Y* defaulting is 5% or 0.05. Using these data, a discrete loss distribution can be derived, as shown in Table 9.1.

The EL for the portfolio is $24.09. The WCL at 99.9% confidence level is $200 (under Basel II, the cutoff cumulative probability must be no less than 0.999). This means that the UL is $175.91.

If default correlation increases to 10% or 0.1, WCL at 99.9% rises to $300 while EL remains unchanged at $24.09. This means that UL increases to $275.91. The interesting result here is that correlation does not affect the EL but impacts on the UL. This is consistent with the need for more economic capital when risk is higher.

The UL/EL relationship provides a potential though still unresearched metric for measuring risk appetite. Under Basel II Pillar 3, banks must disclose a wide range of risk management details. One of this is risk appetite which in the most basic form is the willingness to take risk. Practically all banks will make an informationless statement like "the bank sets a risk appetite commensurate with its capital adequacy". Not only does that not reveal any quantifiable metric, but also it has no value in making a comparison with peer banks on whether too much or too little risk is being taken. Since EL is already accounted for by the loss reserve and invariant to risks like default correlations, a ratio like a portfolio *UL/EL* can offer insights into the tail end risk that the bank is prepared to take. This metric is comparable across banks and can be used by regulators to determine if any is overexposing itself to credit risk. As a consultant, I have proposed this ratio to my client banks to monitor their credit portfolio risk over time.

9.5. Concentration Index

Concentration is the proverbial putting all or most eggs into one basket. Should that basket fail, the loss will be great. Banks are specifically warned against having overexposure to a single customer, region, risk class, etc. In many countries, there is a limit to the percentage of capital that may be concentrated in any of these dimensions.

There are different measures of concentration. One that is popular among economists is the Herfindhal–Hirschman Index (HHI). HHI is simply the sum of the squares of individual shares of the whole. If there are three loans in a credit portfolio of 0.5, 0.3 and 0.2 of the total amount, the HHI will be $0.5^2 + 0.3^2 + 0.2^2 = 0.25 + 0.09 + 0.04 = 0.38$. In a monopsony, the sole entity is also the whole giving a HHI of 1.0. Conversely, this index is close to zero if there are many atomistic shares in the portfolio. By design then, the HHI ranges between 0 and 1 or 0 and 10,000 if the shares are expressed in percentages. The higher the level, the more concentrated is the exposure.

Another measure is the Cn where n of 3 and 4 are most common. $C3$ is the sum of the shares of the three largest exposures. If the three largest entities in a market account for 10%, 7% and 5%, $C3$ will be $0.1 + 0.07 + 0.05 = 0.22$. It is obvious that Cn will be greater than 0 and less than or equal to 1 and the larger the value, the higher the concentration.

From a risk perspective, high concentration has at least two implications. One is equivalent to putting all eggs into too few baskets. This is the case for investment exposures whether credit or securities. Two is the exploitation of market power. A monopoly or monopsony has much more leverage over its counterparties than possible in a highly competitive market. Market economists generally do not favor such a situation as it usually leads to abuse and exploitation.

The R code for HHI or Cn is straightforward. For large n, there is an ineq package available. Following is an illustration of the function conc in this package on distribution across industries. As evident in the code, text values have to be converted to numeric before they can be processed. Another package named HHI can produce the same result, but this requires that the input vector be market shares that sum to 100% unlike ineq which derives them automatically.

```
library(ineq)

# Read FINANCIALS table in data frame Financials
Financials <- dbReadTable(con, "FINANCIALS", schema="RQUSER")

# Remove hard spaces if any with trim function
Financials$Industry  <-ifelse(trim(Financials$INDUSTRY)=='Agriculture',
1, ifelse(trim(Financials$INDUSTRY)=='Education', 2, ifelse(trim(Financi
als$INDUSTRY)=='Finance', 3, ifelse(trim(Financials$INDUSTRY)=='Infor
mation Communication and Technology', 4, ifelse(trim(Financials$INDU
STRY)=='Infrastructure', 5, ifelse(trim(Financials$INDUSTRY)=='Leisure',
6, ifelse(trim(Financials$INDUSTRY)=='Manufacturing', 7, ifelse(trim(Fin
ancials$INDUSTRY)=='Medical', 8, ifelse(trim(Financials$INDUSTRY)=='
Mining and exploration', 9, ifelse(trim(Financials$INDUSTRY)=='Oil and
gas', 10, ifelse(trim(Financials$INDUSTRY)=='Real estate', 11, ifelse(trim
(Financials$INDUSTRY)=='Services', 12, ifelse(trim(Financials$INDUSTR
Y)=='Trading', 13, 14)))))))))))))

# Derive Herfindhal Index
conc(Financials$Industry, type=c("Herfindahl"), na.rm=TRUE)
```

9.6. Operational Loss Distribution

Operational risk has become more prominent with the increasing use of technology. Financial services are especially concerned as theft of $1m is no different from stealing $1 with digitization of money. Besides, securities trading losses can be 100 or 1,000 times more than days before derivatives were invented.

Empirical data suggest that operational losses are distributed with a skew to the right similar to other loss distributions. The Basel Committee suggested that banks could use a joint Poisson–Lognormal Distribution to model the distribution. The frequency of events will be Poisson and the severity of loss for each event will be Lognormal. Other distributions are possible, but these are the most commonly employed.

The R package OpVaR contains many features that are suitable for estimating operational losses. It takes extra effort, however, to install as several of the dependencies are not automatically available and have to be manually downloaded from the R Archive (see the final chapter).

As with credit losses, the main purpose of deriving the operational loss distribution is to determine the level of economic capital to cover operational risk. Under Basel II, international banks have to maintain capital of no less than 99.9% confidence level. With operational loss data, this can be easily derived using the lossdat dataset provided with the OpVaR package:

```
# Read the lossdat dataset
data(lossdat)

# Run simulation and determine 99.9% WCL or VaR
mc_out=mcSim(opriskmodel, 100, verbose=FALSE)
VaR(mc_out, .999)
```

As there are four models in OpVaR, four results are generated as follows:

99.9%	99.9%	99.9%	99.9%
75555.28	85374.02	56870.50	40205.36

Such simulations assume that events are independently distributed. There is a category of Basel II operational loss which is due to external events. An earthquake, for instance, can lead to structural damage of buildings. Beyond that, it can cause increased absenteeism due to illnesses or transportation ruptures. Such secondary losses can be modeled using Bayesian statistics, but that is challenging as empirical data on conditional probabilities are few and hard to come by.

9.7. Stress Testing

One of the more recent developments in risk management is the need for stress testing. Among others, a driver for this is systemic risk largely facilitated by technology. The crash of a stock market in one major developed country can cause a domino effect, resulting in almost similar developments in others. Intricate cross-border relationships, global exposures of credit institutions, instantaneous information transmission and other factors all contribute to a complex network of risks throughout the world.

The global economy is now like a spider web. Disturbance in one corner reverberates throughout the entire structure within a short time. This source of cross-border stress has become prominent requiring close attention.

Stress also occurs within a single economy. A drought leads to serious difficulties and business failures. Socio-political strife often causes economic collapse.

In some respects, stress testing is unnecessary. When VaR was first conceptualized, it was meant to be the measure of estimating large losses with low probability. According to statistics, those losses would be equivalent to those occurring under stress conditions. If historical data for 10 years include a few under stress, a VaR of 99.9% or even 99.0% would have reached those loss levels. Having economic capital at these confidence levels will be equivalent to ensuring solvency under stress conditions. Stress testing then becomes redundant if the data for the VaR estimate included losses under stress conditions.

One argument for stress testing is that VaR data usually do not include stressed losses. This is true by default. If stress is a one in a thousand event, then 99.9% of any sample data will be for normal periods. Stressed losses could easily be missed in most sampling exercises. If care is taken to ensure that these losses are included, a VaR estimate would be good enough to replace stress testing. If the argument is pushed that no sample will cover stressed losses, the legitimate question to ask is when will these losses occur since they never had. There is no limit to hypothesized stress scenarios. With global warming a reality, one can create a scenario where an island nation is sinking into the sea overnight and estimate the losses resulting.

With the extremely negative externalities caused by bank failures, authorities worldwide have made stress testing mandatory. In the USA, stress testing has become so comprehensive that banks had to create new divisions just to manage it.

While operationally demanding, stress testing does not impose new conceptual or coding requirements. What have been developed for regular risk quantifications need only to be tweaked for significantly larger losses. As such, no package has been coded to specifically simplify stress testing.

9.8. Weight of Evidence

In academia, modeling follows what is termed Normative Approach. A theory or hypothesis is first formulated. Sample data are then tested hopefully showing empirical support for the theory. Evidence of support is usually in the form of rejecting the null hypothesis that the theory does not hold. A simple example of this approach is to test the theory that males are taller than females. The null hypothesis is that there is no difference. If a good sample is used and sufficiently strong evidence suggests that males are indeed taller, thus rejecting the null hypothesis, the theory is supported.

Theories have to be consistent with common sense. This is much easier to abide by in hard sciences like engineering. Diamond is harder than copper, so when the two metals interface, it will be copper that gets distorted. The experiment can be repeated endlessly and the result will remain unchanged.

In hard sciences, relationships between factor and outcome are almost always monotonic in nature though not universal. Cooling contracts the volume of matter, but with water, it may be the opposite when becoming ice. Nevertheless, such anomalies can be explained and predicted consistently. The same, however, cannot be said of social sciences where human preferences and decisions are involved. Here, assumptions have to be first made before a theory can be formed.

Normative Economics is based on the assumption of a rational economic agent. Rational means that if offered two envelopes containing $100 and $200, the agent will choose the $200 one. At the most basic level, such assumptions do not pose any major problems. When extended to risk analytics, they may.

Income is closely associated with creditworthiness. It is not unreasonable to assume that the higher the income, the better the creditworthiness. Empirical evidence shows, however, that this need not be true. In one specific country, it is the middle income that incur the highest default rate on bank credit. Any number of reasons can be offered to explain this phenomenon, but there is no theory that can predict it. If one were to employ the Normative Approach to create a credit risk model incorporating Income, the results may be poor.

In practical analytics, theory is not as important as the ability to forecast and predict. Determining how outcomes are caused by a factor regardless of monotonicity is termed the Positive Approach. If the middle-income bracket is the riskiest, accept that reality and build that into the model. There is no need to find an underlying theory. The Weight of Evidence (WoE) approach is based on this philosophy and the name aptly captures the spirit.

WoE is custom-made for binary outcomes like Default, Non-default, for instance. The fundamental idea underlying is to measure how much a factor can discriminate between the two. Unsurprisingly, it is well suited for credit risk modeling since the target is binary in nature.

There is another gem in WoE that is seldom highlighted. Most conventional modeling methods require inputs to be quantitative in nature. Logistic Regression (Logit), Decision Tree, Discriminant Analysis, etc. are widely used for credit risk modeling. Most of these are limited to numeric data values. Potential categorical factors like Industry, Gender, Management, etc. have to be excluded unless there is a way of converting them to quantitative equivalents. With WoE, this is not an issue. In fact, categorical data offer an even better fit into the method.

WoE is often explained as an evaluation of the natural logarithm (log) of the odds. If the outcome Y can only be 0 or 1, then

$$\log \frac{P(Y=1\mid X_i)}{P(Y=0\mid X_i)} = \log \frac{P(Y=1)}{P(Y=0)} + \log \frac{P(X_i\mid Y=1)}{P(X_i\mid Y=0)}.$$

The first term on the right-hand side of the equation is known as the unconditional log-odds and the next term the WoE. A simple example available on the internet to test if gender is a predictor of test outcome can be used to illustrate the method.

Assume that 10 Boys (B) and 10 Girls (G) randomly selected were given a test with Pass (P) or Fail (F). The results are as follows:

Gender	B	B	B	B	B	B	B	B	B	B	G	G	G	G	G	G	G	G	G	G
Result	P	P	F	P	F	F	P	P	F	P	P	P	P	P	F	P	P	P	F	P

The log-odds would then look as in the following table:

Gender	Pass	Fail	Total	% Passes	% Fails	IV	WoE
B	6	4	10	0.4286	0.6667	0.1052	−0.4418
G	8	2	10	0.5714	0.3333	0.1283	0.5390
All	14	6	20	1.0000	1.0000	0.2335	—

Information Value (IV) is defined as (% Passes − % Fails) × log % Passes/ % Fails. The 0.4286 value for Boys is given by 6/14. This metric is always positive by construction.

Unlike for conventional statistical methods, there is no null hypothesis and confidence level in WoE. The purpose here is to determine if there is sufficiently strong empirical evidence to make a certain conclusion which is if gender is a factor in this case. Most practitioners of WoE regard a cumulative IV of 0.3 as good enough evidence. Too high a value is usually suspected as unnatural. In this example, there is some though not strong evidence that boys and girls differ in their performance on the test.

Categorical values suit WoE very well as the categories are already preset. With ordinal or cardinal data that are continuous, there is a need to first use binning or bucketing to facilitate the derivation of log-odds. Size, for example, can be categorized into Large, Medium, Small or more granular strata. This is perhaps the most significant shortcoming of WoE as there is no way to predetermine if bins or buckets are meaningfully discriminating with respect to the target.

Those familiar with Logit will see the resemblance here. As Logit is one of the most popular methods used to develop credit risk models, WoE has gained acceptance among these modelers. This is of no surprise as there are several advantages in WoE. The first and foremost is that it is distribution-free.

Classical Statistics methods like Logit rely on the Normal Distribution which is far from reality. Typical financial ratios are so skewed that extreme values are often discarded through Winsorization which is the removal of $X\%$ of the largest and smallest ones. This reduces the power of discrimination and leads to a lack of statistical significance. WoE is free of this problem. Since continuous data values have to be binned or bucketed, all data points can be included. The extreme values will just become part of the smallest and largest bins. For organizations with precious little data after scrubbing, this is an important consideration.

The second advantage of WoE is the liberation from monotonic relationships. The assumption of a monotonic and even linear relationship between cause and effect is necessary in academic modeling. Theories have to be sufficiently simple to be grasped. Anomalies are then dealt with one at a time. Human behavior is far less easy to fit into this paradigm. Philanthropy and altruism have always posed a challenge to the assumption of rational economic agents trying to maximize their individual utility functions.

By not being bound to monotonic relationships, WoE allows for very flexible models. For instance, the default rates on credit for a specific band of Debt Ratio may be unexpectedly lower than preceding bands along an increasing scale. This will be confounding for conventional methods that require monotonicity. With WoE, this kink in the data is not an issue at all since all the bands are treated as individual categories. The predicted default rate can easily accommodate such data.

Third, WoE can facilitate models with greater power than conventional methods. The default rates of two bands of Debt Ratio may be similar even if they are far apart on the range. These bands can be combined into one to increase the power to discriminate which is not possible for methods like Logit.

Fourth, the number of bins or buckets can be adjusted for the best results. This is essentially the aim of research design which is to develop better models.

WoE is relatively easy to code in R, but its popularity has resulted in packages like woeBinning and IV being created. The woeBinning package offers options to optimize the binning of continuous values like financial ratios. The following R codes illustrate the binning of predictors v1, v2 and v3 for the target Default which has binary values. A more detailed discussion of the package outputs for credit risk modeling is found in Chapter 10.

```
begin
sys.rqScriptCreate('Analytics',
'function() {
library(ROracle)
library(woeBinning)
drv <- dbDriver("Oracle")
con <- dbConnect(drv, username="rquser", password="password",
dbname="ORCLPDB", prefetch=FALSE, external_credentials=FALSE)
df <- dbReadTable(con, "CREDIT", schema="RQUSER")

# Apply woeBinning function
binning <- woeBinning(df, "DEFAULT", c("v1", "v2", "v3"))
}',
v_overwrite => TRUE);
end;
/
Insert into binning (binning)
select * from table(rqEval(NULL, 'select 1 binning from dual', 'Analytics'));
```

Chapter 10

Internal Rating System

Banking is one domain where risk analytics has become prominent. This is largely due to a significantly more demanding risk management regime known as the New Basel Capital Accord or Basel II. More than 100 countries have committed to this standard and implemented local regulations to enforce compliance. It has been estimated that European banks have to spend tens of millions of Euros just to acquire the needed software and hardware to develop the metrics required.

Basel II requires a bank to quantify credit risk along three dimensions. The first is the risk intrinsic to the debtor or obligor. This should be reflected using a risk rating associated with a Probability of Default (PD). The second involves the risk of the credit facility itself. This is measured by the Loss Given Default (LGD) which is the percentage that cannot be recovered in the case of a default. The third is Exposure At Default (EAD) which is the effective amount that could be defaulted beyond what is already on the books. Many adjustments may be made to these metrics, but these three are mandatory.

The modeling of PD or Obligor Risk Rating (ORR) has perhaps attracted the most efforts and resources. One reason is that this metric is not new. Credit Rating Agencies (CRA) like Standard & Poors, Moody's, Fitch, etc. have long offered risk ratings of a similar nature. For investors and decision-makers, a lower rating means a greater risk of default and hence requires a higher level of compensation for risk-bearing in the form of an interest rate premium. Risk rating then serves as a form of quality grade that has helped make debt investment more predictable and widespread. The development of an ORR model provides a good setting to demonstrate the entire process of risk analytics from theory to implementation that is the thrust of this book. Before going into the technical aspects, some requirements of the Basel II ORR are worth elaborating on as they have direct bearing on what needs to be done.

An ORR must have no less than 7 Non-default and 1 Default grade. Under Basel II, default occurs when a payment has not been made for 90 days. The PD for the default grade must be 1.00.

Each risk grade must be associated with a PD. It is not permissible to assign a unique PD to a specific obligor. Risk rating has to be in the form of a grade. The PD of that grade will then be the level of default risk.

The PDs of Non-default grades can theoretically range from more than 0 to less than 1. It is specified in Basel II, however, that the smallest value must not be less than 0.0003 or 0.03% which aligns to the AAA rating of Standard & Poors or Moody's. Though there is no upper limit set, a quirk of Basel II informs modelers to cap it around 0.20 or 20%. In other words, the range of PDs for Non-default grades will be from 0.03% to 20.00% which will guide the development of the ORR system.

Unlike for CRA ratings which are meant to be through an economic cycle, an ORR is designed to last for one year or 18 months ahead in special cases. If the PD of a grade is 0.07, it implies that there is a 7% probability of default for each obligor assigned the same grade. Alternatively, about 7% of these obligors will default within the coming 12 to 18 months.

An ORR has to prove reliable in order for it to be accepted for use. The prescribed validation process is known as backtesting. Although no specific requirements have been stipulated, there is one widely accepted criterion that must be met and this is generally termed the test of consistency.

Backtesting is also known as out of time validation. In conventional empirical research, a model is validated using out-of-sample testing. A data sample is first divided into two or three. They are usually called Training and Testing samples. The Training sample is used to develop the model and the Testing sample also known as Control will be used to test how well the model fits data that have not been used for its creation. All the data employed are from the same sampling period.

The principle underlying backtesting is not different except that the Testing sample must be from a period after the model has been developed. If an ORR model is created using data up to the end of Year 1, only data from Year 2 can be employed to test its reliability. The criterion of consistency must be met here. If risk Grade 1 is better than that of Grade 2, the actual default rate in the backtesting period for Grade 1 must not exceed that of Grade 2. This consistency must hold for all the Non-default grades. A bank must pass the backtesting for three consecutive years before an ORR system is allowed to be used to compute its capital adequacy ratio.

The consistency criterion appears simple in theory but has been a bridge too far for many ORRs. Even seasoned statisticians holding advanced degrees have failed to meet the requirement. A key reason is non-stationarity. Factors that affected credit risk during the modeling period may no longer do so in the backtesting one. New risk determinants emerge in the backtesting period that were non-existent earlier. Even a most robust model developed can fail the consistency test. As such, the Basel Committee advises banks to develop as many models as needed for different credit exposures and banks are submitting specific ones for approval.

10.1. Developing an ORR

There are some regulatory requirements for the ORR. One Wholesale (not consumer or small business) obligor can have only one rating. A model must be developed using no less than three years of historical data. There must be at least 7 Non-default and 1 Default risk grade. An obligor who has defaulted on any exposure must be assigned a Default grade regardless of repayment performance on all other exposures. The PD in a Default grade must be 1. When a credit exposure is cured (all outstanding amounts due have been repaid), the obligor can be returned to a Non-default grade.

A rating must be updated at least annually if there is no default and no less than semiannually if default has occurred. The change in rating must be tracked in a Rating Migration Matrix. Though not critical, these requirements do impose some constraints on the ORR modeling process.

One aspect of the ORR that is seldom addressed is the reageing policy. Reageing is the resetting of the delinquency or Days Past Due (DPD) to zero when the exposure is cured. Basel II explicitly requires a bank to have a consistent and transparent policy in this area. For instance, an obligor with a grade of 2 (1 being the best) defaulted on one of its exposures which chalked up 90 DPD. This obligor has to be downgraded to a

Default grade. After all amounts due have been repaid, the obligor has to be returned to a Non-default grade and the DPD clock is reset to zero. This is reageing and a bank must have a clear policy on how it is done. The obligor is unlikely to be returned to the same risk grade before the default as there is now a blemish on the credit quality. The hard question to be answered is what should the new grade be. While seemingly simple, that requires the formulation of defendable business rules that the regulator is not going to reject. Reageing of a technical default arising from an clerical oversight of repayment need not be the same as that for default due to financial distress. This matter is too subject to bank strategies, culture and management philosophy to be discussed here, but it has been highlighted for the risk professional to be aware of. Banks that I have consulted for take the easy route by returning the obligor to the earlier Non-default grade, but this is not consistent with the purpose of risk rating.

10.2. Data Audit

Real corporate financial data are used in this exercise to best capture the challenges of developing an ORR. As strongly advocated earlier, a data audit is necessary to ensure that any results obtained are not produced or influenced by deficient data.

A sample of 40,000 corporate financial statements is selected from a bank's Wholesale Banking database acquired from a data vendor. Comprising 10,000 records for each year of 2014, 2015, 2016 and 2017, this dataset is transferred to a data table named Sample. Data for 2014 to 2016 would be used to develop the risk model with 2017 data employed for backtesting.

The data comprise 137 columns or variables. The first three are the firm ID, year of financial statement and industry of which there are 14. The remaining are financial figures or derived ratios.

A quick scan of the 14 industries shown in the following suggests that financial data are likely to be quite different among them. The Finance industry has cash and deposits (CashAndDeposits column) which is not found in others. Likewise, land for development (LandForDevelopment) data are predominantly found only in the Real Estate industry. Here, experience and the art of modeling has to come into the picture as there are many ways to classify Industry and a wide range of variables that can be considered.

⬡ INDUSTRY	
1	Agriculture
2	Education
3	Finance
4	Information, Communication and Technology.
5	Infrastructure
6	Leisure
7	Manufacturing
8	Medical
9	Mining and exploration
10	Oil and gas
11	Real estate
12	Services
13	Trading
14	Transport

It is advocated in Basel II that as many models as needed should be developed to ensure that the risk profile derived fits into the class of obligors. For the purpose of a modeling exercise, three sufficiently similar industries are selected. They are Manufacturing, Trading and Transport. Not only does the inclusion of the three industries allows for an adequately large initial sample size that has to be pruned, it also enables a test of difference between industries with respect to credit quality. In research lingo, this is termed developing nested models.

The first step is to extract the desired sample from the dataset. The R code introduced earlier can be used for this purpose:

```
begin
sys.rqScriptCreate('Analytics',
'function() {
library(ROracle)
drv <- dbDriver("Oracle")
con <- dbConnect(drv, username="rquser", password="password",
dbname="ORCLPDB", prefetch = FALSE, external_credentials = FALSE)
df <- dbReadTable(con, "SAMPLE", schema = "RQUSER")
```

```
# Define trim function to remove white spaces
trim <- function (x) gsub("^\\s+|\\s+$", "", x)
sample <-subset(df, trim(INDUSTRY) == "Manufacturing" | trim
(INDUSTRY)=="Trading" | trim(INDUSTRY) == "Transport")
dum <- 1
data.frame(dum = dum)
}',
v_overwrite => TRUE);
end;
/
```

```
# Trigger the script with redundant result
select * from table(rqEval(NULL, 'select 1 dum from dual', 'Analytics'));
```

It should be the noted that the trim function function (x) gsub("^\\ s+|\\s+$", "", x) is necessary for selecting a subset of Sample with Manufacturing, Trading or Transport as the industry criterion. Though the Oracle table uses VARCHAR for the Industry column, leading or trailing spaces can still be generated but remain invisible. Without the trimming function, the trading dataset will return zero rows. The "or" separator in R is |. There are 21,130 records in Sample belonging to these industries and that will be significantly reduced at the end of the data audit. The next step is to deal with invalid values.

Experience suggests that some accounting numbers are technically correct but economically questionable. For instance, a going concern can hardly be operating with zero Current Assets or Current Liabilities though that is not theoretically impossible. Current Assets/Total Assets cannot be negative unless that is Net Current Assets/Total Assets, where the numerator is Current Assets less Current Liabilities which sloppy data recording does not bother to distinguish. For the same reason, Debt is sometimes recorded as negative, giving rise to Debt/Asset being negative. Since a high debt ratio is usually associated with low credit quality, a negative one produces a misleading indication of very high creditworthiness which is accentuated when the value of debt is large. Some firms may even report negative Cash when that is actually Cash less Overdraft which is not stated as such.

The following criteria are used to determine invalidity:

- Cash/Total Assets/Liabilities/Sales/Revenue/Debt is negative
- Current Assets/Liabilities less than or equal to zero

Instead of purging the records, the variable values can be made NA keeping other columns that are still usable as follows:

```
# Replace invalid or unreliable values with NA
sample$CASHNDEPOSITS[sample$CASHNDEPOSITS < 0] <- NA
sample$TOTALCURRENTASSETS[sample$TOTALCURRENTASSETS <= 0]
<- NA
sample$TOTALASSETS[sample$TOTALASSETS < 0] <- NA
sample$TOTALLTLOANS[sample$ TOTALLTLOANS < 0] <- NA
sample$TOTALLIABILITIES[sample$TOTALLIABILITIES < 0] <- NA
sample$TOTALCURRENTLIABILITIES[sample$TOTALCURRENTLIABILITIES
<= 0] <- NA
sample$TOTALREVENUE[sample$TOTALREVENUE < 0] <- NA
valid <- sample
```

The next test is for outdated values. In the country from where the Sample is taken, some active firms submit the same set of financial figures for several years to save accounting fees and these are approved by auditors due to lax regulatory enforcement. The latter year values are certainly outdated. As it is tedious to examine all columns, key ones like Total Assets, Total Revenue, Total Equity and Total Liabilities are selected for testing.

Comparing values across time requires the creation of lags. Revisiting the R script suggested in an earlier chapter, a lag function has to be first defined using the package data.table:

```
library(data.table)

# Create lag function lg
lg <- function(x)c(NA, x[1:(length(x)-1)])
```

After converting data frame into the data.table format, the records have to be sorted chronologically by each firm ID:

```
valid <- data.table(valid)

# Sort records by ID and YEAR
valid <- valid [order(rank(ID), YEAR)]

# Set LAGTOTAL** as the lagged value
```

```
valid [, LAGTOTALASSETS := lg(TOTALASSETS), by = c("ID")]
valid [, LAGTOTALLIABILITIES := lg(TOTALLIABILITIES), by = c("ID")]
valid [, LAGTOTALEQUITY := lg(TOTALEQUITY), by = c("ID")]
```

Unlike for the test of validity, the records with outdated data are removed as all variable values are questionable once the key ones are not updated. Employing the anti_join function, the data frame is pruned of the outdated values:

```
# Use anti_join function to remove record where values are equal
lagged ones
updated<-anti_join(valid,subset(valid,(TOTALASSETS=LAGTOTALASSETS)
& (TOTALLIABILITIES = LAGTOTALLIABILITIES) & (TOTALEQUITY =
LAGTOTALEQUITY)), by = NULL)
```

The updated data frame contains only 8,745 records which suggests that problem of outdatedness is serious in the Sample.

The reliability test will be needed for most modeling approaches. For the Weight of Evidence (WoE) method, however, binning removes the impact of outliers which is one of the biggest advantages so that test will be skipped without material impact on the results.

The final test of consistency is omitted as four years of data are insufficient for a robust test.

It has to be verified that data of the input columns are sufficiently complete before the ratios are derived. A minimum of 75% threshold is set for completeness:

```
# Compute completeness ratio
complete <- 1-data.frame(colSums(is.na(updated))) / nrow(updated)

# Retain only columns with no less than 0.75 complete
complete <- subset(complete, complete[, 1]>=0.75)
complete <- t(complete)

# Transfer data into a new data frame woe
woe <-updated[names(updated) %in% names(complete)]
```

The last data audit data frame complete is then used to extract from updated the columns that meet the completeness threshold to create a data frame woe for the modeling process.

10.3. Predictors and Target

The ORR model aims to develop a profile of credit quality. Even in a bank, credit quality is subjective. It is commonly mistaken that there is an objectively determined state called "Default" which is unequivocally associated with bad credit. Even with the arrival of Basel II which has tried to standardize what amounts to a default, there is a wide variation on how the definitions provided are implemented. This may be trivial for business operations but have material implications on the modeling of credit risk.

Most banks follow the 90 DPD definition for default. What constitutes this 90 DPD is, however, subjective. In a bank that I consulted for, priority is to minimize the amount of Non-Performing Loans (NPL). Keeping 90 DPD to the lowest level possible is desired so the bank designed the system with that objective. A requirement for default in Basel II wholesale obligors is that a default in one exposure must amount to default on all exposures. It implies that restoration to a Non-default status or reageing has to be upon all outstanding credits being settled. This bank's system makes a minor operational adjustment to that requirement. If the minimum amount for an exposure that has reached 90 DPD is repaid, the obligor is reaged. Such a creative implementation allows for two bites of the cherry. Not only does it not require full settlement of the defaulted exposure, it disregards all the other exposures that have not reached 90 DPD. The profile of a defaulter in this banking regime can then be very different from another that tries to comply with the true spirit of the Basel II definition of default. Comparing NPL ratios across regimes is akin to doing so with apples against oranges. This is another facet in business modeling that is not addressed in textbooks as such quirks are only be detected by handling of real data with the requisite domain knowledge and understanding.

The Sample data are from corporate financial statements and not credit facilities, so there is no default state to be determined. The usual alternative is to use the economic definition of "Bankrupt" which is negative equity as elaborated on later.

Conventional analysis suggests that there are five areas associated with corporate financial health. These are Profitability, Liquidity, Indebtedness, Activity and Capitalization. To that may be added the attribute Growth. Many financial ratios have been created to capture these areas. To balance the need for enough predictors with the likelihood that those in the same area are correlated, two are derived for each as follows:

Return on Assets (Profitability)
Gross Profit Margin (Profitability)
Quick Ratio (Liquidity)
Current Ratio (Liquidity)
Equity to Long-term Loan (Indebtedness)
Long-term Loan to Total Assets (Indebtedness)
Total Assets Turnover (Activity)
Property, Plant and Equipment Turnover (Activity)
Equity to Total Assets (Capitalization)
Capital to Total Assets (Capitalization)
Sales Growth (Growth)
Revenue Growth (Growth)

The Long-term Loan variable does not meet the 75% threshold for completeness and was dropped. It has to be replaced by Total Noncurrent Liabilities which is computed as (Total Liabilities minus Total Current Liabilities) due to its unavailability. The codes needed to derive these are straightforward:

```
woe$RoA <- woe$NETINCOME / woe$TOTALASSETS
woe$GrossProfitMargin <- woe$GROSSPROFIT / woe$NETSALES
woe$QuickRatio <- woe$CASHNDEPOSITS /
woe$TOTALCURRENTLIABILITIES
woe$CurrentRatio <- (woe$TOTALASSETS -
woe$TOTALNONCURRENTASSETS) / woe$TOTALCURRENTLIABILITIES
woe$Equity2LTLoans <- woe$TOTALEQUITY /
(woe$TOTALLIABILITIES-woe$TOTALCURRENTLIABILITIES)
woe$LTLoans2TA <- (woe$TOTALLIABILITIES -
woe$TOTALCURRENTLIABILITIES) / woe$TOTALASSETS
woe$TATurnover <- woe$TOTALREVENUE / woe$TOTALASSETS
woe$PPETurnover <- woe$TOTALREVENUE / woe$NETPPE
woe$Equity2TA <- woe$TOTALEQUITY / woe$TOTALASSETS
woe$Capital2TA <- woe$CAPITAL2TA
woe$SalesGrowth <- woe$SALESGROWTH
woe$RevenueGrowth <- woe$REVENUEGROWTH
```

Columns like CAPITAL2TA are pre-existing and simply replicated to create a continual set of columns for easier manipulation. Ratio derivation can result in (negative) infinity values if a denominator is 0 that was previously undetected. This is displayed as Inf or −Inf in the data frame. Unlike NA, such a value causes function failure and has to be replaced by NA:

```
woe[woe == 'Inf'] <- NA
woe [woe == '-Inf'] <- NA
```

It is worth noting that none of the ratios uses Equity as a denominator. Doing so poses a challenge not easily resolvable. Consider ROE, for instance. Textbook discussion of this ratio does not cover the case of negative equity. The issue of both negative equity and negative net income producing a positive ROE has been raised earlier. A negative equity with positive net income is also troubling. The ROE is negative, but the ratio is not reflective of the state of creditworthiness. A firm with a small negative equity achieving a large positive net income for the year would generally be regarded as being on the road to financial health. Instead, the ROE is a large negative associated with high credit risk similar to another firm with a small positive equity and large loss for the year. Manual adjustments can always be made to mitigate the problem, but none is entirely satisfactory. Using Equity as the numerator is a superior approach as the ratio will not be affected by the sign.

10.4. Weight of Evidence (WoE)

As discussed earlier, the WoE approach has increasingly been employed for credit risk modeling. It is especially useful when the distribution of financial ratios widely used as predictors are severely skewed. Besides, WoE is specifically suited for a binary target outcome like "Yes" or "No" to default. There is, however, a minor drawback. WOE predictors have to be categorical in nature and continuous financial ratios have to be first binned to meet that requirement.

Multicollinearity is a perennial thorn in Classical Statistics modeling with financial ratios. As more than one ratio captures one aspect of financial health, it is inevitable that many ratios turn out highly correlated. Return on Assets (RoA) and Return on Equity (RoE) are almost certainly correlated without any test. Classical Statistics require all regressors entered to be evaluated for their predictive powers in the presence of each other. Not only can one cannibalize the power of another that is similar, it can even cause a reversal of the sign of the estimated coefficient. For instance, if both RoA and RoE are used in the same Logistic Regression to predict default, the sign of one coefficient may be large and positive while that of the other negative as compensation for their combined powers. This can be confusing and hard to interpret as both variables should have the same sign, *a priori*. WoE is not plagued by this problem as each variable is evaluated on its own merit in terms of predictive power.

Though WoE is not degraded by multicollinearity, it is still worthwhile to examine correlation among the potential predictors to reduce them to a more manageable number. The rcorr function in the package Hmisc generates the correlation, number of paired values and the *p*-value for a correlation matrix ignoring missing data. A ratio data frame comprising the 10 financial ratios derived earlier (in columns 52 to 61 of woe) is created for the correlation test.

```
library(Hmisc)

# Extract ratio columns 52 to 61 into ratio data frame
ratios <- woe[c(52:61)]

# Compute correlations with p-value
corr <- rcorr(as.matrix(ratios[, unlist(lapply(ratios, is.numeric))]))$P
```

As shown in the code above, only the numeric columns in the woe data frame can be used to derive the correlations and only the *p*-values are extracted (note the $P at the end).

Correlations can be assessed on statistical significance using the p-value which is the column p in the corr data frame. A 5% threshold is set to identify those correlations that are significant:

```
corrsig <- which( corr < 0.05, arr.ind=TRUE )
```

A snapshot of the output is shown as follows:

	row	col
CurrentRatio	2	1
QuickRatio	1	2
TATurnover	4	3
Equity2TA	5	3
Capital2TA	6	3
LTLoans2TA	3	4
Equity2TA	5	4
Capital2TA	6	4
RevenueGrowth	8	4
LTLoans2TA	3	5
TATurnover	4	5
Capital2TA	6	5
LTLoans2TA	3	6
TATurnover	4	6
Equity2TA	5	6
TATurnover	4	8

Current Ratio (column 2) is significantly correlated with Quick Ratio (column 1), Equity to Total Assets (column 5) and Capital to Total Assets (column 6) have the highest number of significant correlations.

The conventional approach to handle highly correlated variables is to drop one of them. Alternatively, orthogonalization can be employed to mitigate the effect. As there are only 12 ratios available, any culling may deprecate the model developed so that option is skipped. Once again, the fact that WoE is not degraded by multicollinearity is a key consideration in the tradeoff between having independent predictors vs a sufficient number for model reliability.

A new column Bankrupt is created to be the target of modeling. Integers are assigned with 1 for bankrupt and 0 otherwise to facilitate later computations. Bankrupt is defined using the accounting standard as total equity being negative:

```
woe$Bankrupt <- ifelse(woe$TOTALEQUITY < 0, "1", "0")
```

The package woeBinning combines the steps needed to arrive at the Information Value of each potential predictor in a data frame ratios which retains only the financial ratios in woe. The code restricts the binning to columns 52–62 where the derived ratios and the column Bankrupt are stored:

```
woe.binning(woe[c(52:62)], "Bankrupt", woe[c(52:62)])
```

The results suggest that only Equity to Long-term Loans and Equity to Total Assets have meaningful IVs which are still rather weak. Though inadequate for a deployable model, all the ratios will be employed to develop one for the purpose of illustration. It should be noted that the issues involving negatives values in Debt to Equity and ROE remain and have to be addressed in developing a model for business use.

It is essential to understand that this chapter is not about developing a reliable credit risk model. Instead, it is meant to explain the process of modeling using R coding and a specific method called WoE. If done in a bank, the IVs must be assessed to determine which variables should be selected. Many suggestions on the threshold IV value to be used as criterion can be found on the internet. Much more care has to be exercised if the model is to be used in credit decision-making.

10.5. Training a Model

To recap, three years of data are used to develop or train a model with those in the fourth year reserved for backtesting. A data frame train is created as follows:

```
# Create train data frame with three years of data before 2017
train <- subset(woe, substring(woe$YEAR, 1, 4) < 2017)
train <- train[c('ID', 'YEAR', 'INDUSTRY', 'RoA', 'GrossProfitMargin',
'QuickRatio','CurrentRatio','Equity2LTLoans','LTLoans2TA','TATurnover',
'PPETurnover','Equity2TA','Capital2TA','SalesGrowth','RevenueGrowth',
'Bankrupt')]
```

Only 5,983 rows or records are available for training. At this point, it is worthwhile to review the purpose of the WoE approach.

WoE is based on the following formula:

$$\log\left(\frac{P(\text{Bankrupt} = \text{"Yes"} \mid X_i)}{P(\text{Bankrupt} = \text{"No"} \mid X_i)}\right) = \log\left(\frac{P(\text{Bankrupt} = \text{"Yes"})}{P(\text{Bankrupt} = \text{"No"})}\right)$$
$$+ \log\left(\frac{f(X_i \mid \text{Bankrupt} = \text{"Yes"})}{f(X_i \mid \text{Bankrupt} = \text{"No"})}\right).$$

The left-hand side is the log-odds of a firm going bankrupt given the values of X_i which are the financial ratio predictors here. The first term on the right-hand side is the unconditional or sample log-odds which is the same for all predictors. The second term $f(X_i \mid Y)$ is the conditional probability density function which is termed the WoE. For a binary outcome like default or bankruptcy, the log-odds of occurrence is the sum of the unconditional log-odds which is equivalent to the intercept value and the log-density ratio or WoE. The larger the sum, the higher is the probability of bankruptcy.

The original financial ratios have to be converted to WoE values. This can be done using the scorecard package function woebin:

```
library(scorecard)
bins = woebin(train, var_skip='ID', y = "Bankrupt")
train_woe = woebin_ply(train, bins)
```

The screenshot of the results is shown as follows:

	ID	BANKRUPT	ROE_woe	DEBTRATIO_woe	DEBT2EQUITYRATIO_woe	EQUITY2TA_woe
1	1001097216	0	0.9061877	0.02719025	0.1198958	-0.126741
2	1001059197	1	0.9061877	0.02719025	0.1198958	-0.126741
3	1001103413	0	0.5156787	0.02719025	0.1198958	-0.126741
4	1001093885	0	-0.8367141	0.02719025	0.1198958	-0.126741
5	1002109940	1	0.9061877	0.02719025	0.1198958	-0.126741
6	1001106403	1	-0.2575112	0.02719025	0.1198958	1.197776
7	1001069910	0	0.5156787	-0.22852366	-2.8842982	-0.126741
8	1001069010	0	0.5156787	0.22852366	2.8842982	0.126741

The sum of the *_woe is equal to the second term WoE on the right-hand side of the formula. The unconditional or sample log-odds is simply the natural log of the percentage of 1 for Bankrupt divided by the percentage of 0. Adding this to the WoE results in the left-hand side value. The output train_woe has to be converted to a data frame before processing:

```
train_woe <- as.data.frame(train_woe)
```

```
# Derive sample log odds
train_woe$samplelogodds <- log(nrow(subset(train_woe, Bankrupt ==
"1"))) / (nrow(subset(train_woe, Bankrupt == "0")))
```

```
# Derive model (left-hand side of equation) log odds
train_woe$logodds  <-  train_woe$samplelogodds  +  train_woe$
INDUSTRY_woe+train_woe$RoA_woe+train_woe$GrossProfitMargin_
woe+train_woe$QuickRatio_woe + train_woe$CurrentRatio_woe +
train_woe$Equity2LTLoans_woe  +  train_woe$LTLoans2TA_woe  +
train_woe$TATurnover_woe + train_woe$PPETurnover_woe + train_
woe$Equity2TA_woe  +  train_woe$Capital2TA_woe  +  train_woe$
SalesGrowth_woe + train_woe$RevenueGrowth_woe
```

The logodds column created should have negative values given that counts for 1 is less than that for 0 in Bankrupt. The final step is to recover P(Bankrupt = 1) which is equivalent to the model PD, not the same as the risk grade PD.

```
train_woe$odds <- exp(train_woe$logodds)
train_woe$prob <- train_woe$odds / (1 + train_woe$odds)
```

A screenshot of the results is as follows:

	ID	BANKRUPT	ROE_woe	DEBTRATIO_woe	DEBT2EQUITYRATIO_woe	EQUITY2TA_woe	samplelogodds	logodds	odds	prob
1	1001097216	0	0.9061877	0.02719025	0.1198958	-0.126741	-0.6587795	0.2677533	1.307024614	0.566541252
2	1001059197	1	0.9061877	0.02719025	0.1198958	-0.126741	-0.6587795	0.2677533	1.307024614	0.566541252
3	1001103413	0	0.5156787	0.02719025	0.1198958	-0.126741	-0.6587795	-0.1227558	0.884479670	0.469349542
4	1001093885	0	-0.8367141	0.02719025	0.1198958	-0.126741	-0.6587795	-1.4751486	0.228744742	0.186161319
5	1002109940	1	0.9061877	0.02719025	0.1198958	-0.126741	-0.6587795	0.2677533	1.307024614	0.566541252
6	1001106403	1	-0.2575112	0.02719025	0.1198958	1.197776	-0.6587795	0.4285714	1.535062908	0.605532472

The value of prob should lie between 0 and 1 if the formula has been correctly processed. To facilitate the next step which is the creation of the risk grades/ratings, two columns are added to the train_woe data frame. woe is the sum of the predictor *_woe and the optional column score is the integer value of prob*10000. This new column is essentially cosmetic but makes it easier to set the thresholds dividing risk grades in the R codes later:

```
train_woe$woe <- train_woe$INDUSTRY_woe + train_woe$RoA_woe +
train_woe$GrossProfitMargin_woe + train_woe$QuickRatio_woe +
train_woe$CurrentRatio_woe + train_woe$Equity2LTLoans_woe +
train_woe$LTLoans2TA_woe + train_woe$TATurnover_woe + train_
woe$PPETurnover_woe + train_woe$Equity2TA_woe + train_woe$
Capital2TA_woe  +  train_woe$SalesGrowth_woe  +  train_woe$
RevenueGrowth_woe
```

```
# Create new column score as prob*10000
train_woe$score <- as.integer(train_woe$prob * 10000)
```

10.6. Risk Grades/Ratings

The probabilities generated and shown in the prob column mark the end of WoE modeling but are not acceptable for a Basel II Internal Rating System (IRS). Projects using the scorecard package usually stop at a scorecard being created as the final outcome. The probabilities obtained up to this point are termed as point estimates as each is unique to the obligor of concern. This is equivalent to the mark obtained by each student and all can be different. Basel II clearly states that such point estimates are disallowed. Instead, bands must be created to group values close to each other. These bands are termed ratings or grades. They are similar to academic grades. Marks between 70 and 79 may be assigned a B grade, etc. A mark of 71 is as good as another of 78 as both are assigned the same grade. At the end of a course, a student achieves a Grade Point Average or GPA rather than X marks in total.

There are several reasons why the IRS requires risk grades instead of point estimates like scores. First, an ORR is not just for a bank's own risk assessment. It is a key input into regulatory capital that banks must maintain. The rating system has to produce at least 7 PDs for obligors who have not defaulted and 1 for defaulters. PD is one of the three key metrics that go into the derivation of economic capital that serves as the basis for regulatory capital.

Second, a PD must reflect the actual default rate. A rate has been be derived from a ratio so a point estimate cannot correspond to a rate. Besides, the WoE probabilities generated are unrealistic. As can be seen from the results later, these probabilities range from near zero to near one which is an artifact of modeling binary outcomes. The third requirement is that a risk grade must be indicative of the credit worthiness of obligors of similar quality. Again, point estimates cannot fulfill these requirements. Finally, there must be no concentration of obligors in any grade. A grade that has too high a proportion has to be divided into more granular segments.

Just like the creation of academic grades from marks, risk grades have to be derived from the WoE probabilities. However, there is a critical difference in the two processes. Marks can be arbitrarily banded into any number of desired grades. A+, A, A−, B+, etc. is just as good as A, B, C and D. That cannot be done for risk grades as there is a necessary condition that needs to be met. The default rate in a better grade cannot be higher than that of a worse one. In practical terms, they cannot even be the same as that would mean that both grades are of equal credit risk. Besides, Basel II disallows any risk grade with a PD of less than 0.03% which means that even the best grade must have some defaults within. And the no less than 7 Non-default grades requirement must be complied with. An ORR system then cannot arise from a mechanical segmentation of the WoE probabilities. With all the criteria to be to be met, creating one is an art as much as a science.

For the sake of this exercise, the minimal requirement of 7 Non-default plus 1 Default grades will be generated. A data frame ratingsystem is created with 8 grades as follows:

```
# Create 8 grades
grade <- c(1, 2, 3, 4, 5, 6, 7, 8)

# Initialise bankruptcy rate, count and WoE to zero
bankruptcyrate <- c(0, 0, 0, 0, 0, 0, 0, 0)
count <- c(0, 0, 0, 0, 0, 0, 0, 0)
WoE <- c(0, 0, 0, 0, 0, 0, 0, 0)
ratingsystem <- data.frame(grade, bankruptcyrate, count, woe)
```

The bankruptcyrate, count and woe columns are initially populated with the value of 0 that will be updated by what is derived from the training sample. Count captures the number of firms in each grade which is useful to evaluate concentration and woe the cutoff value which has to be used for backtesting.

The technical needs for backtesting can be easily overlooked by the inexperienced when creating the ORR. The test involves the comparison of default rates after implementation of the rating system to those derived when developing it. When creating the risk grades, the WoE thresholds can be manipulated to achieve optimal consistencies where the default rate of a better grade is lower than the next. These thresholds have to be applied to the backtesting data to create the same risk grades as those data cannot be used to develop another model. The thresholds then have to be recorded during ORR system creation to facilitate backtesting, else there is no way to assign those data to the risk grades designed earlier.

Creating the eight risk grades requires determining suitable cutoff points to band the obligors. In a Basel II-compliant rating system, the default rate of a lower grade cannot be less than that of a higher grade. If Grade 1 is for the best credit quality, its default rate must be the smallest. Besides, the default rate for the Default grade (Grade 8 in this case) must be 1.0000. In statistical terms, the default rate must be monotonic from the best to the worse grade. In practical rating system development, it is preferable to create grades with increasing default rates.

Using the Basel II requirement that no risk grade must have a default rate of less than 0.03%, the first grade or Grade 1 is created with this threshold as the minimum. The data frame is first sorted in ascending order using the column prob (the probability) derived earlier. Conceptually, the smaller the prob value, the lower the PD which should translate into fewer Bankrupt = 1 records. A column row is created to facilitate a loop to create bands with increasing bankruptcy rates captured in the variable bankruptcyrate. The first band or grade (Grade 1) is set once bankruptcyrate exceeds 0.0003. Rows for the second band starts after the last row of the first and stops when the bankruptcyrate exceeds that of Grade 1. The loop is run for eight bands or until all the rows are exhausted.

With the aim of complying with the Basel II requirement of no concentration in any risk grade, the condition ratingsystem$count[2] > 700 is used except for Grade 1 to ensure that each band has no less than 700 rows. Being the best, Grade 1 should not be constrained to have a minimum number of obligors. There is no theory on the ideal distribution though the bell shape with relatively more obligors being assigned the central grades is often held as ideal. The minimum of 700 is used here as there are nearly 6,000 rows to be distributed to eight grades. The code employed is lengthier than those in the past given the need for repetition:

```
# Sort data frame by ascending order of column prob
train_woe <- train_woe[order(train_woe$prob), ]

# Create column row to track the number of rows assigned to each
band
train_woe$row <- 1:nrow(train_woe)
max <- nrow(train_woe)

# Design loop to create 8 bands as risk grades
for (i in 1:max) {
```

```
# Create first band with no less than 0.0003 bankruptcy rate
bankruptcyrate <- ratingsystem$bankruptcyrate[1] if(bankruptcyrate
>= 0.0003) {break}
ratingsystem$bankruptcyrate  <-  ifelse(ratingsystem$grade  ==  1,
(nrow(subset(train_woe, Bankrupt == "1" & row <= i)) / nrow(subset
(train_woe, row <= i))), ratingsystem$bankruptcyrate)
ratingsystem$count <- ifelse(ratingsystem$grade == 1, nrow(subset
(train_woe, row <= i)), ratingsystem$count)
ratingsystem$woe[1] <- train_woe$woe[train_woe$row == i][1]
j <- i+1
}
K <- j
for (i in j: max) {
bankruptcyrate <- ratingsystem$bankruptcyrate[2]

# Create band 2 and all others with no less than 70 rows each
if(bankruptcyrate > ratingsystem$bankruptcyrate[1] & ratingsystem
$count[2] > 700) {break}
ratingsystem$bankruptcyrate <- ifelse(ratingsystem$grade == 2, nrow
(subset(train_woe, Bankrupt == "1" & row >= k & row <= i)) /
nrow(subset(train_woe, row >= k & row <= i)), ratingsystem$
bankruptcyrate)
ratingsystem$count <- ifelse(ratingsystem$grade == 2, nrow(subset
(train_woe, row >= k & row <= i)), ratingsystem$count)
ratingsystem$woe[2] <- train_woe$woe[train_woe$row == i][1]
j <- i+1
}
K <- j
for (i in j: max) {
bankruptcyrate <- ratingsystem$bankruptcyrate[3]
if(bankruptcyrate > ratingsystem$bankruptcyrate[2] & ratingsystem$
count[3] > 700) {break}
ratingsystem$bankruptcyrate  <-  ifelse(ratingsystem$grade  ==  3,
nrow(subset(train_woe, Bankrupt == "1" & row >= k & row <= i)) /
nrow(subset(train_woe, row >= k & row <= i)), ratingsystem$
bankruptcyrate)
ratingsystem$count <- ifelse(ratingsystem$grade == 3, nrow(subset
(train_woe, row >= k & row <= i)), ratingsystem$count)
ratingsystem$woe[3] <- train_woe$woe[train_woe$row == i][1]
```

```
j <- i+1
}
k <- j
for (i in j: max) {
bankruptcyrate <- ratingsystem$bankruptcyrate[4]
if(bankruptcyrate > ratingsystem$bankruptcyrate[3] & ratingsystem$
count[4] > 70{break}
ratingsystem$bankruptcyrate <- ifelse(ratingsystem$grade == 4, nrow
(subset(train_woe, Bankrupt = ="1" & row >= k & row <= i)) /
nrow(subset(train_woe, row >= k & row <= i)), ratingsystem$
bankruptcyrate)
ratingsystem$count <- ifelse(ratingsystem$grade == 4, nrow(subset
(train_woe, row >= k & row <= i)), ratingsystem$count)
ratingsystem$woe[4] <- train_woe$woe[train_woe$row == i][1]
j <- i+1
}
k <- j
for (i in j: max) {
bankruptcyrate <- ratingsystem$bankruptcyrate[5]
if(bankruptcyrate > ratingsystem$bankruptcyrate[4] & ratingsystem
$count[5] > 700) {break}
ratingsystem$bankruptcyrate <- ifelse(ratingsystem$grade == 5,
nrow(subset(train_woe, Bankrupt == "1" & row >= k & row <= i)) /
nrow(subset(train_woe, row >= k & row <= i)), ratingsystem$
bankruptcyrate)
ratingsystem$count <- ifelse(ratingsystem$grade == 5, nrow(subset
(train_woe, row >= k & row <= i)), ratingsystem$count)
ratingsystem$woe[5] <- train_woe$woe[train_woe$row == i][1]
j <- i+1
}
k <- j
for (i in j: max) {
bankruptcyrate <- ratingsystem$bankruptcyrate[6]
if(bankruptcyrate > ratingsystem$bankruptcyrate[5] & ratingsystem$
count[6] > 700) {break}
ratingsystem$bankruptcyrate <- ifelse(ratingsystem$grade == 6,
nrow(subset(train_woe, Bankrup t== "1" & row >= k & row <= i)) /
nrow(subset(train_woe, row >= k & row <= i)),
ratingsystem$bankruptcyrate)
```

```
ratingsystem$count <- ifelse(ratingsystem$grade == 6, nrow(subset
(train_woe, row >= k & row <= i)), ratingsystem$count)
ratingsystem$woe[6] <- train_woe$woe[train_woe$row == i][1]
j <- i+1
}
k <- j
for (i in j: max) {
bankruptcyrate <- ratingsystem$bankruptcyrate[7]
if(bankruptcyrate > ratingsystem$bankruptcyrate[6] & ratingsystem
$count[7] > 700) {break}
ratingsystem$bankruptcyrate <- ifelse(ratingsystem$grade == 7, nrow
(subset(train_woe, Bankrupt == "1" & row >= k & row <= i)) / nrow
(subset(train_woe, row >= k & row <= i)), ratingsystem$bankruptcyrate)
ratingsystem$count <- ifelse(ratingsystem$grade == 7, nrow(subset
(train_woe, row >= k & row <= i)), ratingsystem$count)
ratingsystem$woe[7] <- train_woe$woe[train_woe$row == i][1]
j <- i+1
}
k <- j
for (i in j: max) {
bankruptcyrate <- ratingsystem$bankruptcyrate[8]
if(bankruptcyrate > ratingsystem$bankruptcyrate[7]) {break}
ratingsystem$bankruptcyrate <- ifelse(ratingsystem$grade == 8, nrow
(subset(train_woe, Bankrupt == "1" & row >= k & row <= i)) / nrow
(subset(train_woe, row >= k & row <= i)), ratingsystem$bankruptcyrate)
ratingsystem$count <- ifelse(ratingsystem$grade == 8, nrow(subset
(train_woe, row >= k & row <= i)), ratingsystem$count)
ratingsystem$woe[8] <- train_woe$woe[train_woe$row == i][1]
j <- i+1
}
```

The ratingsystem data frame created to store the results look as follows:

```
  grade bankruptcyrate count      woe
1     1   0.003906250    256 -8.132533
2     2   0.004087193    734 -7.056821
3     3   0.005706134    701 -6.171603
4     4   0.007132668    701 -5.298325
5     5   0.014265335    701 -4.363344
6     6   0.032810271    701 -3.281601
7     7   0.088445078    701 -1.833972
8     8   1.000000000      1 -1.830856
```

It is not perfect but achieves two important objectives. First, the bankruptcyrate increases from the best (Grade 1) to the worst Non-default grade (Grade 7). Second, the bankruptcyrate for default grade (Grade 8) is 1.00000000 which fits perfectly into the regulatory PD required for this grade.

It should be noted that the rating system created here is not the only one possible. The permutations are endless. This is where the art of development coupled with experience have to guide the science. The entire process may have to be repeated with different parameters if the backtesting standard cannot be met.

Several conceptual issues of an ORR that are both challenging and easily misunderstood are worth discussing here.

In theory, a perfect model will assign all the bankrupts the highest probabilities (PD) based on the WoE formula. Even an imperfect but powerful one will result in most bankrupts falling to the bottom of the probability ranked data frame. Though this outcome is desired for most other models, it creates a problem for the ORR. Under Basel II, a rating system cannot have zero defaults (or bankruptcies in this case) in any risk grade. If all or most of the bankrupts are concentrated at the highest PDs, it will be difficult and even impossible to create bands with bankruptcy rates before reaching the end of the data set. Ironically, a perfect or even near-perfect model will result in the inability to develop an ORR. This is where the pursuit of academic ideals in modeling can confound practical requirements. It is the very imperfection where bankrupts are spread along the PD sorted dataset that allows for an ORR to be created. That may be an uncomfortable contradiction to a purely academic modeler.

The use of bankruptcy here as proxy for default obscures a challenge in the use of data. Bankruptcy is defined as negative equity derived using annual financial returns. In any of the three years used for model development, a firm is either bankrupt or not. This does not pose a problem to the Basel II definition of PD being a measure of risk of default over the next 12 months. Consider a model developed with quarterly bank credit data. With four times the volume of annual ones, this immediately appears to be an improvement. However, the issue of Default/Non-default is not straightforward. If firm X defaults in Q2 and gets reaged in Q3 after full repayment, should it be classified as Default in Q3 or Non-default with respect to Q1 data used for modeling? Under the Basel II definition, default within the following 12 months of a rating should be classified as such. Technically, the Q1 data predicts if the firm would default from Q1 to Q4. On the other hand, default due to 90 DPD can be due to transient financial stress which is quickly rectified over two quarters.

Classifying X as either Default or Non-default can impact on the quality of the model as the two states are essentially opposite.

10.7. Backtesting

Conventional model development requires a holdout or testing subsample to be carved out from the main. Some software automate this by splitting the sample into 70% and 30%, the former used for training the model and the latter for testing. The underlying principle is that a model should be validated by data that have not been used in its development. This is also termed out-of-sample testing. Experienced modelers will know that such validation often yield impressive results with high overall accuracy rates. Unfortunately, theoretical principles may not be good enough for actual use.

A credit rating system is only as good as its predictions. Out-of-sample testing results may be perfect but if ratings based on actual use are inconsistent, the model is useless. Recognizing this, Basel II states that backtesting is the only approach acceptable for approving a rating system. The following figure captures the spirit of this method.

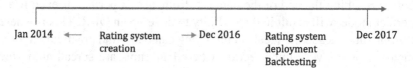

| Jan 2014 | ⟵ | Rating system creation | ⟶ Dec 2016 | Rating system deployment Backtesting | Dec 2017 |

A minimum of three years of data must be used to develop the model. The model is used to create the rating system. The exercise just completed fulfill this requirement as data from 2014 to 2016 were employed and a rating system of 7 Non-default and 1 Default grade was created. In business application, this rating system is deployed from the start of 2017. Credit applicants are assigned a rating based on the WoE model. Backtesting is to evaluate how well the ratings assigned in 2017 match the credit risk of the new obligors.

Two parameters are used for the evaluation. One is accuracy and the other is consistency. They are also termed as the sufficient and necessary conditions. If the default rates are exactly or even nearly the same as those in the rating system, it would be sufficient to pass the test. In the exercise, the default (bankruptcy) rate for Grade 7 is 0.088445078 or around 8.84%. If the default rate for obligors in 2017 assigned Grade 7 is close to 8.84%, that would be considered as accurate. Achieving such accuracy for all grades would be sufficient which is why this is known as the sufficient condition test.

It is almost impossible to achieve accuracy even if a reasonably wide band of variation around the rating system PDs is used. Facing this reality, a minimum standard must then be set for rating system acceptance and this is the necessary condition. Failure to achieve it means that the system is simply not good enough for actual use. This condition is consistency.

At the minimum, a rating system must be able to distinguish between credit qualities. An obligor in a lower grade should not have a lower PD than another in a higher grade. Basel II states that this must be evidenced by the default rates. If the default rate in a lower grade is lower than that of a higher grade, the rating system is inconsistent. Any occurrence between two grades will cause the rating system to fail. The following simple illustration explains this in greater detail:

Risk grade	Model PD	Actual default rate
2	0.15%	0.17%
3	0.22%	0.13%

The actual default rate for Grade 3 computed from the deployment year is lower than that of Grade 2 which fails the consistency test.

Before embarking on the backtesting process, a few issues have to be addressed else the test can be manipulated to achieve results desired. First is if all obligors in the deployment year 2017 should be used in the test dataset.

A grade default rate is meant to be used as proxy for PD of obligors within that grade. Basel II PD is defined as the probability of default within the next calendar year. As known in Statistics, that probability is non-decreasing over time. Since PD is for one year, the probability over half a year or one month should be no higher and actually lower in reality. Computing the default rate of obligors existing before 2017 accords with the backtesting intent. For credit applicants who become new obligors in 2017, the matter is less straightforward. For those approved at the beginning of the year, it is still quite reasonable to include them in deriving the default rate as there is still an entire year for that to happen. For obligors new from the second half of the year and especially near year end, the decision is less clear cut. Even for one assigned the lowest Non-default grade in December, the likelihood of default in 2017 itself is close to zero as few do so just after being made a customer. Including new obligors in the backtesting period then biases the default rates downward and may cause inconsistency.

The second issue relates to those who defaulted in the rating system development period. Under Basel II, an obligor who has defaulted must be automatically assigned to the Default grade. A defaulter who repays all outstanding is then reassigned a Non-default grade. This is known as reageing where the DPD is reset to zero. There is no clear principle if such obligors should be included in the backtesting dataset. Exclusion will mean that the default rates derived in 2017 do not accurately reflect the actual business conditions. Inclusion, on the other hand, distorts the predictions of the model since the obligor has been reassigned a grade based on reageing policy rather than model parameters.

Ideally, the backtesting carried out should be based on Non-default obligors existing up to end 2016. These are assigned risk grades using the rating system created. The bankruptcy rates in 2017 for these obligors are then computed:

```
# Create data frame of Non-defaults
nondefault <- subset(train_woe, Bankrupt == 0)

# Copy grade column and copy value from ratingsystem data frame
nondefault$grade <- ifelse(nondefault$woe <= ratingsystem$woe[1],
"1", ifelse(nondefault$woe > ratingsystem$woe[1] & nondefault$woe
<= ratingsystem$woe[2], "2", ifelse(nondefault$woe > ratingsystem$
woe[2] & nondefault$woe < =ratingsystem$woe[3], "3", ifelse
(nondefault$woe > ratingsystem$woe[3] & nondefault$woe <= rating
system$woe[4], "4", ifelse(nondefault$woe > ratingsystem$woe[4] &
nondefault$woe <= ratingsystem$woe[5], "5", ifelse(nondefault$woe >
ratingsystem$woe[5] & nondefault$woe <= ratingsystem$woe[6], "6",
ratingsystem$woe[7]))))))
```

A data frame **test** is created using 2017 data. This data frame is then updated as an intersection with nondefault with the firm ID as reference. As ID may be repeated throughout 2014 to 2016, the nondefault data frame is pruned keeping only the 2016 data to ensure that only unique IDs are used for the intersection:

```
# Keep on 2016 data
nondefault <- subset(nondefault, nondefault$YEAR == 2016)
```

```
# Create test data frame
test <- subset(woe, substring(woe$YEAR, 1, 4) == 2017)
test <- merge(test, nondefault[, c('ID', 'grade')], by = 'ID')
```

A check shows, however, that there are only six IDs in 2017 found in 2016 despite the test data frame having 2,762 rows. This makes the preferred approach of computing the 2017 bankruptcy rates among firms in the dataset till end 2016 infeasible. The alternative is to assign grades to all 2017 obligors using the WoE thresholds derived earlier. This is less than ideal as it does not capture the spirit of backtesting which is to evaluate how well the ratings assigned during model development hold up at deployment.

Panels for each of the financial ratio WoE has to be first extracted from the bins output:

```
Industry <- bins$INDUSTRY
RoA <- bins$RoA
GrossProfitMargin <- bins$GrossProfitMargin
QuickRatio <- bins$QuickRatio
CurrentRatio <- bins$CurrentRatio
Equity2LTLoans <- bins$Equity2LTLoans
LTLoans2TA <- bins$LTLoans2TA
TATurnover <- bins$TATurnover
PPETurnover <- bins$PPETurnover
Equity2TA <- bins$Equity2TA
Capital2TA <- bins$Capital2TA
SalesGrowth <- bins$SalesGrowth
RevenueGrowth <- bins$RevenueGrowth
```

As will be demonstrated later, saving the data frames into Oracle tables will facilitate later automation of assigning ratings:

```
# Write data frame to Oracle data table using the same name
dbWriteTable(con, "Industry", Industry, field.types = NULL, row.names =
TRUE, overwrite = FALSE, append = TRUE, allow.keywords = FALSE)
dbWriteTable(con, "RoA", RoA, field.types = NULL, row.names = TRUE,
overwrite = FALSE, append = TRUE, allow.keywords = FALSE)
dbWriteTable(con, "GrossProfitMargin", GrossProfitMargin, field.types =
NULL, row.names = TRUE, overwrite = FALSE, append = TRUE, allow.
keywords = FALSE)
```

```
dbWriteTable(con, "QuickRatio", QuickRatio, field.types = NULL, row.
names = TRUE, overwrite = FALSE, append = TRUE, allow.keywords =
FALSE)
dbWriteTable(con, "CurrentRatio", CurrentRatio, field.types = NULL,
row.names = TRUE, overwrite = FALSE, append = TRUE, allow.keywords =
FALSE)
dbWriteTable(con, "Equity2LTLoans", Equity2LTLoans, field.types =
NULL, row.names = TRUE, overwrite = FALSE, append = TRUE, allow.
keywords = FALSE)
dbWriteTable(con, "LTLoans2TA", LTLoans2TA, field.types = NULL, row.
names = TRUE, overwrite = FALSE, append = TRUE, allow.keywords =
FALSE)
dbWriteTable(con, "TATurnover", TATurnover, field.types = NULL, row.
names = TRUE, overwrite = FALSE, append = TRUE, allow.keywords =
FALSE)
dbWriteTable(con, "PPETurnover", PPETurnover, field.types = NULL,
row.names = TRUE, overwrite = FALSE, append = TRUE, allow.keywords =
FALSE)
dbWriteTable(con, "Equity2TA", Equity2TA, field.types = NULL, row.
names = TRUE, overwrite = FALSE, append = TRUE, allow.keywords =
FALSE)
dbWriteTable(con, "Capital2TA", Capital2TA, field.types = NULL, row.
names = TRUE, overwrite = FALSE, append = TRUE, allow.keywords =
FALSE)
dbWriteTable(con, "SalesGrowth", SalesGrowth, field.types = NULL,
row.names = TRUE, overwrite = FALSE, append = TRUE, allow.keywords
= FALSE)
dbWriteTable(con, "RevenueGrowth", RevenueGrowth, field.types =
NULL, row.names = TRUE, overwrite = FALSE, append = TRUE, allow.
keywords = FALSE)
```

If necessary, another column Industry has to be created that has spaces trimmed from the INDUSTRY name. A nested ifelse function is then applied to extract the woe for each bin:

```
# Trim Industry column of hard spaces before and after
test$Industry <- trim(test$INDUSTRY)
test$Industry_woe <- ifelse(test$Industry == "Transport", Industry
$woe[1], ifelse(test$Industry == "Manufacturing", Industry$woe[2],
Industry$woe[3]))
```

```
test$RoA_woe <- ifelse(test$RoA == "NA", RoA$woe[1], ifelse(test$
RoA < RoA$breaks[2], RoA$woe[2], ifelse(test$RoA < RoA$breaks[3],
RoA$woe[3], ifelse(test$RoA < RoA$breaks[4], RoA$woe[4], ifelse(test$
RoA < RoA$breaks[5], RoA$woe[5], RoA$woe[6])))))
test$GrossProfitMargin_woe <- ifelse(test$GrossProfitMargin == "NA",
GrossProfitMargin$woe[1], ifelse(test$GrossProfitMargin < GrossProfit
Margin$breaks[3], GrossProfitMargin$woe[3], ifelse(test$GrossProfit
Margin < GrossProfitMargin$breaks[4], GrossProfitMargin$woe[4],
ifelse(test$GrossProfitMargin < GrossProfitMargin$breaks[5], Gross
ProfitMargin$woe[5], ifelse(test$GrossProfitMargin < GrossProfit
Margin$breaks[6], GrossProfitMargin$woe[6], GrossProfitMargin$
woe[7])))))
test$QuickRatio_woe <- ifelse(test$QuickRatio == "NA", QuickRatio$
woe[1], ifelse(test$QuickRatio < QuickRatio$breaks[3], QuickRatio$
woe[3], ifelse(test$QuickRatio < QuickRatio$breaks[4], QuickRatio$
woe[4], QuickRatio$woe[5])))
test$CurrentRatio_woe <- ifelse(test$CurrentRatio == "NA", Current
Ratio$woe[1], ifelse(test$CurrentRatio < CurrentRatio$breaks[3],
CurrentRatio$woe[3],ifelse(test$CurrentRatio<CurrentRatio$breaks[4],
CurrentRatio$woe[4], CurrentRatio$woe[5])))
test$Equity2LTLoans_woe <- ifelse(test$Equity2LTLoans == "NA", Equity
2LTLoans$woe[1], Equity2LTLoans$woe[3])
test$LTLoans2TA_woe <- ifelse(test$LTLoans2TA == "NA", LTLoans2
TA$woe[1], ifelse(test$LTLoans2TA < LTLoans2TA$breaks[2], LTLoans2
TA$woe[2], ifelse(test$LTLoans2TA < LTLoans2TA$breaks[3], LTLoans2
TA$woe[3], LTLoans2TA$woe[4])))
test$TATurnover_woe <- ifelse(test$TATurnover == "NA", TATurnover$
woe[1], ifelse(test$TATurnover < TATurnover$breaks[2], TATurnover$
woe[2], ifelse(test$TATurnover < TATurnover$breaks[3], TATurnover$
woe[3], ifelse(test$TATurnover < TATurnover$breaks[4], TATurnover$
woe[4], ifelse(test$TATurnover < TATurnover$breaks[5], TATurnover$
woe[5], TATurnover$woe[6])))))
test$PPETurnover_woe <- ifelse(test$PPETurnover == "NA", PPETurnover
$woe[1], ifelse(test$PPETurnover < PPETurnover$breaks[2], PPE
Turnover$woe[2], ifelse(test$PPETurnover < PPETurnover$breaks[3],
PPETurnover$woe[3],ifelse(test$PPETurnover<PPETurnover$breaks[4],
PPETurnover$woe[4],ifelse(test$PPETurnover<PPETurnover$breaks[5],
PPETurnover$woe[5], PPETurnover$woe[6])))))
test$Equity2TA_woe<-ifelse(test$Equity2TA=="NA",Equity2TA$woe[1],
Equity2TA$woe[2])
```

```
test$Capital2TA_woe <- ifelse(test$Capital2TA == "NA", Capital2TA
$woe[1], ifelse(test$Capital2TA < Capital2TA$breaks[2], Capital2TA
$woe[2], ifelse(test$Capital2TA < Capital2TA$breaks[3], Capital2TA$
woe[3], ifelse(test$Capital2TA < Capital2TA$breaks[4], Capital2TA$
woe[4], Capital2TA$woe[5]))))
test$SalesGrowth_woe <- ifelse(test$SalesGrowth == "NA", Sales
Growth$woe[1], ifelse(test$SalesGrowth < SalesGrowth$breaks[2],
SalesGrowth$woe[2], ifelse(test$SalesGrowth<SalesGrowth$breaks[3],
SalesGrowth$woe[3], ifelse(test$SalesGrowth<SalesGrowth$breaks[4],
SalesGrowth$woe[4], ifelse(test$SalesGrowth<SalesGrowth$breaks[5],
SalesGrowth$woe[5], SalesGrowth$woe[6]))))))
test$RevenueGrowth_woe <- ifelse(test$RevenueGrowth == "NA",
RevenueGrowth$woe[1], ifelse(test$RevenueGrowth < Revenue
Growth$breaks[2], RevenueGrowth$woe[2], ifelse(test$Revenue
Growth < RevenueGrowth$breaks[3], RevenueGrowth$woe[3], ifelse
(test$RevenueGrowth < RevenueGrowth$breaks[4], RevenueGrowth$
woe[4], RevenueGrowth$woe[5]))))
```

As with the training data frame, the ratio WoE values are summed and used to assign risk grades to each obligor:

```
# Sum predictor WoE values
test$woe <- test$Industry_woe + test$RoA_woe + test$GrossProfit
Margin_woe + test$QuickRatio_woe + test$CurrentRatio_woe + test$
Equity2LTLoans_woe + test$LTLoans2TA_woe + test$TATurnover_woe
+ test$PPETurnover_woe + test$Equity2TA_woe + test$Capital2TA_
woe + test$SalesGrowth_woe + test$RevenueGrowth_woe
test$grade <- ifelse(test$woe <= ratingsystem$woe[1], "1", ifelse(test$
woe > ratingsystem$woe[1] & test$woe <= ratingsystem$woe[2], "2",
ifelse(test$woe > ratingsystem$woe[2] & test$woe <= ratingsystem$
woe[3], "3", ifelse(test$woe > ratingsystem$woe[3] & test$woe
<= ratingsystem$woe[4], "4", ifelse(test$woe > ratingsystem$woe[4]
& test$woe <= ratingsystem$woe[5], "5", ifelse(test$woe > rating
system$woe[5] & test$woe <= ratingsystem$woe[6], "6", ifelse(test$
woe > ratingsystem$woe[6] & test$woe <= ratingsystem$woe[7], "7",
"8")))))))
```

The backtesting results are as follows:

Grade	Bankruptcy rate
1	NA
2	NA
3	NA
4	0.00000000
5	0.01244813
6	0.02600000
7	0.24698800

Technically, the consistency requirement has not been breached, so the rating system developed has not failed. This can be regarded as encouraging as more often than not, rating systems do not meet the necessary condition. However, the results are not ideal as there are no obligors assigned the first three grades and the default rate for Grade 4 is 0.00000000 which is lower that the Basel II minimum. Securing approval for business use will require further model development. Nevertheless, the exercise suggests that the WoE approach is robust even with the limited quantity and quality of the data available. The R codes for the entire IRS development process using WoE are shown in the Annex with accompanying comments.

Chapter 11

Deployment

Desktop analytics are useful for planning. R itself is now embedded in Microsoft Excel as Basic Excel R Toolkit or BERT, enhancing the use of the already popular business utility. What has been covered in the earlier chapters could be replicated in Excel and there are some types of analytics well suited to that platform. These are discussed in later chapters. The efforts incurred would, however, have gained limited returns if analytics like a rating system cannot be deployed in an automated process to support intensive and time-critical operational decision-making. In many developed countries, there is a demand for retail credit approval decisions to be made in no more than five seconds from the time of application. With today's level of digital data flow, any financial institution that is too slow in making the necessary analysis will find itself outcompeted soon. The ORR development process described earlier will be used to discuss the merits of deployment for automation.

The backtesting carried out provides some insight on how an ORR can be deployed. Just as all the obligors in 2017 can be assigned a risk grade based on the system developed using 2014 to 2016 data, a new credit applicant in 2017 providing the necessary financial ratios could be rated the same way. Ideally, a deployed ORR will turn an electronic application into a customized credit analysis report leading to an Approve/ Reject decision before any manual intervention. A bank can then manage by exception, focusing on borderline cases.

Assuming that an ORR has been approved for use. Tables can be first created for the rating system and the rating output. The relevant parts of the backtesting codes can be saved as a SQL script and run with a trigger or stored procedure to derive a credit rating once an application is received. The following script processes the application with the latest time stamp which is automatically generated:

```
begin
sys.rqScriptCreate('IRS',
'function() {
library(ROracle)
drv <- dbDriver("Oracle")
con <- dbConnect(drv, username = "rquser", password="password",
dbname = "ORCLPDB", prefetch = FALSE,external_credentials = FALSE)

# Create trim function to remove spaces
trim <- function (x) gsub("^\\s+|\\s+$", "", x)
# Select the latest applicant from the Oracle data table using maximum
DateTime
applicant <- dbGetQuery(con,"select * from loanapplication where
DateTime = (select max(DateTime) from loanapplication)")
applicantrating <- dbReadTable(con,"APPLICANTRATING",schema =
"RQUSER")

# Keep only 1 row
applicantrating <- applicantrating[1,]
ratingsystem <- dbReadTable(con,"RATINGSYSTEM",schema = "RQUSER")
Industry <- dbReadTable(con,"Industry",schema = "RQUSER")
RoA <- dbReadTable(con,"RoA",schema = "RQUSER")
GrossProfitMargin <- dbReadTable(con,"GrossProfitMargin",schema =
"RQUSER")
QuickRatio <- dbReadTable(con,"QuickRatio",schema = "RQUSER")
CurrentRatio <- dbReadTable(con,"CurrentRatio",schema = "RQUSER")
Equity2LTLoans <- dbReadTable(con,"Equity2LTLoans",schema = "RQUSER")
LTLoans2TA <- dbReadTable(con,"LTLoans2TA",schema = "RQUSER")
TATurnover <- dbReadTable(con,"TATurnover",schema = "RQUSER")
PPETurnover <- dbReadTable(con,"PPETurnover",schema = "RQUSER")
Equity2TA <- dbReadTable(con,"Equity2TA",schema = "RQUSER")
Capital2TA <- dbReadTable(con,"Capital2TA",schema = "RQUSER")
SalesGrowth <- dbReadTable(con,"SalesGrowth",schema = "RQUSER")
RevenueGrowth <- dbReadTable(con,"RevenueGrowth",schema =
"RQUSER")
```

```
applicantrating$ID <- applicant$ID
applicantrating$Industry <- applicant$INDUSTRY


# Derive financial ratios
applicantrating$RoA<-applicant$NETINCOME/applicant$TOTALASSETS
applicantrating$GrossProfitMargin  <-  applicant$GROSSPROFIT  /
applicant$NETSALES
applicantrating$QuickRatio <- applicant$CASHNDEPOSITS / applicant
$TOTALCURRENTLIABILITIES
applicantrating$CurrentRatio <- (applicant$TOTALASSETS-applicant$TO
TALNONCURRENTASSETS) / applicant$TOTALCURRENTLIABILITIES
applicantrating$Equity2LTLoans   <-   applicant$TOTALEQUITY   /
(applicant$TOTALLIABILITIES-applicant$TOTALCURRENTLIABILITIES)
applicantrating$LTLoans2TA <- (applicant$TOTALLIABILITIES-applicant$
TOTALCURRENTLIABILITIES) / applicant$TOTALASSETS
applicantrating$TATurnover <- applicant$TOTALREVENUE / applicant$
TOTALASSETS
applicantrating$PPETurnover <- applicant$TOTALREVENUE / applicant$
NETPPE
applicantrating$Equity2TA  <-  applicant$TOTALEQUITY  /  applicant$
TOTALASSETS
applicantrating$Capital2TA <- applicant$CAPITAL2TA
applicantrating$SalesGrowth <- applicant$SALESGROWTH
applicantrating$RevenueGrowth <- applicant$REVENUEGROWTH
applicantrating$Industry <- trim(applicantrating$Industry)
applicantrating$Industry_woe  <-  ifelse(applicantrating$Industry  ==
"Transport",  Industry$woe[1],  ifelse(applicantrating$Industry  ==
"Manufacturing", Industry$woe[2], Industry$woe[3]))


# Determine the WoE band for each predictor
applicantrating$RoA_woe  <-  ifelse(applicantrating$RoA  ==  "NA",
RoA$woe[1], ifelse(applicantrating$RoA < RoA$breaks[2], RoA$woe[2],
ifelse(applicantrating$RoA  <  RoA$breaks[3],  RoA$woe[3],  ifelse
(applicantrating$RoA  <  RoA$breaks[4],  RoA$woe[4],  ifelse
(applicantrating$RoA < RoA$breaks[5], RoA$woe[5], RoA$woe[6]))))))
applicantrating$GrossProfitMargin_woe  <-  ifelse(applicantrating$
GrossProfitMargin == "NA", GrossProfitMargin$woe[1], ifelse(applicant
rating$GrossProfitMargin < GrossProfitMargin$breaks[3], GrossProfit
```

```
Margin$woe[3], ifelse(applicantrating$GrossProfitMargin < GrossProfit
Margin$breaks[4], GrossProfitMargin$woe[4], ifelse(applicantrating$G
rossProfitMargin < GrossProfitMargin$breaks[5], GrossProfitMargin$
woe[5], ifelse(applicantrating$GrossProfitMargin < GrossProfitMargin$
breaks[6],     GrossProfitMargin$woe[6],      GrossProfitMargin$
woe[7]))))) 
applicantrating$QuickRatio_woe   <-   ifelse(applicantrating$Quick
Ratio == "NA", QuickRatio$woe[1], ifelse(applicantrating$QuickRatio <
QuickRatio$breaks[3], QuickRatio$woe[3], ifelse(applicantrating$Quick
Ratio < QuickRatio$breaks[4], QuickRatio$woe[4], QuickRatio$
woe[5]))) 
applicantrating$CurrentRatio_woe <- ifelse(applicantrating$CurrentRa
tio == "NA", CurrentRatio$woe[1], ifelse(applicantrating$CurrentRatio
< CurrentRatio$breaks[3], CurrentRatio$woe[3], ifelse(applicantrating$
CurrentRatio < CurrentRatio$breaks[4], CurrentRatio$woe[4], Current
Ratio$woe[5]))) 
applicantrating$Equity2LTLoans_woe   <-   ifelse(applicantrating$
Equity2LTLoans == "NA", Equity2LTLoans$woe[1], Equity2LTLoans$
woe[3]) 
applicantrating$LTLoans2TA_woe <- ifelse(applicantrating$LTLoans2
TA == "NA", LTLoans2TA$woe[1], ifelse(applicantrating$LTLoans2TA <
LTLoans2TA$breaks[2], LTLoans2TA$woe[2], ifelse(applicantrating$
LTLoans2TA < LTLoans2TA$breaks[3], LTLoans2TA$woe[3], LTLoans2TA
$woe[4]))) 
applicantrating$TATurnover_woe   <-   ifelse(applicantrating$TATurn
over == "NA", TATurnover$woe[1], ifelse(applicantrating$TATurnover <
TATurnover$breaks[2], TATurnover$woe[2], ifelse(applicantrating$
TATurnover < TATurnover$breaks[3], TATurnover$woe[3], ifelse(applica
ntrating$TATurnover < TATurnover$breaks[4], TATurnover$woe[4],
ifelse(applicantrating$TATurnover < TATurnover$breaks[5], TATurnover
$woe[5], TATurnover$woe[6]))))) 
applicantrating$PPETurnover_woe   <-   ifelse(applicantrating$PPE
Turnover == "NA", PPETurnover$woe[1], ifelse(applicantrating$PPETur
nover < PPETurnover$breaks[2], PPETurnover$woe[2], ifelse(applicantr
ating$PPETurnover < PPETurnover$breaks[3], PPETurnover$woe[3],
ifelse(applicantrating$PPETurnover < PPETurnover$breaks[4], PPE
Turnover$woe[4], ifelse(applicantrating$PPETurnover < PPETurnover$
breaks[5], PPETurnover$woe[5], PPETurnover$woe[6])))))
applicantrating$Equity2TA_woe <- ifelse(applicantrating$Equity2TA ==
"NA", Equity2TA$woe[1], Equity2TA$woe[2])
```

```
applicantrating$Capital2TA_woe  <-  ifelse(applicantrating$Capital
2TA == "NA", Capital2TA$woe[1], ifelse(applicantrating$Capital2TA <
Capital2TA$breaks[2],  Capital2TA$woe[2],  ifelse(applicantrating$
Capital2TA < Capital2TA$breaks[3], Capital2TA$woe[3], ifelse(applicant
rating$Capital2TA  <  Capital2TA$breaks[4],  Capital2TA$woe[4],
Capital2TA$woe[5]))))
applicantrating$SalesGrowth_woe <- ifelse(applicantrating$SalesGro
wth == "NA", SalesGrowth$woe[1], ifelse(applicantrating$SalesGrowth
< SalesGrowth$breaks[2], SalesGrowth$woe[2], ifelse(applicantrating
$SalesGrowth < SalesGrowth$breaks[3], SalesGrowth$woe[3], ifelse
(applicantrating$SalesGrowth < SalesGrowth$breaks[4], SalesGrowth$
woe[4], ifelse(applicantrating$SalesGrowth < SalesGrowth$breaks[5],
SalesGrowth$woe[5], SalesGrowth$woe[6]))))))
applicantrating$RevenueGrowth_woe  <-  ifelse(applicantrating$
RevenueGrowth == "NA", RevenueGrowth$woe[1], ifelse(applicant
rating$RevenueGrowth < RevenueGrowth$breaks[2], RevenueGrowth$
woe[2], ifelse(applicantrating$RevenueGrowth < RevenueGrowth$
breaks[3], RevenueGrowth$woe[3], ifelse(applicantrating$Revenue
Growth  <  RevenueGrowth$breaks[4],  RevenueGrowth$woe[4],
RevenueGrowth$woe[5]))))
applicantrating$woe <- applicantrating$Industry_woe + applicant
rating$RoA_woe + applicantrating$GrossProfitMargin_woe + applicant
rating$QuickRatio_woe  +  applicantrating$CurrentRatio_woe  +
applicantrating$Equity2LTLoans_woe + applicantrating$LTLoans2TA_
woe + applicantrating$TATurnover_woe + applicantrating$PPETurn
over_woe  +  applicantrating$Equity2TA_woe  +  applicantrating$
Capital2TA_woe  +  applicantrating$SalesGrowth_woe  +  applicant
rating$RevenueGrowth_woe
applicantrating$grade  <-  ifelse(applicantrating$woe  <=  rating
system$woe[1], "1", ifelse(applicantrating$woe > ratingsystem$woe[1]
& (applicantrating$woe <= ratingsystem$woe[2]), "2", ifelse(applicant
rating$woe > ratingsystem$woe[2] & (applicantrating$woe <= rating
system$woe[3]), "3", ifelse(applicantrating$woe > ratingsystem$woe
[3] & (applicantrating$woe <= ratingsystem$woe[4]), "4", ifelse
(applicantrating$woe > ratingsystem$woe[4] & (applicantrating$
woe <= ratingsystem$woe[5]), "5", ifelse(applicantrating$woe >
ratingsystem$woe[5] & (applicantrating$woe <= ratingsystem$woe[6]),
"6", ifelse(applicantrating$woe > ratingsystem$woe[6] & (applicant
rating$woe <= ratingsystem$woe[7]), "7", "8")))))))
applicantrating <- applicantrating[c(1,16:28,43)]
```

```
dbWriteTable(con, "APPLICANTRATING", applicantrating, field.types =
NULL, row.names = FALSE, overwrite = FALSE, append = TRUE, allow.
keywords = FALSE)
dum <- 1
data.frame(dum = dum)
}',
v_overwrite => TRUE);
end;
/
select * from table(rqEval(NULL,'select 1 dum from dual', 'IRS'));
```

Technically, ORR parameters can be manually entered into an Oracle database. An SQL script can be written to derive the WoE values and arrive at a risk grade of a credit applicant as done in the backtesting. This could have been the only option in earlier days when languages like R (or Python) have not been embedded into databases. Though the same logic can be replicated using SQL, speed may be compromised if the training dataset is large. With R having been made a free utility, integrating development and deployment is desirable for two reasons. The first is documentation and the second is updating.

Despite all the advances in file management technology, documentation remains dismal in most organizations including government agencies. This is perhaps more so in modeling and analytics as those involved are more interested in the methods, techniques and results. Assumptions and rationale may be well-understood to them but little effort is made to explain these to the non-professionals. Over time, even the modeler may forget these aspects and have difficulty presenting them to an auditor or regulator.

Program codes are not easy to comprehend to begin with. It is said that in the fund management industry, a new hire will simply rewrite codes rather than try to understand existing ones to make improvements. That is possible if there is no need to demonstrate a model's reliability to regulators before obtaining approval for use. Under Basel II, an IRS has to pass three consecutive years of backtesting before it can be employed to derive regulatory capital requirements. Documentation of the logic is not an option. Simply inserting ORR parameters into a data table for automated credit rating will fall far short of a bank examiner's expectations.

Again in Basel II, models have to be updated regularly. The recommended interval is yearly. This is reasonable. Modelers in social sciences are well aware of non-stationarity. Parameters derived may be outdated even a short time later. The poverty line is one good example. In a developed economy, this line can creep upward more quickly than realized simply due to inflation. The same goes for financial ratios. Leverage used to be considered undesirable. With low interest rates, that has been turned into strategic advantage. Non-stationarity is not only a given, it is unpredictable. For that reason, academics often joke that any credit risk model is good only for the year in which it is developed. This explains why it is the norm and not the exception that most fail backtesting.

The WoE approach has proven to be robust in modeling binary outcomes. Any deficiency lies in the choices of variables as predictors. Typically, credit risk models are developed or updated once a year. If a specific model has proven reliable, it can be refined more regularly if the process is automated. In countries with quarterly financial reports, ratios and other inputs are available at least four times a year. A bank with a WoE ORR can automatically feed such data into the codes and generate updated WoE values. This can be termed Updated WoE approach.

11.1. Default and Reageing

It was briefly mentioned in the earlier chapter that a defaulter who makes good all repayments must be assigned to a Non-default risk grade. In banking jargon, the loan is said to be cured. Recognizing the challenges of reageing in practice, Basel II requires banks to implement an explicit policy on this area. The policy must be transparent and applied consistently to all credit exposures.

Reageing is not of academic interest as no theory is involved. The practical considerations needed though are not trivial as they impact on the regulatory capital required of a bank with an approved IRS. As reageing is unlikely to be widespread else a bank would have failed, automation is unnecessary. Nevertheless, there are implications on the IRS especially in the backtesting.

In a bank, default is not a scientifically determined state. It is not even defined by regulators though most follow the Basel II prescription of 90 DPD. That may seem deterministic, but banks have a wide latitude in interpretation. Take credit card, for instance. A minimum amount is required for repayment to keep the cardholder from defaulting. While usually small relative to the credit outstanding, it can still be larger than the interest incurred. Some generous banks choose to consider repayment of the interest alone as sufficient with the principal rolled over. This policy is extended even to a defaulter as described earlier. While Basel II has not explicitly stated the requirements for a loan to be cured, it is implicit that all amounts outstanding should be repaid before reageing can be applied. Once again, banks may choose to be less demanding and accept repayment of all interest outstanding as sufficient. Such variations can impact on the robustness of models and decision-making since they concern the very definition of the target which is default.

The next issue is what grade should a reaged obligor be placed in. Conceptually, default would have impaired credit quality so the obligor should not be returned to the same grade as before. This creates two other issues that have to be properly addressed. The first relates to ratings update and the second to modeling.

It is not uncommon that ratings are updated using an upgraded WoE model. The latest financial ratios are used. If such data are not available for a reaged obligor, earlier ratios will be employed. They can be those before the default and hence, the resultant risk grade will also be pre-default. To illustrate, consider an obligor rated Grade 2 prior to default. Upon being reaged, it is assigned to Grade 4. Grade 2 is derived from a WoE model while Grade 4 is a reageing policy decision. An updated WoE model may still assign the obligor to Grade 2 if the financial ratios used remain unchanged. A seemingly easy solution is to remove the obligor from the training sample used. In practice, this is an ideal seldom feasible. In a sizable bank, those responsible for reageing operations are unlikely in the same room or even same building as the modelers. The agendas of both parties are so divergent that reageing staff have little or no interest in the concerns of the modelers. When that happens, the ORR is degraded.

In developing a credit risk model, the question of when default occurred is rarely asked. Predictor variable data and default status within the same year are used. This is generally accepted as being consistent with the Basel II requirement that a PD should be valid for 12 months ahead. It becomes less clear if a model is updated quarterly. As discussed earlier, should an obligor who defaulted in the first quarter but reaged in the second be categorized as Default or Non-default when the model is updated? Technically, second-quarter data are associated with credit status in the same quarter. However, these are unlikely to deviate significantly from those of the previous quarter. Very similar financial ratios are then predicting Default and Non-default. This actually confounds the model.

11.2. Enterprise Data Warehouse or Data Mart

By this point, it is evident that operational deployment of analytics cannot be done using the core banking system. An enterprise data warehouse is not the ideal option largely due to the data stewardship challenges. As most banks have eventually realized, a risk data mart is the only sustainable way to deploy risk analytics. Even then, extensive architecting and continual maintenance are a necessity. Aside from credit risk which has been most extensively covered in this book, there is also the interest rate in the banking book, market risk, operational risk and liquidity risk. The basic task of creating and maintaining a universal ID or UID for all wholesale banking counterparties is one that has consumed immeasurable human resources in practically all banks. Even a global bank known for its data warehousing accomplishments had to manually merge different IDs from different legacy systems when warehousing the data.

R models cannot be coded in core banking systems. They can only be done after data are warehoused. A data mart allows for much more flexibility if it is under direct control of the Risk Management Unit. Even relatively minor concerns like updating of R versions or installation of packages are less of a hassle as compared to doing it in an enterprise data warehouse.

A final note on deployment — it cannot be left to IT. All the stakeholders, especially users, must be involved from conceptualization to design and creation of the data mart. Those responsible for modeling have to provide their inputs on matters like how and where models are to be stored, employed and updated.

Chapter 12

Through The Cycle (TTC) Updating

The use of periodic data like financial ratios to develop credit risk models is known as Point In Time (PIT) modeling. Theoretically, such models are good enough for predictions around the time of the data. They can be viewed as snapshots of financial health. Due to practical limitations, such models are used for a significant period, usually a year, before being recalibrated.

Credit Rating Agencies (CRAs) like Standard & Poors and Moody's carry out similar PIT modeling for their clients. A letter grade is then assigned for the credit rating. That letter is supposed to reflect credit quality at the bottom of an entire business cycle which is why they are termed Through The Cycle (TTC) ratings. For example, an A rating corresponds to approximately 0.1% chance of default if it is for a corporate bond. This probability applies to the lowest point of the coming business cycle or economically worst-case scenario. A business cycle can easily last 10 years. Any PIT prediction that can remain good for the next 10 years will be magical and CRAs are fully aware of that. To ensure that their ratings remain valid, they update them as soon as information is sufficiently material to do so. Rating upgrade or downgrade are often announced, especially for listed firms or government issued debt. Such continual recalibration is necessary to keep a rating relevant to changes in the business environment. The same can be applied to ORR in a bank.

Studies have shown that trade credit management behavior is a strong predictor of default. How well a firm is able to service its Accounts Payable and how much Accounts Receivable turn into cash are reliable indicators of financial health. Recent global financial crises suggest that liquidity may be a more critical determinant of solvency than profitability. Banks can easily find a parallel to this in the form of repayment delinquency or DPD which is automatically generated in almost every core banking system. If 90 DPD is the threshold for default, 60 and 30 DPD must precede this state. A pattern or model can be developed using DPD to predict default. Like trade credit, this approach which is also known as behavioral modeling has been proven so robust that leading rating agencies have employed it for commercial ratings. This approach can be regarded as TTC since the initial PIT rating is upgraded or downgraded based on new information which is DPD here. Unlike PIT methods, there is no theory involved so heuristics is perhaps the best way forward. The rest of this chapter describes a paid engagement to develop a TTC model for one of the largest banks in the country that needed to upgrade its IRS.

As delinquencies is a result of repayment behavior independent of the obligor profile, modeling with such data can be termed Behavioral Scoring. The bank concerned had been relying on a PIT model for its consumer credit card risk profiling. Like typical banks, that is a credit scoring method where points are assigned to selected demographics when the card application is made. Under Basel II, consumers belong to the Retail category of obligors and do not have to be individually risk rated. However, this is a bank catering only to consumers and it wants to have a reliable credit rating system.

The existing ratings are first backtested for consistency. The results are shown in Table 12.1.

Table 12.1.   Results of backtesting of existing ratings.

Risk grade	Number of obligors	Default rate in percentage
1	2757	8.27
2	4327	11.16
3	5307	12.06
4	7305	12.76
5	4526	11.27
6	3340	10.60
7	2814	11.80
8	1298	11.94
9	821	13.15
10	1367	16.97

It is evident that the 10 Non-default ratings used do not exhibit a consistent degree of credit risk from the best to the worst. The default rates for Grade 5 is lower than that of Grade 4 and for Grade 6 lower than that of Grade 5. Though the default rates appear to increase in the right direction overall, the rating system would not have passed the consistency criterion of backtesting.

The bank wants to retain its 10 Non-default risk grades so that serves as the starting point of modeling. To facilitate a more granular transition from one risk grade to another akin to the upgrading or downgrading practiced by CRAs, a scorecard is developed. This is shown in Table 12.2.

Score ranges are assigned to each risk grade. There is no theoretical or conceptual basis for these ranges. Except for Grades 1 and 10, a 15-point interval is used. A set of heuristics based on delinquencies will be employed to adjust the score of an obligor. One who started at 636 and ends with 631 will be downgraded from Grade 4 to Grade 5.

The risk grades assigned by the bank for the 30,000 obligors selected after data cleansing are used as the starting point. DPD are recorded in the core banking system at the end of every month. This lack of daily capture compromises the quality of the model but does not critically undermine it. The system uses a XDays count if X is less than 15 and 30 DPD otherwise. If due date is on the 4th of the month, for instance, a 30 DPD will be recorded if no repayment is received by the end of the month. On the other hand, 4 XDays would the count if due date is on the 27th of a 31-day month. The bank requested to use 120 DPD as the threshold for default as

Table 12.2. Score range and risk grade.

Score	Risk grade
0–559	10
560–574	9
575–589	8
590–604	7
605–619	6
620–634	5
635–649	4
650–664	3
665–679	2
680–1000	1

a 90 DPD may actually mean a less than 90-day delinquency given the system design.

A scoring system based on heuristics is developed to adjust an obligor's grade. It is unquestionable that it will take at least one 30 DPD and one 60 DPD to reach 90 DPD. Since a 30 DPD count is closer to default than no DPD, it is reasonable to deduct points from an obligor's score to reflect an elevated credit risk. On the other hand, an obligor who has consistently repaid on or before due date should be rewarded with points indicating a credit quality improvement.

Single counts of 30, 60 or 90 DPD are straightforward indicators. Each larger number corresponds with increased credit risk. The challenge arises in comparing two 30 DPD counts vs. one 60 DPD. Should the former be regarded as riskier behavior than the latter or vice versa. This is where an iterative process of deciding on the scoring system that yields the best results is needed as there is no theory to guide its formulation. After evaluating several different approaches with backtesting, the scoring system shown in Table 12.3 was selected.

Delta is a metric to subtract from or add to an obligor's score. A limit is set for each type of behavior so as not to over-penalize or over over-reward resulting in volatile grade transitions. Based on the bank's requirements, a 120 DPD count immediate removes the obligor from the 10-grade system and be assigned to Defaults. R codes for such a scoring system is relatively simple and are not elaborated on here.

The bank has set a semi-annual interval to review risk grades and changes if any. The results of applying the scoring system to a random sample of 20 obligors are shown in Table 12.4.

An * marks the case where there is a change in risk grade over six months. Only one of the 20 grades has changed which suggests that the scoring system does not lead to volatile grade transitions. It can be expected that the number will be higher over a one-year period.

Table 12.3.   Scoring system.

Delinquencies	Delta	Limit	Impact
Every count of XDays	−1	−5	Negative
Every count of 30 DPD	−2	−10	Negative
Every count of 90 DPD	−3	−15	Negative
Every two consecutive 0 DPD	+1	+3	Positive
No DPD for past 12 times	+5	+5	Positive

Table 12.4.   Results of a random sample of 20 obligors.

Obligor	Start score	Start grade	Delta	End score	End grade
10001	560	9	−3	557	10*
10002	634	4	3	637	4
10003	594	7	−4	590	7
10004	500	10	0	500	10
10005	620	5	0	620	5
10006	616	6	0	616	6
10007	615	6	3	618	6
10008	645	4	2	647	4
10009	651	3	3	654	3
10010	638	4	1	639	4
10011	562	9	2	564	9
10012	515	10	2	517	10
10013	609	6	−2	607	6
10014	542	10	3	545	10
10015	598	7	3	601	7
10016	625	5	−2	623	5
10017	579	8	−1	578	8
10018	668	2	3	671	2
10019	627	5	5	632	5
10020	587	8	0	587	8

An IRS must pass the backtesting criterion of consistency to be acceptable for deployment. Results of this test are shown in Table 12.5.

There are several noteworthy aspects of the results. First, it passes the consistency test. As discussed earlier, achieving such an outcome has been a challenge for most PIT models. The superiority of behavioral data is once again demonstrated. The second aspect is the distribution of obligors across the grades. It is quite close to the ideal of a bell shape despite the slight skew to the right. Third, there is no concentration in any grade which is another Basel II requirement of a robust IRS.

The outcome of this modeling exercise has succeeded on all counts even if not perfect. Nevertheless, it remains a legitimate question if the results are simply due to the chips falling in place because of the bank's own initial ratings and the nature of the data or behavioral scoring

Table 12.5.   Consistency found in backtesting.

Risk grade	Number of defaults	Number of obligors	Default rate in percentage
1	189	4634	4.08
2	393	4997	7.86
3	593	6116	9.7
4	791	7778	10.17
5	611	5796	10.54
6	452	4238	10.67
7	401	3383	11.85
8	284	2093	13.57
9	203	1275	15.92
10	332	1875	17.71

Table 12.6.   Simulation results.

Risk grade	Default rate in percentage			
	Year 1	Year 2	Year 3	Year 4
1	0.15	2.34	1.05	0.00
2	0.17	0.75	1.69	1.75
3	0.17	0.75	3.47	3.51
4	0.16	1.47	3.03	4.62
5	0.00	2.92	1.59	5.13
6	0.17	2.07	2.86	0.00
7	0.16	13.33	25.00	15.38

with DPD. To answer the question, a simulation is conducted with ratings randomly assigned at the beginning and actual DPD data to change them over the course of four years. Here, 90 DPD is the threshold for default. The regrading system is deliberately kept simple with every two counts of 30 DPD or one count of 60 DPD resulting in a downgrade while prompt payment for the whole year leads to an upgrade. This lack of granularity should handicap the model.

Results of the simulation are shown in Table 12.6.

In Year 1, the default rate was evenly distributed across all risk grades except Grade 5. As these grades were randomly assigned, the result is not unexpected. The heuristic is applied from Year 2 onwards and a clear trend emerges. Default rates for the better grades decrease while that of the lower ones increase. By Year 4, the distribution is nearly monotonic except for Grade 6. It is almost certain that if the process is run for more years, a monotonic one will be achieved.

Consistency in backtesting is mandatory, but a desirable feature of a reliable rating system is a stable transition matrix. CRAs take pride in such matrices as they reflect the rather glacial pace at which most credit risks migrate except for those that fell off the cliff with sudden default. Under Basel II, a proven transition matrix can be used as the basis to update a grade where information is unavailable to do so. The percentages in the matrix proxy for probabilities of transition.

The one-year transition matrix of the model developed for the bank is shown in Table 12.7.

There are two features of a stable matrix. The first is that the percentages in the top-left to bottom-right diagonal should be the largest in each row. Those are the percentages of risk grades remaining unchanged from the past year. Second is that percentages spreading from the diagonal should be systematically smaller. This means that there should be relatively more being regraded from 3 to 4 than 3 to 5. While credit risks do change, large transitions from one level to another within a period of a year should be less than minor adjustments.

Table 12.7. One-year transition matrix.

To / From	**Risk grade**										
	1	**2**	**3**	**4**	**5**	**6**	**7**	**8**	**9**	**10**	**D**
1	0.976	0.024	—	—	—	—	—	—	—	—	—
2	0.001	0.975	0.023	—	—	—	—	—	—	—	0.001
3	—	0.000	0.968	0.030	—	—	—	—	—	—	0.002
4	—	—	0.000	0.966	0.033	—	—	—	—	—	0.001
5	—	—	—	0.001	0.951	0.044	—	—	—	—	0.004
6	—	—	—	—	0.001	0.959	0.039	—	—	—	0.001
7	—	—	—	—	—	0.002	0.953	0.044	—	—	0.002
8	—	—	—	—	—	—	0.005	0.936	0.055	—	0.005
9	—	—	—	—	—	—	—	0.013	0.925	0.050	0.013
10	—	—	—	—	—	—	—	—	0.167	0.833	—
D	—	—	—	—	—	—	—	—		—	1.000

In Table 12.7, D is for default. The numbers are consistent with that of a stable transition matrix. The default rates may not be monotonic as they are only derived for one specific year.

The power of modeling credit risk with behavioral data like DPD has been proven by both an actual paid engagement and simulation. This is a major boost to risk analytics, at least for credit products, as delinquency data are organic to core banking systems. Not only are they easily available, but they are also less prone to errors than financial ratios or demographics that have to be diligently collected. Besides, there is no need for updating as they are system generated. It is unsurprising then that banks have come to value this approach to risk modeling.

Chapter 13

Desktop Analytics

So far, the book has advocated development of deployable risk analytics integrated with a database. One or more models can process new data and produce results without the need for manual extraction and subsequent reinsertion of outputs. Assigning a risk rating to a new credit applicant is a business process that this design is well-suited for. Not only does complete automation save time and effort, it reduces the possibilities for errors and enhance competitiveness if processing is time critical like in the retail credit business. There was a time when this was known as Decision Support System (DSS) when IT was leveraged to expedite decision-making. There is, however, a wide range of risk analytics that can be done at a more considered pace on a desktop and presented at meetings. These are used to support strategic and even tactical decisions that do not have to be made soon. In fact, such analytics benefit from the typical "what-if" analysis where parameters are tweaked to evaluate the range of outcomes possible, usually at a meeting of corporate planners. In most business environments, Microsoft Excel or spreadsheet equivalents have been widely used for this purpose. With R now embedded as a free add-in, Excel is a useful tool for risk analytics that are not time critical. This chapter will cover some of the common topics.

13.1. Basic Excel R Toolkit (BERT)

This is a free Excel add-in that can be downloaded from https://bert-toolkit.com/. It should be automatically incorporated into a supported version of Excel else the usual adding and activation of an add-in

Figure 13.1.   Add-ins drop down option.

BERT Console

File Edit View Packages Help

excel-scripting.r ✕   functions.r ✕   R

```
1
2  #                                    R version 3.5.0 (2018-04-23) -- "Joy in Playing"
3  # add all arguments                  Copyright (C) 2018 The R Foundation for Statistical Computing
4  #                                    Platform: x86_64-w64-mingw32/x64 (64-bit)
5  TestAdd <- function(...){
6    sum(...)                           R is free software and comes with ABSOLUTELY NO WARRANTY.
7  }                                     You are welcome to redistribute it under certain conditions.
8                                        Type 'license()' or 'licence()' for distribution details.
9  #
10 # eigenvalues for matrix (returns a vector)   R is a collaborative project with many contributors.
11 #                                     Type 'contributors()' for more information and
12 EigenValues <- function(mat){         'citation()' on how to cite R or R packages in publications.
13   eigen(mat)$values
14 }                                     Type 'demo()' for some demos, 'help()' for on-line help, or
15                                       'help.start()' for an HTML browser interface to help.
                                         Type 'q()' to quit R.

                                         ---
                                         BERT Version 2.4.4 (http://bert-toolkit.com).

                                         Loading script file: C:\Users\edwar\Documents\BERT2\functions\functions.r
                                         > []
```

Figure 13.2.   Bert Console window.

has to be carried out. If BERT is successfully added, a new tab Add-ins should appear on the ribbon and clicking that will lead to a drop down like that in Fig. 13.1.

A click on the BERT Console opens another window like Fig. 13.2 for R coding.

As can be seen from the figure, the R version in BERT is 3.5.0 or even later which has more functions and packages than that of 3.3.0 used in the ORE. The benefit of having advanced routines surfaces when more complex analytics are required. How Excel can be leveraged for desktop analytics follows after a brief coverage of topics suited for that.

13.2. Probabilities and PD

In the recent years, the Accounting profession has recognized the need to incorporate risk into valuations. Prior to that, unrealized market value cannot be accepted as they do not conform with Accounting standards. The change resulted in International Accounting Standards (IAS) 36 generally termed impairment accounting. The key principle in this standard is that an asset cannot be carried in the financial statements at more than its recoverable value if sold. If the book value is higher than the recoverable one, the asset must be regarded as impaired.

A key driver for this change in Accounting philosophy is derivatives. Not only are their valuations susceptible to minor fluctuations in pricing factors, they have become such significant components of balance sheets that they pose existential threats if not properly accounted for. The global financial crisis of 2008–2010 showed clear evidence of that.

The term "recoverable value" implies uncertainty and uncertainty can only be quantified with probabilities. By itself, probabilities are difficult to estimate. Just consider the two recent presidential elections in the USA. Despite all the polling, the final outcomes were significantly different from or even opposite of predictions based on data. Unfortunately, there is yet to be a science better than probabilities in forecasting the future.

Impairment accounting requires the estimation of probabilities of a loss in value. This is not confined to default. It can be associated with many drivers like a depreciation of the currency which the asset is dominated in. As such, probabilities of different events have to be estimated differently.

13.2.1. *Cumulative and marginal probabilities*

An asset in the form of a forward position is due to mature in 2.5 years. How should the probability that its value will remain unchanged from today be estimated if there are no historical probability data for a holding period of 2.5 years available? The most common approach to answering this question is to use cumulative probabilities.

Assume that there are only two possible outcomes for the asset's value in the next six months or 0.5 year. The probability that it will remain unchanged is 0.8 and the probability that it will fall is 0.2. This is a deliberately asymmetric distribution of future values to eliminate the possibility of negative followed by positive changes to return the value to its original after five periods. The only way for the value to remain unchanged over 2.5 years then is it does not change over each of the five 6-month periods. The probability of that happening is $0.8^5 = 0.3277$. That is less than half of the probability for the same outcome over six months.

The use of cumulative probability is near inevitable when the time to recovery is long. As probabilities are less than one, the probability over a longer period will inevitably be lower than that for a shorter one. The shortest one-period probability is usually considered the marginal probability. If six months is the shortest period where historical data or basis is available, the marginal probability for asset value remaining unchanged is 0.8.

The relationship between marginal and cumulative probabilities become material over the holding period of the asset. If asset value has not changed by the end of the second year, the marginal probability that it will remain unchanged for the last 6 months till eventual disposal and recovery will be 0.8 and not 0.3277. This dynamic evolution of probabilities mean that impairment accounting is more challenging than the more conventional forms of asset valuation in financial accounting.

13.2.2. *Joint, conditional and unconditional probabilities*

Events or developments that affect economic values rarely occur in isolation. Just like the weather, a myriad of factors act in concert or contradiction to shape outcomes. Pricing models attempt to incorporate the most significant ones but fall far short of being able to capture all relevant drivers. Similar to weather forecasts, predicting the market price for any actively traded asset even for the next day remains a hit and miss.

Consider the simple case of a Call option to buy a basket of foreign securities. This is a common strategy to seeking an exposure to the foreign country without having to make actual investments there. Such options are usually sold by global investment banks which can hedge the risk involved with other derivatives. The value of this Call is affected by too many factors to be completely accounted for. Domestic and foreign interest rates are immediately obvious. These, in turn, affect the exchange rate. And then there are the drivers of each of the securities' prices. Add the returns correlations between pairs of securities and the number of factors explode exponentially. A simplistic response to such complexity is to ignore all the cross influences and enumerate each probability as a stand-alone metric. That, however, is not acceptable where there is fiduciary accountability to the public for valuations.

More realistic modeling considers the probability of two or more events happening together. The probability of that occurrence is termed joint probability. A common example is the joint probability of domestic inflation exceeding that of a foreign country and depreciation of local currency against the foreign one. As it is already challenging to quantify the joint probability of two events happening, there is little or no attempt to estimate the same for three or more events.

Joint probability leads to conditional probability. The former is associated with two events occurring simultaneously while the latter is the chance of one event occurring given that the other has happened. Conditional probability can exist independent of joint probability and is widely used in Bayesian statistics. Under Basel II operational risk management, there is a category for events caused by external developments. A breakdown in the securities exchange can lead to transaction failures and losses.

A related kind of probability is unconditional probability. This is the chance of an event happening regardless of how related events turn out. In a sense, unconditional probability is closest to the singular probability of occurrence.

13.2.3. Binomial lattice

A widely accepted approach to modeling with probabilities is the use of a binomial lattice or tree. Based on the standard assumption that the prevailing market price is at equilibrium, there is an equal chance that it will rise or fall and by equal proportions. Figure 13.3 illustrates this concept.

Starting at $100, an asset's price can rise to $101, commonly denoted as u or fall to $99, denoted as d, with equal probabilities over the next period. The end of each state is then extended with the same projection. This is a reasonable assumption. If price changes are serially uncorrelated, the probability that price will reach $102 is 0.5×0.5 or 0.25 which is the

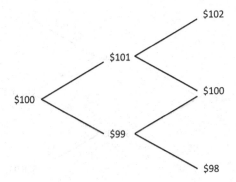

Figure 13.3.   Binomial lattice or tree approach.

cumulative probability over two periods. The probability of price reaching $102 in the second period after having risen to $101 in the first is 0.5. This is the conditional probability.

The probability that it will remain at $100 is 2(0.5)(0.5) = 0.5 which is the unconditional probability that price remains unchanged. The probability that it will fall to $98 is 0.25. The sum of probabilities in each period must equal one.

Though easy to comprehend and compute, this method has a critical deficiency which is the price falling to zero or even negative if the rise and fall are applied repetitively. To overcome this, the common industry practice is to use a modified form of d as being equal to $1/1+u$. Instead of a change of $1 in each period, a percentage growth is applied. For the illustration, $u = 0.01$ or 1%. The price fall d will then be $1/1+0.01 = 0.9901$. Price fall is 0.009901 or 0.9901% which is slightly less than 1%. This modification sacrifices the symmetry in change or return for the certainty that price will not reach zero or negative. Figure 13.3 will be changed to Fig. 13.4.

Another approach to avoid the zero or negative price possibility is to use the lognormal distribution.

A lognormal distribution is one where the natural logarithm of the original value follows a Normal distribution. If $X \sim \log n(\mu, \sigma^2)$ then $\log(X) \sim N(\mu, \sigma^2)$. This also means that X itself is skewed to the right and not bell-shaped.

The antilog of a value is the exponential, commonly denoted as "e". If the rate of change or return is normally distributed, the level or price is can be expressed as a series of exponential values. Securities returns are often assumed to follow the normal distribution which makes their prices

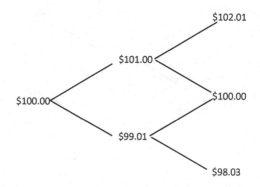

Figure 13.4.   Binomial tree with percent growth applied.

lognormally distributed. For example, $X_1 = X_0 e^{rt}$ where X_i is the level or price at period i, r is the normally distributed rate of return per period and t is the number of periods. Following the illustration, the rate of price change is 1%. The price after one period is $\$100e^{0.01(1)} = \$101.005$ or $\$100e^{-0.01(1)} = \$99.005$. There are two differences between using exponential and absolute percentages. First is the slight difference in the final value. For the rise, the change is a little more than 1% and for the fall, it is a little less than 1%. This difference is normally immaterial as there is no requirement that change must be precisely at 1% and 1.005% is unacceptable. Second is the asymmetry in changes. The rise is 1.005% while the fall is 0.995%. This is systematic and inconsistent with the original assumption that the starting price is at equilibrium with equal rises and falls. For this reason, the exponential approach is applied to very short periods to limit the asymmetry. At a return of 0.01%, price will rise to $100.01 or fall to $99.99 resulting in $0.01 change for both outcomes which is nearly symmetric.

The use of lognormal changes is discussed in greater detail in the section on Credit or Debit Valuation Adjustment.

13.3. Loss Given Default (LGD)

This metric was introduced earlier as one of the three main quantifications together with PD and EAD required under Basel II to estimate credit losses. Though simple in concept, LGD is an area of well suited to desktop analytics. Not only is it not time critical, it benefits from sensitivity analyses that can be explored and documented on a worksheet.

LGD is defined as the percentage of economic loss when there is a default. While easy to comprehend in words, translating this into figures is far more challenging than first impressions. It opens up wide vistas for moral hazard where a financial institution can choose the most favorable definitions to minimize its LGDs. It is for this reason that the Basel Committee established a minimum LGD for credit exposures.

Under Basel II, a bank should develop a workout process to track default costs and recoveries. All material cash flows are to be captured and discounted to the present value at the time of default. The percentage that cannot be recovered from the EAD will then be the LGD. For instance, an obligor defaults on a loan of $100,000. Costs like legal expenses were incurred over the workout process to recover the loan. Discounted to the present value, this amounted to $10,000. Eventually, the present value equivalent of $50,000 was repaid by the obligor. The LGD for this exposure will be $100,000 − $50,000 + $10,000 or $60,000 which is 0.6 or 60% of the EAD.

LGDs are very different over the typical range of credit facilities. Some like residential mortgage which is usually secured by the underlying property may have a negligible LGD. Others like unsecured revolving credit may have LGDs at the other end of the continuum. Basel II encourages banks to have as many LGDs as needed for better precision.

The LGD for a defined credit facility is the exposure weighted LGDs of each default for that facility. This LGD is then applied to all exposures for that facility to derive the Expected Loss $EL = PD \times LGD \times EAD$.

There is a host of measurement issues to address in deriving an LGD. First is the definition of default which has been briefly discussed before.

In a large bank that I consulted for, the regulator permits a creative way to keep the default rate low. When the 90 DPD threshold is reached, a bank can extend a bridging loan to help the obligor make partial repayment, similar to what Japanese banks did in the past which possibly led to the paralysis of its banking industry. It is essentially the bank paying itself but the exposure DPD is reset to zero though the exposure amount is increased by the bridging loan. This is termed as a friendly approach to dealing with some customers, but it distorts both the default rate and LGD for the facility.

Technically, the bridging should be treated as a recovery expense instead of additional credit granted. A reclassification which I proposed pushed the LGDs of nearly all such defaulted exposures to 100% or more in some cases. The bank, however, was not agreeable to doing so.

The second issue is how a default is considered cured. With another bank in the same country, another creative treatment is permitted.

For card credit, a minimum payment is required, but that is only valid if there is no default. Basel II requires that all amounts outstanding have to be repaid after a default for a loan to be cured and reaged. In this country, however, a payment of minimum sum is sufficient for that. This truncates the workout process and produces LGDs that are unrealistically low since the workout process has barely started.

Third, there is the matter of what interest rate is appropriate to discount the workout process cash flows to the present value. In finance theory, interest rate reflects risk. Junk bonds pay significantly higher rates than Treasuries. It is termed a risk premium. Default is at the extreme end of credit risk and cash flows associated with the event should be discounted at a very high interest rate. As there is no consensus on what that rate should be, most practitioners have chosen to apply the risk-free rate. This may be for convenience but it also minimizes the LGD if recoveries are minimal.

The fourth issue is when the workout process should stop. Not only is there no theoretical guidance on this, the regulatory regime has a measurable impact. In some countries, a non-performing loan has to be written off before recovery can be initiated. In others, write-off is only permitted after all reasonable attempts at recovery have been made. Culture also makes difference in whether recoveries are possible. In one where defaults are purely impersonal business decisions, it is left to the creditor to try its best to recover anything available. In others where default is tied to personal reputation or has legal implications on decision-makers, obligors try to repay whenever it is possible. It is said that during the 1997 Asian Financial Crisis, defaulters in Thailand honor their obligations even after more than 10 years.

Academics have tried to provide inputs on when the workout process should stop. One suggestion is when any remaining recoverable amount is not likely to exceed 5% of the total. This sounds reasonable but the challenge is how to estimate that amount.

13.4. Credit Valuation Adjustment (CVA), Debit Valuation Adjustment (DVA) and xVA

The value of a derivative is dependent not only on the factors driving the underlying commodity's price, it is also a function of the counterparty's ability to fulfill the contract at settlement. This understanding underlies the need for impairment accounting. For banks, it impacts on regulatory capital requirements which take into account any adjustments needed to factor in the possibility of adverse developments. As the range of such adjustments continue to widen, it is now generally termed xVA.

Under Basel II, the failure of the counterparty does not necessarily result in a complete loss. There is also the LGD to be considered. Since the global financial crisis of 2008–2010, there has been intense scrutiny on the valuation of derivative positions. It is particularly important for commercial banks as they have to provide regulatory capital against risk exposures. CVA became a necessity to account for the deterioration in a counterparty's creditworthiness or an adverse turn in key

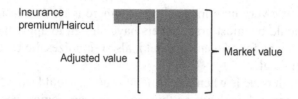

Figure 13.5.   Insurance premium/haircut.

pricing parameters. This aligns market risk with credit risk where allowance must be made for the Expected Loss. Some have argued that if the negative implications of CVA must be accounted, it is only right to consider DVA which is the opposite outcome. This argument has yet to gain traction in determining Basel II regulatory capital requirement.

In a nutshell, CVA marks down the value of a derivative position based on the degree of counterparty risk. The amount to discount is also termed a haircut and can be viewed as an insurance premium, as shown in Fig. 13.5.

The market value is what the position will be worth if there is no counterparty risk. Since this is untrue in reality, insurance can be purchased to cover the loss from a counterparty default. Credit Default Swap or CDS has become a popular instrument for large exposures. The insurance premium needed is equivalent to the CVA haircut resulting in the adjusted value being less than the market value.

The commonly used example to illustrate CVA is an interest rate swap and it will be employed here. More details on this illustration can be found in *Understanding CVA, DVA and FVA: Examples of Interest Rate Swap Valuation, 2016, Donald J. Smith, Journal of Accounting and Finance, Vol. 16(8), pp. 11–31.* It should be noted, however, that the paper published rounded figures which differ a little from the those obtained using the R codes shown later. The swap illustration is as follows.

A bank entered into a seven-year interest rate swap with a firm two years ago which means that the contract has another five years to maturity. The bank pays a fixed rate of 4.00% once a year and receives the London Interbank Offer Rate (LIBOR) in return. LIBOR is the international benchmark floating rate used to value nearly all derivative positions. LIBOR is set at the beginning of the year and if it is more than 4.00%, the bank receives a net payment of (LIBOR − 4.00%) at the end of the that year.

It is worthwhile to take a short detour to understand why swaps are the most heavily traded derivatives globally. Though a zero-sum game like all derivatives, swap is underpinned by an economic driver not found in others and, that is, it can be beneficial to both transacting parties. The reason is the Law of Comparative Advantage that also underpins international trade.

Assume that the bank is of better creditworthiness than the firm and can borrow from the market at 4.20% fixed or LIBOR + 10%. The firm's market funding cost is be 4.50% and LIBRO + 0.60%. On the surface, it will appear the bank could not benefit from any swap with the firm since it already enjoys absolute advantage in debt funding. This observation, however, is inaccurate. If the bank borrows at LIBOR + 10% from the market and enters the swap, it will end up paying 4.10% (4.00% for the swap payment and a net of 0.10% after the LIBOR received). This is less than the 4.20% fixed cost of the market. The firm in turn borrows at 4.50% fixed from the market and ends up with LIBOR + 0.50% which is lower than its market cost. Both parties have borrowed at that which they have comparative advantage and exchanged for that which they do not, increasing the welfare of both in the process.

Being of better creditworthiness, the bank has a PD of 0.5% compared to 2.5% for the firm. On the other hand, LGD for the bank is 90% while only 60% for the firm. This example illustrates how LGD is an important parameter of credit risk. A bank has few tangible assets unless it has invested heavily in other lines of businesses like real estate, for instance. It may have a low PD but once insolvent, there is little for its creditors to make recoveries from.

Risk management regulations require the bank to estimate a CVA for this swap so computations are from the bank's perspective. This impetus frames the parameters of the process which may not be the same as how a firm or investor would do it.

Banks are concerned with a material loss arising from risk taking. An unfavorable change in interest rate results in a loss of value to the swap position. There is no theoretical threshold for what amounts to material but it should be sufficiently large to warrant attention. In statistics, the standard deviation is often used to demarcate what can normally be expected and that which is less likely. This is an important consideration in modeling the CVA for banks as it informs the interest rate path to be developed. Otherwise, CVA can be derived from any change in interest rate resulting in endless possibilities on the quantification.

Several assumptions are needed to derive the CVA. Current LIBOR is assumed to be 1.00%. This is also termed the spot rate which is the

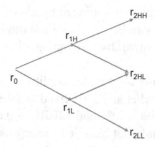

Figure 13.6.   Rise or fall of rates.

interest cost of a one-year debt without any cash payments in between. Rates are assumed to rise or fall, as shown in Fig. 13.6.

Unlike for securities prices discussed earlier, there is no assumed rate of return for interest. Instead, future rates are assumed to follow a lognormal distribution which prevents a rate from becoming negative. The high state (H) and the low state (L) occur with equal probabilities.

With r_0 at 1.00%, interest rate moves up and down by one standard deviation. Since the distribution is lognormal, log(s.d.) = σ, where s.d. stands for standard deviation. If σ is 0.2 or 20%, the standard deviation will be $e^{0.2} = 1.2214$.

13.4.1. *Spot, forward and par rates*

To develop the binomial tree for interest rate paths, a short tutorial on the different forms of interest rates is helpful.

Spot rate which is usually annualized is regarded as the true cost of debt as it is finance theory that there cannot be more than a one spot rate for one period and risk class. If that happens, arbitrage will force all transacted rates to a single equilibrium in the absence of transaction costs. Though spot rates are real in the sense that they are paid by the borrower, most are actually not directly observable in the business world. Rates are inferred from traded bonds of the same risk class and because only Treasuries have a sufficient spread across maturities and are regarded as risk-free, their prices are the main inputs for computation. The result is a yield curve which plots the spot rates of different maturities.

Spot rates over different maturities produce forward or implied forward rates. As the term reveals, the forward rate is implied so it is not even

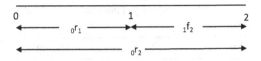

Figure 13.7. Derivation of the simplest forward rate using a one-period and a two-period spot rate.

indirectly observable. The simplest forward rate is derived using a one-period and a two-period spot rate, as shown in Fig. 13.7.

Spot rate for one period from 0 to 1 is $_0r_1$ and spot rate for two periods is $_0r_2$. Under a strict assumption that there is no premium for investing over a longer period and no arbitrage $(1 + {_0r_2})^2 = (1 + {_0r_1})(1 + {_1f_2})$, where $_1f_2$ is the forward rate from period 1 to 2. The left-hand side of the equation is sometimes known as the buy-and-hold strategy and the right-hand side the rollover strategy. Both must yield the same total return over two periods to prevent arbitrage. The forward rate is often regarded as the expected spot rate. As shown shortly, forward rates provide a reference for the interest rate paths to be developed.

A less used form is the par rate which is more relevant here than in other forums. This is the value of the coupon expressed as a rate needed to price the bond at par. Continuing with the assumption that the one-year LIBOR is 1.00%, the two-year LIBOR is assumed to be 2.0101%. The annual coupon for a two-year bond to be priced at par is 2.00% which is $2.00 if the par value is $100. This can be derived as $100 = C/1.01 + 100+C/1.020101^2$, where C is the coupon. Solving the equation gives C equal to 2. As spot rates are traded and observable even if indirectly, the par rate will be used to develop the path of future interest rates.

13.4.2. *Interest rate binomial lattice*

The first step in developing the lattice is the extraction of coupon rates from the spot rates. Banks would typically subscribe to financial information services like Thomson Reuters or Bloomberg where yield curve data are readily available. With such rates, the forward and par rates can be derived, as explained earlier and shown in Table 13.1.

Both the forward and par rates can be derived from the spot rate. As explained, the forward rate is only implied, so it cannot be presumed that the rate from period Date 1 to Date 2 will be 3.0303%. The aim of the

Table 13.1.   Forward and par rates derived from spot rates

Par	Spot	Forward
1.00%	1.0000%	—
2.00%	2.0101%	3.0303%
2.50%	2.5212%	3.5512%
2.80%	2.8310%	3.7658%
3.00%	3.0392%	3.8765%

binomial lattice is to allow for different possible outcomes and evaluate how they can affect the value of the swap for the bank.

The 1.00% spot rate for Date 0 is established. The next step is to develop the possible outcomes for Date 1. Using one standard deviation as metric for constant rate volatility, it means that r_{1H} will be two standard deviations from r_{1L}. Mathematically, this translates into $\log(r_{1H}) = \log(r_{1L}) + 2\sigma$ or $r_{1H} = e^{2\sigma}r_{1L}$. Since $\sigma = 0.20$, $r_{1H} = 1.491825r_{1L}$. Using the par rate derived and the equal probabilities of a rate rise or fall, the properties of expectations can be used to set the equation $100 = 0.5\ (102/(1+ r_{1H})(1.01) + 2/(1.01))\ 0.5\ (102/(1+ r_{1L})(1.01) + 2/(1.01))$. This means that the expected value of two-year 2.00% annual coupon bond discounted using the possible forward rates r_{1H} and r_{1L} and the spot rate of 1.00% should equal the par value of 100 to meet the no-arbitrage condition. Substituting r_{1H} with $1.491825r_{1L}$, the equation becomes quadratic and can be solved giving $r_{1L} = 2.435\%$ and $r_{1H} = 3.6326\%$. The average of these two results is 3.0338% which is slightly higher than the forward rate of 3.0303% derived using the spot rates. This means that the model does not create a symmetric distribution centered on the forward rate and if the forward rate is an unbiased predictor of the spot rate, there is a built-in bias here. As discussed earlier, the use of a lognormal distribution induces an upward bias where a rate rise is slightly larger than a rate fall similar to that of up and down states of securities returns discussed earlier.

The same approach is repeated for Dates 2 to 4 but the calculations become much more complex as the number of branches increases systematically. As will be shown later, R packages like uniroot can be employed to bypass the need for manual computations. The binomial lattice will look like Fig. 13.8, if completed.

The weight is the probability for an interest rate to be realized.

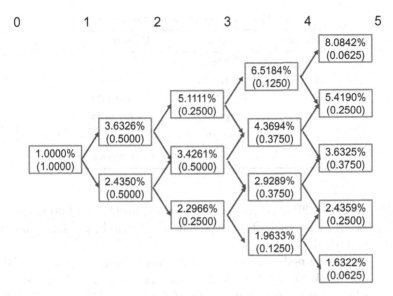

Figure 13.8. Binomial tree over five periods, with weights in parentheses.

13.4.3. *Counterparty default*

The goal of the CVA is to estimate the loss should the firm default when the swap is in the bank's favor. This happens when LIBOR is above 4.00%. To derive that, the implication of LIBOR is first considered.

LIBOR is floating rate which changes in response to market forces and is regarded as the equilibrium cost of debt. It is set by a panel of banks that are members of the British Bankers' Association for a specific currency. The highest and lowest 25% of quotes are removed and the most competitive rate is announced at 11am London time to the world. As such, a bond paying LIBOR is always priced at par. The value of the swap to the bank then is the price difference between a bond paying 4.00% coupon and a par bond. The price of a 4.00% coupon bond $V_{4\%}$ can be obtained by discounting the coupon and final payment with the spot rate for each date. The discount factor for each spot rate is provided in Table 13.2.

The result is $V_{4\%}$ = 4(0.990099) + 4(0.960978) + 4(0.928023) + 4(0.894344) + 104(0.860968) = 104.6344. Since the par value of a bond is $100, the swap to the bank at Date 0 is worth $100 − $104.6344 = −$4.6344. It can be considered the value of a no-default swap V_{ND}. If the bank wishes to terminate the swap at that time, it has to pay the firm $4.6344. Over time, however, there is the possibility of interest rate

Table 13.2.   Discount factors for spot rates.

Period	Spot	Discount factor
0	1.0000%	—
1	2.0101%	0.990099
2	2.5212%	0.960978
3	2.8310%	0.928023
4	3.0392%	0.894344
5	—	0.860968

rising beyond 4.00%. When that happens, the swap turns into a positive value for the bank. Each of these possibilities has to be evaluated and the value quantified.

Consider the node on Date 3 where interest rate is 4.3694%. If this occurs, the bank gains 0.3694%. This gain can only be collected at Date 4 according to the terms of the swap. If the rate on Date 3 is 4.3694%, there are equal chances that it will be 5.4190% or 3.6325% in Date 4. These translate into a gain of 1.4190% or −0.3675% but they are settled only at Date 5. To value these payoffs at Date 4, they must be discounted using the relevant spot rates for each outcome which result in $1.4190/1.05419 = 1.3461\%$ or $-0.3675/1.036325 = -0.3547\%$. So at Date 3, the value of the swap to the bank should interest rate be at 4.3694% will be $V_{\mathrm{ND}} = 0.3694 + 0.5(1.3461+)0.5(-0.3675)/1.043694 = 0.8289$.

The CVA for the bank is the loss in the positive value of the swap should the firm default. This is the summation of the product of probability of positive expected exposure, positive expected exposure, the PD and the LGD, all discounted to Date 0. It can be expressed as CVA = $\Sigma(+\text{Expected Exposure}) \times \text{LGD} \times \text{PD} \times \text{Discount factor}$. This derivation has to be backward recursive to account for all possible positive exposures to the end of the swap. At Date 4, there are two such outcomes, when rates are 6.5184% and 4.3694%. Applying the process explained above, the Expected Exposure (EE) = $[0.125(6.5184 - 4.0000) + 0.375(4.3694 - 4.0000)] + [[0.0625(8.0842 - 4.0000/1.080842) + 0.25(5.4190 - 4.0000/1.054190)] = 1.026$. This EE has to be multiplied by the PD, LGD and discount factor to bring it to the value at Date 0. When applied to all EEs, the results will be as in Table 13.3.

The CVA for the bank will be $0.0583. Added to the market value of −$4.6344, the fair value of the swap will be −$4.6927 if the DVA

Table 13.3.   Results after application to all EEs.

Date	EE	LGD	PD	Discount	CVA
1	0.4550	0.6	0.025	0.990099	0.0068
2	0.9301	0.6	0.025	0.960978	0.0134
3	1.1848	0.6	0.025	0.928023	0.0165
4	1.0260	0.6	0.025	0.894344	0.0138
5	0.6100	0.6	0.025	0.860968	0.0079
					0.0583

is ignored. Derived using the same process, the DVA will be $0.0503 which will translate into a fair value of −$4.6424 for a third party.

Another type of adjustment that has gained traction is FVA which is Funding Valuation Adjustment. As this adjustment is essentially domain sensitive, it is most widely employed only in the U.S.A. where there are many options to source for and invest funds. The net result can be positive or negative.

A short discussion on the inputs to the CVA derivation may be worthwhile. First, the PD employed by a bank is usually the one that has been estimated based on Basel II guidelines. This is the one-year probability of default or at most 18 months for permitted exceptions. This is a marginal probability. Strictly speaking, CVA is meant to account for the loss should the counterparty default at any time for the remainder of the contract. The PD of the firm over the next five years should then be $(1 - 0.975^5)$ or 0.1189 or 11.89%. The 5-year cumulative probability is substantially higher than the one-year marginal one. Second, the summation across all positive Expected Exposures may be an overestimation. If the firm defaulted on Date 2, potential losses from Date 3 to Date 5 are irrelevant.

13.5. R with Excel

BERT has been introduced earlier. Though it adds value to Excel to have R integrated, embedding is not to the same extent as with databases like SQL Server and Oracle. BERT requires its own R syntax that can be quite different from that widely used. For instance, a data frame cannot be displayed by typing its name alone. The BERT code is df$get_Value() where df is the data frame name. Every function has to be based on BERT's proprietary syntax. Besides, data frame rows and columns cannot be easily accessed like in regular R using df[r,c] where r and c are the row and column numbers. Finally, where BERT functions can be viewed using ls(EXCEL$Application), documentation whether organic or from third parties is sparse. With packages developed for R to interface with Excel directly, it is possible and easier to use an R editing tool to leverage on the additional capabilities that Excel provides for desktop risk analytics. This section provides a couple of illustrations on complementary use of Excel with R especially for presentations and what-if analysis.

Some preparations are needed to access Excel from R. First is the installation of the Java Runtime Environment JRE. At the time of this writing, the latest version is 8. It is essential to note that the default JRE downloaded is 32-bit and that would not work with a 64-bit Excel. The 64-bit JRE has to be specifically installed. A convenient website where it can currently be found is https://download.cnet.com/Java-Runtime-Environment-JRE-64-Bit/3000-2213_4-75317067.html. Next, the Windows operating system environment has to be updated to run the JRE. This is done by editing the system environment to add a JAVA_HOME which the directory set to the JAVA program folder and the adding a new path pointing to \\...\bin\server in the same folder. This is similar to the adding of R_HOME when R was installed.

The second step is to edit the Rprofile.site file to enable permanent R access to JRE by adding the line Sys.setenv(JAVA_HOME = "//.../bin/server"). If this is not done, the command must be issued at the start of each R session.

Finally, the package rJava has to be installed. Without it, other packages used to access Excel will throw an error message.

The first example is examining how different discount rates affect the LGD derived according to Basel II requirements. To recap, LGD starts with a workout process at the point of default. The amount due from the obligor is the Exposure At Default (EAD). Recovery expenses incurred are offset by recoveries with each cash flow discounted to the present value as on the day of default. The net recovered amount is subtracted from the EAD and becomes the LGD. For comparability, LGD is divided by the EAD and turned into a ratio. For a credit facility, the LGD is the EAD-weighted LGDs of individual exposures to that facility.

Figure 13.9 shows an Excel worksheet named Workout consisting of workout data extracted from a recovery unit database. It is the first

⬛	A	B	C	D	E	F	G
1	Date	Idx	L101	L102	L103	L104	L105
2	1/1/2017	1					
3	1/2/2017	2	643174				
4	1/3/2017	3					
5	1/4/2017	4		1494986			
6	1/5/2017	5					
7	1/6/2017	6					
8	1/7/2017	7			1146727		
9	1/8/2017	8					
10	1/9/2017	9					
11	1/10/2017	10	3677				
12	1/11/2017	11				933612	
13	1/12/2017	12					
14	1/13/2017	13					
15	1/14/2017	14					
16	1/15/2017	15					
17	1/16/2017	16					669169
18	1/17/2017	17					
19	1/18/2017	18			-821		
20	1/19/2017	19					

Figure 13.9.   Workout data extracted from a recovery unit database.

worksheet of the workbook LGD.xlsx. The process of extraction is skipped as it is widely known.

The figure is for illustrative purpose and comprises only five defaulted exposures in early 2017 with workout to the end of 2018. Each exposure is prefixed with a "L" for coding convenience as will be shown shortly.

The first number in an exposure is the EAD. Subsequent positive numbers are recoveries while negative ones are expenses incurred in the workout process. For exposure L101, for instance, the EAD is $643,174 and the first cashflow is a recovery of $3,677. For exposure L103, the first cashflow is an expense of $821.

The Date column indicates when each cashflow occurred. Next to it is a column named Idx which is an index of running numbers. If this is not already in the spreadsheet, it can be created in R. As will be shown in the derivation of present value later, it is needed for the function to be employed.

The second worksheet is named Rates as shown in Fig. 13.10.

	A
1	Rate
2	0.02
3	0.03
4	0.04
5	0.05

Figure 13.10.   Rates worksheet

The rates in the Rate column will be used to discount the cashflows to present value. Four rates are preset but a key purpose of this exercise is to facilitate a what-if analysis by changing the rates or the intervals. Corporate decision-makers often want to be presented with different scenarios and outcomes before finalizing their decisions. A buzzword once popular is Online Analytical Programming or OLAP where real-time analysis is made possible by data and applications.

A third worksheet called Results can either be created in the workbook LGD or with R codes. For convenience, it is included in the workbook.

The R editor used here is RStudio. More about customizing this utility is explained in the next chapter. An advantage of using R instead of BERT is the possibility of employing the latest version. At the time of this writing, R version 4.0.3 is used.

Several packages are available for connecting R to Excel. The most widely used are xlsx and openxlsx. It has been reported and verified in this exercise that there may be conflicts between the two packages. After some experimentation, openxlsx is the package used.

The LGD workbook is first loaded into R and the worksheets extracted:

```
# Read Excel workbook and extract worksheets
library(rJava)
library(openxlsx)

# Load Excel workbook and read worksheets as data frames
wb_LGD <- loadWorkbook(file = ".../LGD.xlsx")
workout <- readWorkbook(xlsxFile = wb_LGD,sheet = "Workout")
rates <- readWorkbook(xlsxFile = wb_LGD,sheet = "Rates")
```

As the Results worksheet is needed only later to store the outputs, it is not read in here.

The empty cells in the Workout worksheet are converted to NA in the workout data frame. With the present value function to be used later, NA cannot be processed and has to be removed. A loop is created to systematically do that:

```
# Remove NA from workout data frame for each default
i = 3
for (i in j:ncol(workout)) {
x <- i-2

# Omit all NAs in workout data frame
tmp <- na.omit(select(workout, 2, i))

# Concatenate the prefix "L10" and number then assign the data frame
tmp
assign(paste('L10', x, sep = ""), tmp)
}
```

It may be worth noting that the codes developed here can be applied to any number of exposures and days of the workout process. Besides, the use of sequential column names prefixed by "L10" facilities the employment of a loop. If the exposures came with different labels, a set of sequential column names can be created in R to serve the same purpose.

The NA removal has created individual data frames for each exposure. The exposure data frame comprises only the index in the first column and the cashflows in the second for that exposure alone. This allows for each exposure to be processed separately to derive its LGD. Before doing so, the total amount of the defaulted exposures is computed to enable the computation of weights:

```
# Compute total defaulted exposure amount
i = 1
total = 0
for (i in 1:5) {
tmp <- get(paste('L10', i, sep = ""))
total <- total + first(tmp[1, 2])
}
```

The LGD for each exposure is derived using the presentValue function of the package lifecontingencies. Surprisingly, there are few packages that compute the present value of a stream of random cashflows though a number are available for annuity functions. The interest rate in the rates data frame are used to discount the cashflows but each has to be divided by 365 as the rates are annual and the cashflows are recorded by the day. Each present value is then divided by the total computed earlier to obtain the weighted LGD. It should be noted that the present value function includes the first cashflow which is the EAD and this has to be removed to arrive at the percentage LGD:

```
library(lifecontingencies)
# Compute exposure weighted LGD
i = 1
j = 1
loss = 0
LGD = c(0, 0, 0, 0)
for (j in 1:4) {
r = rates/365
for (i in 1:5) {
def <- get(paste('L10', j, sep = ""))
exp <- first(def[1, 2])
wt <- exp / total
pv <- presentValue(cashFlows = def[, 2], timeIds = def[, 1], interestRates
= r$Rate[j])
loss = loss + (wt * (pv/exp - 1))
}
LGD[j] <- loss
}
```

As mentioned earlier, the presentValue function relies on the Idx column in the argument timeIds to enumerate the number of days from the point of default that a cash flow occurs. The exposure weighted LGD is combined with the interest rates into a data frame and saved to workbook before being updated to Excel:

```
# Combine interest rates and exposure weighted LGD
results <- cbind(rates,LGD)

# Write data to worksheet
writeData(wb_LGD, "Results", results)
```

```
# Save workbook to Excel
saveWorkbook(wb_LGD, ".../LGD.xlsx",overwrite = TRUE)
```

The Results worksheet appears as in Fig. 13.11.

The output reveals some interesting results. LGD is lower with a smaller discount rate. However, the change in value is not linear though monotonic. The difference in LGD between using 4% and 5% as discount rate is much smaller than that between 2% and 3%. For a more granular analysis on the relationship between discount rate and LGD, the cell values in Rates can be easily revised and the codes rerun for a new set of outputs.

The second example shows how a lognormally distributed binomial tree can be constructed. This is perhaps the most challenging aspect of CVA derivation. The purpose here is to perform what-if analyses of assumptions like the volatility of interest rates as proxied by the standard deviation which is suited for a utility like Excel.

A workbook named BinomialTree.xlsx is first read in. The worksheet Spot comprises a column of spot rate and another of standard deviations. The worksheet is shown in Fig. 13.12.

	A	B
1	Rate	LGD
2	0.02	0.07101025
3	0.03	0.42141422
4	0.04	0.4549616
5	0.05	0.51028326

Figure 13.11. Results worksheet.

	A	B
1	spot	sd
2	0.01000000	0.15
3	0.02010098	0.20
4	0.02520832	0.25
5	0.02830909	
6	0.03037733	

Figure 13.12. Spot worksheet.

It should be noted that the spot rates have been deliberately set to produce par rates similar to those in the paper discussed above. Using the rounded spot rates shown there will not result in the rounded par rates when run with the R codes:

```
# Read Excel workbook and extract worksheets
library(rJava)
library(openxlsx)
bt <- loadWorkbook(file = ".../BinomialTree.xlsx")
spot <- readWorkbook(xlsxFile = bt,sheet = "Spot")
```

The next step is to derive the par rates from the spot rates. To recap, a par rate is the coupon rate such that the discounted cash flows equal the par value of the bond. The rate c for a two-year bond can be obtained from the equation $100 = 100 + c/1.02010098^2 + c/1.01$ which can be re-expressed as $100 + c/1.02010098^2 + c/1.01 - 100 = 0$. The R function uniroot is very useful for solving such and more complex equations instantaneously:

```
# Derive par rate
f <- function(c) (100 + c)/1.02010098^2 + c/1.01 - 100
answer <- uniroot(f, interval = c(0, 100))
print(answer$root)
```

The function expression is set to equal 0 as shown above. The output will be 1.999998 which is perhaps as close to 2 as possible as the two-year spot rate of 0.02010098 was originally derived using 2 as the coupon rate.

To simplify the iterative process of obtaining the par rates, the discount factor df for each year is first derived as $1/(1+r)^t$ where r is the spot rate and t is the number of years:

```
# Derive discount factor
df <- c(0,0,0,0,0)
for (i in 1:5) {
df[i] <- 1/(1 + spot$spot[i])^i
}
```

The par rates can be obtained as follows:

```
# Obtain par rate
par <- c(0,0,0,0,0)
for (i in 1:5) {
f <- function(c) (100 + c)*df[i] + c*sum(df[1:i-1])-100
answer <- uniroot(f, interval = c(0, 100))
par[i] <- answer$root
}
```

These interim results can be viewed and verified by exporting them to the Excel workbook with a new worksheet named Rates added:

```
# Combine spot and par rates
Rates <- cbind(spot$spot,par)

# Add a worksheet
addWorksheet(bt, "Rates")

# Write data to worksheet
writeData(bt, "Rates", rates)

# Save workbook to Excel
saveWorkbook(bt, ".../BinomialTree.xlsx",overwrite = TRUE)
```

The output in Fig. 13.13 shows that the par rates are close to the round figures but not exactly those shown in the paper.

This is the result despite the spot rates being deliberately derived from the rounded par rates. Inverting the derivations should produce the original inputs but negligible differences remain.

	A	B
1	spot	par
2	0.01	1
3	0.02010098	1.99999753
4	0.02520832	2.49960987
5	0.02830909	2.79994099
6	0.03037733	2.9985956

Figure 13.13.   Rates worksheet.

Precision is not essential in CVA as it is subject to key assumptions like volatility which have more significant effects. To construct the binomial tree, the par rates used will be the rounded ones shown in Table 13.1, so a manual replacement is made:

```
# Replace par rates with rounded numbers
par<-c(0.01,0.02,0.025,0.028,0.03)
```

From the binomial tree shown in Fig. 13.8, it appears that there are two forward rates at Date 1, three at Date 2, five at Date 3, etc. In construction, there are actually four rates in Date 2, six rates in Date 3. On Date 2, the higher rate extending from the lower half is set to be the same as the lower rate extending from the upper half. For the binomial tree, the two rates have to be processed separately despite being identical as they have to be discounted by different prior rates. So, two rates have to be constructed for Date 1 and four for Date 2.

This R code for this example will cover only up to Date 2 but it can be quite easily extended to all the five years. To differentiate forward rates for each period, a subscript is attached to a new variable f, with f1 being forward rate at Date 1 and f2 forward rate at Date 2, etc. Each forward rate is further divided into f11 being the lower for f1 and f24 being the highest for f2, etc.:

```
# Create forward rate columns
f1 <- c(0, 0)
f2 <- c(0, 0, 0, 0)
```

To simplify coding, a coefficient m is created such that $m = e^{2\sigma}$ where σ is the standard deviation to be used. As σ changes, m changes accordingly. A worksheet Results is added to the workbook and a data frame results is created to store all the outputs:

```
# Add a Results worksheet
addWorksheet(bt, "Results")

# Set a data frame to store all results
results <- data.frame()
```

To evaluate all three values of σ, a loop is constructed to iteratively process each of them. In each iteration, the forward rates from Date 1 to Date 2 are first derived as column f1 with two values followed by the four forward rates from Date 2 to 3 denoted as f2. As discussed earlier, the second and third values of f2 are identical but the they still have to be separately processed to obtain the results. All outputs are appended, written to the Results worksheet and finally saved to the BinomialTree Excel workbook. The R script used is as follows:

```
# Add a Results worksheet
addWorksheet(bt, "Results")

# Set a data frame to store all results
results <- data.frame()

for (i in 1:3) {
# Set m
m = exp(2 * spot$sd[i])

# Derive Date 1 forward rates
f <- function(r) 0.5 * ((100 + 100 * par[2])/(1 + r) * df[1] + 100 * par[2]
* df[1]) + 0.5 * ((100 + 100 * par[2])/(1 + m * r) * df[1] + 100 * par[2] *
df[1]) - 100
answer <- uniroot(f, interval = c(0, 1))
f1[1] <- answer$root
f1[2] <- m * answer$root

# Derive Date 2 forward rates
f <- function(r) 0.25 * ((100 + 100 * par[3])/((1 + r) * (1 + f1[1])) * df[1]
+ 100 * par[3]/(1 + f1[1]) * df[1] + 100 * par[3] * df[1]) + 0.25 * ((100 +
100 * par[3])/((1 + m * r) * (1 + f1[1])) * df[1] + 100 * par[3]/(1 + f1[1])
* df[1] + 100 * par[3] * df[1]) + 0.25 * ((100 + 100 * par[3])/((1 + m * r)
* (1 + f1[2])) * df[1] + 100 * par[3]/(1 + f1[2]) * df[1] + 100 * par[3] *
df[1]) + 0.25 * ((100 + 100 * par[3])/((1 + m^2 * r) * (1 + f1[2])) * df[1]
+ 100 * par[3]/(1 + f1[2]) * df[1] + 100 * par[3] * df[1]) - 100
answer <- uniroot(f, interval = c(0, 1))
f2[1] <- answer$root
f2[2] <- m * answer$root
f2[3] = f2[2]
f2[4] <- m * f2[3]

# Combine two Dates
result <- cbind(f1, f2)
```

```
# Append results to data frame results
results <- rbind(results, result)

# Add empty row to each set of results
results[nrow(results)+1,] <- NA

# Write data frame to worksheet
writeData(bt, "Results", results)


}


# Save workbook
saveWorkbook(bt, ".../BinomialTree.xlsx", overwrite = TRUE)
```

The first function f which derives the forward rate on Date 1 is relatively straightforward as there are only two branches extending from a single Date 0 spot rate of 1.00%. The second f function for the Date 2 forward rates is more complex though. There are four branches of two each

	A	B
1	f1	f2
2	0.02583427	0.0257405
3	0.03487261	0.03474604
4	0.02583427	0.03474604
5	0.03487261	0.04690225
6		
7	0.02437699	0.0229289
8	0.0363662	0.0342059
9	0.02437699	0.0342059
10	0.0363662	0.0510292
11		
12	0.02295018	0.02033681
13	0.03783845	0.03352973
14	0.02295018	0.03352973
15	0.03783845	0.05528118

Figure 13.14.   Results worksheet.

extending from the high and low Date 1 forward rates. To obtain the forward rate for a branch, the par coupon of 2.50 must be discounted by the appropriate prior forward rate of Date 1. Each forward rate after the lowest is larger by the multiple m so the largest will be m^2 times the smallest as the middle two are identical. The Results worksheet appears as in Fig. 13.14 with f1 being repeated due to the binding of columns.

Unsurprisingly, the spread of the forward rates is wider for a larger σ. The middle group of four rows is derived using σ as 0.2 or 20% which is value employed in the paper. Once again, the forward rates obtained are similar but not identical to those published due to rounding errors.

Being able to carry out desktop analytics can help a bank present its models for acceptance as part of the Basel II regulatory requirements. More than largely data-driven ones like credit risk ratings, models like CVA are assumption dependent. As Excel is ubiquitous, it makes for easier presentation to regulators when worksheet cell values can be instantaneously modified to evaluate how outcomes can change.

Chapter 14

Resources

With the increasingly widespread use of R, resources continue to be added to the ecosystem. Packages have already been mentioned in earlier chapters. Though this book is largely devoted to the use of Oracle R Enterprise (ORE), tools like an R editor can be very helpful in the coding process.

14.1. RStudio

There are several R editors available. Among these, RStudio is arguably the most well known. The features of this tool have been described in an earlier chapter so will not be repeated here.

Unlike ORE, RStudio allows for immediate viewing of results and provides more feedback on coding errors. Practically, all the R codes in the preceding chapters were validated that way. The error messages can be fairly cryptic and require some research to understand, but they are still helpful in reaching correctness eventually.

One issue needs to be addressed in using RStudio as an aid to ORE. At the time of this writing, ORE is compatible with up to R 3.3.0 only (Fig. 14.1). RStudio is always downloaded with the latest version of R which is 4.0.3. Unlike some software, R is not backward compatible. Codes written for R 4.0.3 cannot be run on R 3.3.0. That applies to packages. R codes created in RStudio may not be usable in ORE and an error

Figure 14.1.   R 3.3.0.

message will be thrown to state this. One way to avoid such an outcome is to change the R version used to 3.3.0 and the library for the packages to be installed. Version change can be done with the Tools menu item followed by Global Options.

If this is the only version of R downloaded, that would be automatic. Otherwise, a conscious change has to be made.

By default, RStudio uses the R-3.3.0 library which is usually ...\Documents\R\win-library\3.3. This location is outside of the ORE environment so packages installed cannot be found and used when codes are implemented in the Oracle server. To breach this gap, the RStudio library can be changed to that used by ORE. That can be accomplished by editing the Rprofile SITE file to reconfigure the library location to (ORACLE_HOME)\R\(ORE folder)\library using a text editor.

14.2. Packages

R packages are not backward compatible with the R version. Some are written after 3.3.0 and cannot be employed in ORE. Most are updated versions of existing ones but even these are unusable if a later version of R has been used for coding. To ensure compatible, only packages written for R 3.3 should be installed. These can be found in the Packages hyperlink of The Comprehensive R Archive Network site. A screenshot of the /bin/windows/contrib/3.3 folder following the Package link is shown in Fig 14.2.

Name	Last modified	Size	Description
Parent Directory		-	
@ReadMe	2018-04-22 14:52	5.9K	
A3_1.0.0.zip	2018-04-23 13:46	69K	
ABC.RAP_0.9.0.zip	2018-04-23 13:46	4.6M	
ABCanalysis_1.2.1.zip	2017-12-09 17:59	54K	
ABCoptim_0.15.0.zip	2018-04-23 13:46	566K	
ABCp2_1.2.zip	2018-04-23 13:47	35K	
ABHgenotypeR_1.0.1.zip	2018-04-23 13:46	123K	

Figure 14.2.   Index of /bin/windows/contrib/3.3.

All package names starting with a lower-case letter are listed at the end of the page shown in Fig. 14.2.

14.3. Free Data

Most R packages come with sample data. All such free data can be easily listed by executing **data()** in RStudio. They are often used for the R tutorials found in different sites.

Annex A: Meeting of Minds Questionnaire

Business Problem and Solution

1. As concisely as possible, describe the business problem that the solution is meant to address (A one-sentence answer would be best).

   _____

   _____

   _____

   _____

2. Information produced by this solution can be broadly proportioned for the following uses (Please provide an estimated percentage for each category):

   | | | % Corporate policy-making

   | | | % Strategic planning

   | | | % Operational decision-making

   | | | % General internal analysis

   | | | % Value add to clients

3. If this project involves analytics, the following solutions are needed (Please tick appropriate boxes):

☐ Customer profiling

☐ Cross-selling analysis

☐ Database marketing

☐ Mass customization

☐ Targeted promotion

☐ Loyalty analysis

☐ Attrition analysis

☐ Credit scoring

☐ Behavioral scoring

☐ Application scoring

☐ Others (please describe)

4. Information produced by this solution can be broadly proportioned to the following (Please provide an estimated percentage for each category):

☐☐☐ % Increasing revenue

☐☐☐ % Decreasing cost

☐☐☐ % Reducing risk

5. The following are types of outputs that the solution is expected to produce (Please tick the appropriate boxes):

☐ Analysis tables

☐ Analysis graphs and charts

☐ Action reports

☐ Color coding

☐ Others (Please describe)

6. This is a standalone solution, i.e. it would not be part of a larger solution in future.

☐ Yes   ☐ No

Departments and Individual Users

7. The main user department of this solution would be (Please provide the complete name of department or unit)

_____

8. The main individual users of this solution are (Please provide job titles only)

_____

_____

_____

_____

_____

9. Other departments that would be immediate users are (Please provide the complete name of department or unit)

_____

_____

_____

_____

_____

10. Other departments that are likely to use this solution within the next two years are (Please provide the complete name of department or unit)

_____

_____

_____

_____

11. The department that would maintain and update the solution is (Please provide the complete name of department or unit)

_____

12. Staff who have to directly interface with the computer for the purpose of this solution can be broadly proportioned as follows (Please provide an estimated percentage for each category):

%   IT savvy

%   Proficient computer user

%   Average computer user

%   Computer phobic

Budget

13. The intended or approved financial budget for this project is $ _____ .

14. The amount of time budgeted for this project is _____ months.

Working Mode

15. Dren Analytics normally prefers to work with a project manager designated by the client. All internal coordination within the client's organization is left to the discretion of this manager. It helps productivity if this manager has the requisite knowledge bases for the project. For this project, the designated manager would have the following knowledge bases (Please tick the appropriate boxes):

☐ Business problem domain

☐ Statistics

☐ Research design

☐ Relevant operating system

- [ ] Relevant application software

- [ ] Database modeling

- [ ] Data warehousing

- [ ] Client/server system

16. The project manager would be able to meet with Dren Analytics staff on a week/fortnightly basis.

- [ ] Yes   [ ] No

Data Collection and Storage

17. The following types of data are required (Please tick the appropriate boxes):

- [ ] Primary external data to be collected

- [ ] Public data to be collected

- [ ] Commercial market data

- [ ] OLTP data

- [ ] Customer registration data

- [ ] Internally derived data

- [ ] Data captured by other portals

18. The firm already has in place a system to collect primary external data.

- [ ] Yes   [ ] No

19. The firm does not have a primary data collection system, but its corporate website can easily integrate such an interface if necessary.

- [ ] Yes   [ ] No

20. If data are to be captured, checked and integrated to an existing database, the task would be undertaken by a/an

    ☐ Officer   ☐ Clerk

21. There is an existing data warehouse/mart storing the necessary data.

    ☐ Yes   ☐ No

22. There is no existing data warehouse/mart, but the firm is prepared to build one for this solution.

    ☐ Yes   ☐ No

23. If a data warehouse/mart is to be built, it is expected to be shared with other departments for their application solutions.

    ☐ Yes   ☐ No

24. If the data warehouse/mart were to be shared with other departments, it would remain under the control and management of the main user department of this solution.

    ☐ Yes   ☐ No

Analytics Tool

25. The firm has an analytics tool which it prefers to use. The name of the tool is _____

    _____

26. The firm does not have an analytics tool and is open to the following products (Please tick the appropriate boxes):

    ☐ SAS Enterprise Miner

    ☐ IBM Intelligent Miner

    ☐ SPSS Clementine

    ☐ Others

27. Analytics tool recommendation by Dren Analytics is a requirement.

    ☐ Yes   ☐ No

OLAP and Front-End Tools

28. The firm has an OLAP tool which it prefers to use. The name of the tool is _____

   _____

29. The firm has its own front end reporting tool which it prefers to use. The name of the tool is _____

   _____

30. The firm would like Dren Analytics to recommend OLAP and front end reporting tools.

   ☐ Yes   ☐ No

Other Information

31. It would be helpful to Dren Analytics if there are any factors specific to this firm that has to be understood and taken into consideration in framing the objectives and scope of this project. Kindly provide such in point form if possible.

   _____

   _____

   _____

   _____

   _____

   _____

   _____

   _____

   _____

   _____

   _____

   _____

- END -

Annex B

```
begin
sys.rqScriptCreate('Analytics',
'function() {
library(ROracle)
drv <- dbDriver("Oracle")
con <- dbConnect(drv, username = "rquser", password="password",
dbname = "ORCLPDB", prefetch = FALSE, external_credentials = FALSE)
df <- dbReadTable(con, "SAMPLE", schema = "RQUSER") # Fetch data
from Oracle SAMPLE table
trim <- function (x) gsub("^\\s+|\\s+$", "", x) # Create trim function to
remove spaces from labels
sample <-subset(df, trim(INDUSTRY) == "Manufacturing" | trim
(INDUSTRY) == "Trading" | trim(INDUSTRY) == "Transport") # Select
only Manufacturing, Trading and Transport industries
dbWriteTable(con, "COMPLETE", complete, field.types = NULL, row.
names = TRUE, overwrite = FALSE, append = TRUE, allow.keywords =
FALSE) # Save COMPLETE into Oracle database

# Replace invalid values with NA# Replace invalid values with NA
sample$CASHNDEPOSITS[sample$CASHNDEPOSITS < 0] <- NA
sample$TOTALCURRENTASSETS[sample$TOTALCURRENTASSETS <= 0]
<- NA
sample$TOTALASSETS[sample$TOTALASSETS < 0] <- NA
sample$TOTALLTLOANS[sample$ TOTALLTLOANS < 0] <- NA
sample$TOTALLIABILITIES[sample$TOTALLIABILITIES < 0] <- NA
```

```
sample$TOTALCURRENTLIABILITIES[sample$TOTALCURRENTLIABILITIES
<= 0] <- NA
sample$TOTALREVENUE[sample$TOTALREVENUE < 0] <- NA
valid <- sample # Create valid data frame after invalid values replacement
dbWriteTable(con, "VALID", valid, field.types = NULL, row.names =
TRUE, overwrite = FALSE, append = TRUE, allow.keywords = FALSE) #
Save VALID into Oracle database

# Identify outdated rows# Remove outdated rows
library(data.table)
lg <- function(x)c(NA, x[1:(length(x)-1)]) # Create lag function
valid <- data.table(valid)
valid <- valid [order(rank(ID), YEAR)]
valid [, LAGTOTALASSETS := lg(TOTALASSETS), by = c("ID")] # Create lag
value
valid [, LAGTOTALLIABILITIES := lg(TOTALLIABILITIES), by = c("ID")]
valid [, LAGTOTALEQUITY := lg(TOTALEQUITY), by = c("ID")]
updated  <-  anti_join(valid,  subset(valid,  (TOTALASSETS=LAGTOTAL
ASSETS) & (TOTALLIABILITIES=LAGTOTALLIABILITIES) & (TOTALEQUITY=
LAGTOTALEQUITY)), by=NULL) # Created updated data frame by elimi-
nating outdated rows
dbWriteTable(con, "UPDATED", updated, field.types = NULL, row.names
= TRUE, overwrite = FALSE, append = TRUE, allow.keywords = FALSE) #
Save UPDATED into Oracle database

# Remove columns with low completeness
complete <- 1-data.frame(colSums(is.na(updated))) / nrow(updated)
complete <- subset(complete, complete[, 1]>=0.75)
complete <- t(complete)
woe <-updated[names(updated) %in% names(complete)]
dbWriteTable(con, "COMPLETE", woe, field.types = NULL, row.names =
TRUE, overwrite = FALSE, append = TRUE, allow.keywords = FALSE) #
Save COMPLETE into Oracle database

# Derive financial ratios# Derive financial ratios for WoE
woe$RoA <- woe$NETINCOME / woe$TOTALASSETS
woe$GrossProfitMargin <- woe$GROSSPROFIT / woe$NETSALES
woe$QuickRatio  <-  woe$CASHNDEPOSITS  /  woe$TOTALCURRENT
LIABILITIES
```

```
woe$CurrentRatio  <-  (woe$TOTALASSETS-woe$TOTALNONCURRENT
ASSETS) / woe$TOTALCURRENTLIABILITIES
woe$Equity2LTLoans <- woe$TOTALEQUITY / (woe$TOTALLIABILITIES-
woe$TOTALCURRENTLIABILITIES)
woe$LTLoans2TA  <-  (woe$TOTALLIABILITIES-woe$TOTALCURRENT
LIABILITIES) / woe$TOTALASSETS
woe$TATurnover <- woe$TOTALREVENUE / woe$TOTALASSETS
woe$PPETurnover <- woe$TOTALREVENUE / woe$NETPPE
woe$Equity2TA <-  woe$TOTALEQUITY / woe$TOTALASSETS
woe$Capital2TA <- woe$CAPITAL2TA
woe$SalesGrowth <- woe$SALESGROWTH
woe$RevenueGrowth <- woe$REVENUEGROWTH


# Replace infinite values by NA# Replace infinity values due to division
by zero
woe[woe == 'Inf'] <- NA
woe [woe == '-Inf'] <- NA


# Create target for model
woe$Bankrupt <- ifelse(woe$TOTALEQUITY < 0, "1", "0") # Define
Bankrupt as negative equity


# Create train data frame
train <- subset(woe, substring(woe$YEAR, 1, 4) < 2017) # Leave 2017 for
backtesting
train <- train[c('ID', 'YEAR', 'INDUSTRY', 'RoA', 'GrossProfitMargin',
'QuickRatio', 'CurrentRatio', 'Equity2LTLoans', 'LTLoans2TA', 'TATurnover',
'PPETurnover', 'Equity2TA', 'Capital2TA', 'SalesGrowth', 'RevenueGrowth',
'Bankrupt')] # Select only columns needed


# Binning with scorecard package and derive logodds
library(scorecard)
bins = woebin(train, var_skip='ID', y = "Bankrupt")
train_woe = woebin_ply(train, bins)
train_woe <- as.data.frame(train_woe)
train_woe$samplelogodds <- log(nrow(subset(train_woe, Bankrupt ==
"1"))) / (nrow(subset(train_woe, Bankrupt == "0")))
train_woe$logodds <-  train_woe$samplelogodds +  train_woe$
INDUSTRY_woe + train_woe$RoA_woe + train_woe$GrossProfitMargin_
```

```
woe+train_woe$QuickRatio_woe + train_woe$CurrentRatio_woe +
train_woe$Equity2LTLoans_woe + train_woe$LTLoans2TA_woe + train_
woe$TATurnover_woe + train_woe$PPETurnover_woe + train_woe$
Equity2TA_woe+train_woe$Capital2TA_woe+train_woe$SalesGrowth_
woe + train_woe$RevenueGrowth_woe
train_woe$odds <- exp(train_woe$logodds)
train_woe$prob <- train_woe$odds / (1 + train_woe$odds) # Derive
probability according to WoE fomula

# Derive WoE and Score for each row
train_woe$woe <- train_woe$INDUSTRY_woe + train_woe$RoA_woe +
train_woe$GrossProfitMargin_woe + train_woe$QuickRatio_woe +
train_woe$CurrentRatio_woe + train_woe$Equity2LTLoans_woe +
train_woe$LTLoans2TA_woe + train_woe$TATurnover_woe + train_
woe$PPETurnover_woe + train_woe$Equity2TA_woe + train_woe$
Capital2TA_woe + train_woe$SalesGrowth_woe + train_woe$Revenue
Growth_woe
train_woe$score <- as.integer(train_woe$prob * 10000) # Create Score
for easier sorting

# Create rating system
grade <- c(1, 2, 3, 4, 5, 6, 7, 8)
bankruptcyrate <- c(0, 0, 0, 0, 0, 0, 0, 0) # Initialize all values to zero
count <- c(0, 0, 0, 0, 0, 0, 0, 0)
WoE <- c(0, 0, 0, 0, 0, 0, 0, 0)
ratingsystem <- data.frame(grade, bankruptcyrate, count, woe)

# Derive rating system parameters
train_woe <- train_woe[order(train_woe$prob), ]
train_woe$row <- 1:nrow(train_woe)
max <- nrow(train_woe)
for (i in 1:max) {
    bankruptcyrate <- ratingsystem$bankruptcyrate[1] if(bankruptcyrate
    >= 0.0003) {break}
    <- ifelse(ratingsystem$grade == 1, (nrow(subset(train_woe,
    Bankrupt == "1" & row <= i)) / nrow(subset(train_woe, row <= i))),
    ratingsystem$bankruptcyrate)
    ratingsystem$count <- ifelse(ratingsystem$grade == 1, nrow(subset
    (train_woe, row <= i)), ratingsystem$count)
```

```
  ratingsystem$woe[1] <- train_woe$woe[train_woe$row == i][1]
  j <- i+1
}
K <- j
for (i in j: max) {
    bankruptcyrate <- ratingsystem$bankruptcyrate[2]
    if(bankruptcyrate > ratingsystem$bankruptcyrate[1] & ratingsystem$
    count[2] > 700) {break}
    ratingsystem$bankruptcyrate <- ifelse(ratingsystem$grade == 2,
    nrow(subset(train_woe, Bankrupt == "1" & row >= k & row <= i)) /
    nrow(subset(train_woe, row >= k & row <= i)), ratingsystem$
    bankruptcyrate)
    ratingsystem$count <- ifelse(ratingsystem$grade == 2, nrow(subset
    (train_woe, row >= k & row <= i)), ratingsystem$count)
    ratingsystem$woe[2] <- train_woe$woe[train_woe$row == i][1]
    j <- i+1
}
K <- j
for (i in j: max) {
    bankruptcyrate <- ratingsystem$bankruptcyrate[3]
    if(bankruptcyrate > ratingsystem$bankruptcyrate[2] & ratingsystem$
    count[3] > 700) {break}
    ratingsystem$bankruptcyrate <- ifelse(ratingsystem$grade == 3,
    nrow(subset(train_woe, Bankrupt == "1" & row >= k & row <= i)) /
    nrow(subset(train_woe, row >= k & row <= i)), ratingsystem$
    bankruptcyrate)
    ratingsystem$count <- ifelse(ratingsystem$grade == 3, nrow(subset
    (train_woe, row >= k & row <= i)), ratingsystem$count)
    ratingsystem$woe[3] <- train_woe$woe[train_woe$row == i][1]
    j <- i+1
}
k <- j
for (i in j: max) {
    bankruptcyrate <- ratingsystem$bankruptcyrate[4]
    if(bankruptcyrate > ratingsystem$bankruptcyrate[3] & ratingsystem
    $count[4] > 70{break}
    ratingsystem$bankruptcyrate <- ifelse(ratingsystem$grade == 4,
    nrow(subset(train_woe, Bankrupt = ="1" & row >= k & row <= i)) /
```

```
    nrow(subset(train_woe, row >= k & row <= i)), ratingsystem$
    bankruptcyrate)
    ratingsystem$count <- ifelse(ratingsystem$grade == 4, nrow(subset
    (train_woe, row >= k & row <= i)), ratingsystem$count)
    ratingsystem$woe[4] <- train_woe$woe[train_woe$row == i][1]
    j <- i+1
}
k <- j
for (i in j: max) {
    bankruptcyrate <- ratingsystem$bankruptcyrate[5]
    if(bankruptcyrate > ratingsystem$bankruptcyrate[4] & ratingsystem$
    count[5] > 700) {break}
    ratingsystem$bankruptcyrate <- ifelse(ratingsystem$grade == 5,
    nrow(subset(train_woe, Bankrupt == "1" & row >= k & row <= i)) /
    nrow(subset(train_woe, row >= k & row <= i)), ratingsystem$
    bankruptcyrate)
    ratingsystem$count <- ifelse(ratingsystem$grade == 5, nrow(subset
    (train_woe, row >= k & row <= i)), ratingsystem$count)
    ratingsystem$woe[5] <- train_woe$woe[train_woe$row == i][1]
    j <- i+1
}
k <- j
for (i in j: max) {
    bankruptcyrate <- ratingsystem$bankruptcyrate[6]
    if(bankruptcyrate > ratingsystem$bankruptcyrate[5] & ratingsystem
    $count[6] > 700) {break}
    ratingsystem$bankruptcyrate <- ifelse(ratingsystem$grade == 6,
    nrow(subset(train_woe, Bankrup t== "1" & row >= k & row <= i)) /
    nrow(subset(train_woe, row >= k & row <= i)), ratingsystem$
    bankruptcyrate)
    ratingsystem$count <- ifelse(ratingsystem$grade == 6, nrow(subset
    (train_woe, row >= k & row <= i)), ratingsystem$count)
    ratingsystem$woe[6] <- train_woe$woe[train_woe$row == i][1]
    j <- i+1
}
k <- j
for (i in j: max) {
    bankruptcyrate <- ratingsystem$bankruptcyrate[7]
```

```
    if(bankruptcyrate > ratingsystem$bankruptcyrate[6] & ratingsystem$
    count[7] > 700) {break}
    ratingsystem$bankruptcyrate <- ifelse(ratingsystem$grade == 7,
    nrow(subset(train_woe, Bankrupt == "1" & row >= k & row <= i)) /
    nrow(subset(train_woe, row >= k & row <= i)), ratingsystem$
    bankruptcyrate)
    ratingsystem$count <- ifelse(ratingsystem$grade == 7, nrow(subset
    (train_woe, row >= k & row <= i)), ratingsystem$count)
    ratingsystem$woe[7] <- train_woe$woe[train_woe$row == i][1]
    j <- i+1
}
k <- j
for (i in j: max) {
    bankruptcyrate <- ratingsystem$bankruptcyrate[8]
    if(bankruptcyrate > ratingsystem$bankruptcyrate[7]) {break}
    ratingsystem$bankruptcyrate <- ifelse(ratingsystem$grade == 8,
    nrow(subset(train_woe, Bankrupt == "1" & row >= k & row <= i)) /
    nrow(subset(train_woe, row >= k &  row <= i)), ratingsystem
    $bankruptcyrate)
    ratingsystem$count <- ifelse(ratingsystem$grade == 8, nrow(subset
    (train_woe, row >= k & row <= i)), ratingsystem$count)
    ratingsystem$woe[8] <- train_woe$woe[train_woe$row == i][1]
    j <- i+1
}

# Insert rating system into Oracle database
dbWriteTable(con, "RATINGSYSTEM", ratingsystem, field.types = NULL,
row.names = TRUE, overwrite = FALSE, append = TRUE, allow.keywords
= FALSE) # Save UPDATED into Oracle database

# Select non-Bankrupts and assign risk grade
nondefault <- subset(train_woe, Bankrupt == 0) # data frame of
non-Bankrupts
nondefault$grade <- ifelse(nondefault$woe <= ratingsystem$woe[1],
"1", ifelse(nondefault$woe > ratingsystem$woe[1] & nondefault$woe
<= ratingsystem$woe[2], "2", ifelse(nondefault$woe > ratingsystem$
woe[2] & nondefault$woe < =ratingsystem$woe[3], "3", ifelse(non
default$woe > ratingsystem$woe[3] & nondefault$woe <= rating
```

```
system$woe[4], "4", ifelse(nondefault$woe > ratingsystem$woe[4] &
nondefault$woe <= ratingsystem$woe[5], "5", ifelse(nondefault$woe >
ratingsystem$woe[5] & nondefault$woe <= ratingsystem$woe[6], "6",
ratingsystem$woe[7])))))

# Backtest bankruptcy rates on final year of training period
nondefault <- subset(nondefault, nondefault$YEAR == 2016) # Final
year of training period
test <- subset(woe, substring(woe$YEAR, 1, 4) == 2017)
test <- merge(test, nondefault[, c('ID', 'grade')], by = 'ID') # Match IDs of
training and backtesting periods

# Extract data frames from bins output
Industry <- bins$INDUSTRY
RoA <- bins$RoA
GrossProfitMargin <- bins$GrossProfitMargin
QuickRatio <- bins$QuickRatio
CurrentRatio <- bins$CurrentRatio
Equity2LTLoans <- bins$Equity2LTLoans
LTLoans2TA <- bins$LTLoans2TA
TATurnover <- bins$TATurnover
PPETurnover <- bins$PPETurnover
Equity2TA <- bins$Equity2TA
Capital2TA <- bins$Capital2TA
SalesGrowth <- bins$SalesGrowth
RevenueGrowth <- bins$RevenueGrowth

# Save model tables into Oracle for later rating# Save to Oracle as tables
for later use in rating
dbWriteTable(con, "Industry", Industry, field.types = NULL, row.names =
TRUE, overwrite = FALSE, append = TRUE, allow.keywords = FALSE)
dbWriteTable(con, "RoA", RoA, field.types = NULL, row.names = TRUE,
overwrite = FALSE, append = TRUE, allow.keywords = FALSE)
dbWriteTable(con, "GrossProfitMargin", GrossProfitMargin, field.types
= NULL, row.names = TRUE, overwrite = FALSE, append = TRUE, allow.
keywords = FALSE)
dbWriteTable(con, "QuickRatio", QuickRatio, field.types = NULL, row.
names = TRUE, overwrite = FALSE, append = TRUE, allow.keywords =
FALSE)
```

```
dbWriteTable(con, "CurrentRatio", CurrentRatio, field.types = NULL,
row.names = TRUE, overwrite = FALSE, append = TRUE, allow.keywords
= FALSE)
dbWriteTable(con, "Equity2LTLoans", Equity2LTLoans, field.types =
NULL, row.names = TRUE, overwrite = FALSE, append = TRUE, allow.
keywords = FALSE)
dbWriteTable(con, "LTLoans2TA", LTLoans2TA, field.types = NULL, row.
names = TRUE, overwrite = FALSE, append = TRUE, allow.keywords =
FALSE)
dbWriteTable(con, "TATurnover", TATurnover, field.types = NULL, row.
names = TRUE, overwrite = FALSE, append = TRUE, allow.keywords =
FALSE)
dbWriteTable(con, "PPETurnover", PPETurnover, field.types = NULL,
row.names = TRUE, overwrite = FALSE, append = TRUE, allow.keywords
= FALSE)
dbWriteTable(con, "Equity2TA", Equity2TA, field.types = NULL, row.
names = TRUE, overwrite = FALSE, append = TRUE, allow.keywords =
FALSE)
dbWriteTable(con, "Capital2TA", Capital2TA, field.types = NULL, row.
names = TRUE, overwrite = FALSE, append = TRUE, allow.keywords =
FALSE)
dbWriteTable(con, "SalesGrowth", SalesGrowth, field.types = NULL,
row.names = TRUE, overwrite = FALSE, append = TRUE, allow.keywords
= FALSE)
dbWriteTable(con, "RevenueGrowth", RevenueGrowth, field.types =
NULL, row.names = TRUE, overwrite = FALSE, append = TRUE, allow.
keywords = FALSE)

# Derive test data frame ratio WoE values# Assign WoE based on rating
system WoE thresholds
test$Industry <- trim(test$INDUSTRY)
test$Industry_woe <- ifelse(test$Industry == "Transport", Industry$
woe[1], ifelse(test$Industry == "Manufacturing", Industry$woe[2],
Industry$woe[3]))
test$RoA_woe <- ifelse(test$RoA == "NA", RoA$woe[1], ifelse(test$RoA
< RoA$breaks[2], RoA$woe[2], ifelse(test$RoA < RoA$breaks[3], RoA$
woe[3], ifelse(test$RoA < RoA$breaks[4], RoA$woe[4], ifelse(test$RoA
< RoA$breaks[5], RoA$woe[5], RoA$woe[6]))))))
```

```
test$GrossProfitMargin_woe <- ifelse(test$GrossProfitMargin == "NA",
GrossProfitMargin$woe[1], ifelse(test$GrossProfitMargin < GrossProfit
Margin$breaks[3], GrossProfitMargin$woe[3], ifelse(test$GrossProfit
Margin < GrossProfitMargin$breaks[4], GrossProfitMargin$woe[4],
ifelse(test$GrossProfitMargin < GrossProfitMargin$breaks[5], Gross
ProfitMargin$woe[5], ifelse(test$GrossProfitMargin < GrossProfit
Margin$breaks[6], GrossProfitMargin$woe[6], GrossProfitMargin$
woe[7])))))
test$QuickRatio_woe <- ifelse(test$QuickRatio == "NA", QuickRatio$
woe[1], ifelse(test$QuickRatio < QuickRatio$breaks[3], QuickRatio$
woe[3], ifelse(test$QuickRatio < QuickRatio$breaks[4], QuickRatio$
woe[4], QuickRatio$woe[5])))
test$CurrentRatio_woe <- ifelse(test$CurrentRatio == "NA", Current
Ratio$woe[1], ifelse(test$CurrentRatio < CurrentRatio$breaks[3],
CurrentRatio$woe[3],ifelse(test$CurrentRatio<CurrentRatio$breaks[4],
CurrentRatio$woe[4], CurrentRatio$woe[5])))
test$Equity2LTLoans_woe <- ifelse(test$Equity2LTLoans == "NA",
Equity2LTLoans$woe[1], Equity2LTLoans$woe[3])
test$LTLoans2TA_woe <- ifelse(test$LTLoans2TA == "NA", LTLoans
2TA$woe[1], ifelse(test$LTLoans2TA < LTLoans2TA$breaks[2], LTLoans
2TA$woe[2], ifelse(test$LTLoans2TA < LTLoans2TA$breaks[3], LTLoans
2TA$woe[3], LTLoans2TA$woe[4])))
test$TATurnover_woe <- ifelse(test$TATurnover == "NA", TATurnover
$woe[1], ifelse(test$TATurnover < TATurnover$breaks[2], TATurnover$
woe[2], ifelse(test$TATurnover < TATurnover$breaks[3], TATurnover$
woe[3], ifelse(test$TATurnover < TATurnover$breaks[4], TATurnover$
woe[4], ifelse(test$TATurnover < TATurnover$breaks[5], TATurnover$
woe[5], TATurnover$woe[6])))))
test$PPETurnover_woe <- ifelse(test$PPETurnover == "NA", PPETurn
over$woe[1], ifelse(test$PPETurnover < PPETurnover$breaks[2], PPE
Turnover$woe[2], ifelse(test$PPETurnover < PPETurnover$breaks[3],
PPETurnover$woe[3],ifelse(test$PPETurnover<PPETurnover$breaks[4],
PPETurnover$woe[4],ifelse(test$PPETurnover<PPETurnover$breaks[5],
PPETurnover$woe[5], PPETurnover$woe[6])))))
test$Equity2TA_woe<-ifelse(test$Equity2TA=="NA",Equity2TA$woe[1],
Equity2TA$woe[2])
test$Capital2TA_woe <- ifelse(test$Capital2TA == "NA", Capital
2TA$woe[1], ifelse(test$Capital2TA < Capital2TA$breaks[2], Capital
2TA$woe[2], ifelse(test$Capital2TA < Capital2TA$breaks[3], Capital
```

```
2TA$woe[3], ifelse(test$Capital2TA < Capital2TA$breaks[4], Capital2TA$
woe[4], Capital2TA$woe[5]))))
test$SalesGrowth_woe  <-  ifelse(test$SalesGrowth  ==  "NA",  Sales
Growth$woe[1],  ifelse(test$SalesGrowth  <  SalesGrowth$breaks[2],
SalesGrowth$woe[2], ifelse(test$SalesGrowth < SalesGrowth$breaks[3],
SalesGrowth$woe[3], ifelse(test$SalesGrowth < SalesGrowth$breaks[4],
SalesGrowth$woe[4], ifelse(test$SalesGrowth < SalesGrowth$breaks[5],
SalesGrowth$woe[5], SalesGrowth$woe[6]))))))
test$RevenueGrowth_woe  <-  ifelse(test$RevenueGrowth  ==  "NA",
RevenueGrowth$woe[1],  ifelse(test$RevenueGrowth  <  Revenue
Growth$breaks[2],  RevenueGrowth$woe[2],  ifelse(test$Revenue
Growth < RevenueGrowth$breaks[3], RevenueGrowth$woe[3], ifelse
(test$RevenueGrowth  <  RevenueGrowth$breaks[4],  RevenueGrowth
$woe[4], RevenueGrowth$woe[5]))))

# Derive row WoE value and risk grade
test$woe <- test$Industry_woe  +  test$RoA_woe + test$GrossProfit
Margin_woe  +  test$QuickRatio_woe  +  test$CurrentRatio_woe  +
test$Equity2LTLoans_woe + test$LTLoans2TA_woe + test$TATurnover_
woe + test$PPETurnover_woe + test$Equity2TA_woe + test$Capital2TA_
woe + test$SalesGrowth_woe + test$RevenueGrowth_woe
test$grade <- ifelse(test$woe <= ratingsystem$woe[1], "1", ifelse(test$
woe > ratingsystem$woe[1] & test$woe <= ratingsystem$woe[2], "2",
ifelse(test$woe  >  ratingsystem$woe[2]  &  test$woe  <=  rating
system$woe[3], "3", ifelse(test$woe > ratingsystem$woe[3] & test$woe
<= ratingsystem$woe[4], "4", ifelse(test$woe > ratingsystem$woe[4] &
test$woe  <=  ratingsystem$woe[5],  "5",  ifelse(test$woe  >  rating
system$woe[5] & test$woe <= ratingsystem$woe[6], "6", ifelse(test$woe
> ratingsystem$woe[6]  &  test$woe  <=  ratingsystem$woe[7],  "7",
"8")))))))

# End with ORE codes to run
dum <- 1
data.frame(dum = dum)
}',
v_overwrite => TRUE);
end;
/
select * from table(rqEval(NULL, 'select 1 dum from dual', 'Analytics'));
```

Index

A

absolute advantage, 179
absolute VaR, 102
academics, 37
access to data, 39
accounting, 170
accuracy rates, 142
acquisition process, 17
actual default rate, 135
add-in, 169
algorithms, 16, 18
analytical codes, 5
analytical data, 3, 74
analytical data sphere, 79
analytical sphere, 79
analytics, 204, 208
analytics professionals, 40
analytics space, 3
annuity, 190
application software, 207
arbitrage, 180
architecting, 42
archive, 81
artificial intelligence, 5
Asset Liability Committee (ALCO), 43

Asset Liability Management (ALM), 43
assumption, 156, 181
asymmetry, 175
audited financial statements, 38
automated, 47

B

backtesting, 33
Banker's Trust, 105
bankrupt, 127
bankruptcy, 27
Basel II, 9, 119
Basic Excel R Tool (BERT), 108
Bayesian statistics, 113
behavioral modeling, 162
behavioral scoring, 162
big data, 5
binary outcome, 29
binning, 126
binomial lattice, 173
Black Swan event, 1
Bloomberg, 181
British empiricism, 32
business analytics, 43
business cycle, 161

business information system, 40
business problem, 203, 206
business rules, 41
business software, 16
business understanding, 26
business units, 25

C

*C*3, 111
call option, 27, 172
capital adequacy ratio, 102
cardinal, 28
cardinal rule, 93
cashflow, 187
categorical, 28
categories, 24, 83
cbind, 66
central kitchen, 43
Chief Risk Officer, 74
CIO, 80
classical statistics, 28
Classification and Regression Tree
  (CART), 29, 33
cleansing, 77
cloud-based, 69
code execution, 21
coding, 47
coding errors, 199
collateral, 71
collection scoring, 17
compliance, 71
Compliance Officer, 8
Comprehensive R Archive Network,
  200
concentration risk, 8, 97
conceptual framework, 32
conditional probability, 173
conditional VaR, 108
confidence level, 32, 100
confounds, 159
confusion matrix, 33
consistency, 121

consultancy experience, 24
control measures, 43
core banking, 9
core banking system, 43, 94
corporate default rate, 34
corporate financial data, 122
correlated returns, 106
cost center, 35
cost-centered, 107
counterparties, 111, 159, 177
country, 7
coupon, 181
credit, 2, 7
credit application system, 9
credit approval model, 35
Credit Default Swap (CDS), 178
credit institutions, 113
credit model, 61
credit portfolio, 36
credit portfolio diversification, 82
credit quality, 122
Credit Rating Agencies (CRA), 94,
  119
credit ratings, 10
credit scoring, 25
Credit Valuation Adjustment (CVA),
  177
credit worthiness, 94, 115
CRISP-DM, 26
criterion, 64
criticality, 38
CRO, 90
cross-border relationships, 113
cumulative probability, 171
cured, 121
customerID, 72

D

Daily Earnings at Risk (DEAR),
  103
data assets, 79
data audit, 57

data audit report, 65
database, 2
data cleansing, 74, 163
data dictionary, 18
data entry forms, 92
data flow, 37
data frame, 58, 125
data inadequacy, 57
data mart, 39, 72
database modeling, 207
data preparation, 30
data stewardship, 12, 72
data table, 21, 58
data.table, 63, 104
data type, 21, 71
data understanding, 28
data warehouse, 39, 69, 207
data warehouse/mart, 208
DateTime, 78
Days Past Due (DPD), 77
Debit Valuation Adjustment (DVA),
    177
debtors, 94
decision-makers, 79
decision-making, 3, 40
decision support, 41
Decision Support System (DSS),
    169
decision tree, 116
default, 25
default correlations, 82
default grade, 120
delinquency, 77
deliverables, 17
delta-normal, 104
deployable analytics, 5
deployable risk solutions, 47
deployment, 2, 37, 41, 151
depository, 10
deposit-taking, 13
derivatives, 171
derived data, 12

desktop analytics, 169
digital data flow, 151
digital forms, 10
direct invoiceable loss, 97
direct non-invoiceable loss, 97
discriminant analysis, 116
Disk Operating System (DOS), 93
diversification, 91
documentation, 48, 156
dplyr, 63
Dren Analytics, 206
drilldown, 40
dropdown, 82
dummy variables, 29
duration, 43
duration gap, 43

E
Early Warning System (EWS), 7
economic capital, 8, 101
economic cycle, 120
embedded, 53
embedded R, 48
empirical approach, 32
empirical VaR, 103
end-to-end automation, 14
end users, 21, 85
enterprise data warehouse, 72
enterprise-level, 18
Enterprise Risk Management (ERM),
    25, 42
environmental risk, 8
error-checking, 10
error-checking algorithm, 24
evaluation, 33
E-views, 15
existing database, 208
Expected Loss (EL), 99
expected shortfall, 108
exposure, 95
Exposure at Default (EAD), 106
external data, 10

external environment, 91
external warning indicators, 95
Extraction, Transfer, Load (ETL), 74

F
facility rating, 17
factor, 29, 93
financial health, 161
financial institution, 17
financial ratio analysis, 31
financial ratios, 25
financial stress, 141
flat files, 18
foreign key (FK), 23, 76
forward rate, 180
Forward Risk, 8
frequency, 43
fundamentals, 94
funding gap, 43

G
G20, 105
Garbage In Garbage Out (GIGO), 37
Gartner Report, 17
global banks, 44
global financial crisis, 177
global options, 200
good governance, 67
good-to-have, 13
governance, risk and compliance
  (GRC), 17
granular, 135
GRC, 17

H
hardcoded, 18
Herfindhal–Hirschman Index (HHI),
  111
heuristics, 162
high-frequency trading, 92
historical data, 103
historical simulation, 104

historical values, 81
Hmisc, 130
hypothesis, 114
hypothesis testing, 32

I
illustration, 143
impairment accounting, 87, 170
inconsistent, 64
index, 71
indirect loss, 96
inference, 67
Information Value (IV), 116
inherent risk, 7
insolvency, 2
insolvent, 179
insurance premium, 178
interest rate premium, 119
interest rate swap, 178
interface, 206
internal audit, 43
Internal Rating System (IRS), 9
International Financial Corporation
  (IFC), 41, 48
International Monetary Fund (IMF),
  105
interpolation, 29, 66
intrinsic, 7
intrinsic information, 28
invalid data values, 59
invalidity, 124
IT, 3

J
Java Runtime Environment (JRE),
  186
joint probability, 172

K
Key Performance Indicators (KPI),
  46
knowledge base, 48

known distribution, 30
Know Your Customer (KYC), 92
kurtotic, 104

L

lag function, 63
law of comparative advantage, 179
legacy systems, 22
legal, 7
lending, 13
level of confidence, 32
library, 52
lines of responsibilities, 44
liquidation, 39
liquidity, 162
logistic regression (Logit), 116
lognormally distributed, 175
log-odds, 133
London Interbank Offer Rate
  (LIBOR), 178
loop, 137
Loss Given Default (LGD), 17, 22,
  106
loss reserve, 99

M

machine learning, 15
maintain, 206
mandatory data fields, 10
manual extraction, 169
mappings, 76
marginal probability, 172
marginal risk, 8
market, 7
market values, 39
meeting of minds, 40, 203
metric, 101
migration matrix, 81
mindset change, 24
misclassification matrix, 34
model, 2, 7, 157
modeling, 12, 24, 31, 61

money laundering, 92
monotonic, 137
monotonous relationship, 29
Monte Carlo Simulation, 104
multicollinearity, 129
must-have, 13

N

99.9% confidence level, 113
Naïve Model, 26
Nassim Nicholas Taleb, 1
nested modeling, 29
nested models, 123
New Basel Capital Accord, 119
nominal, 28
nonparametric, 32
non-proprietary databases, 18
non-stationarity, 121, 157
normal distribution, 32
normative approach, 114
NULL, 24
null hypothesis, 32

O

obligor, 93
obligor rating, 17
obligor risk rating, 119
OLTP data, 207
one-size-fits-all, 25
online, 24
Online Analytical Programming
  (OLAP), 40, 209
open source, 4
openxlsx, 188
Operational, 7
operational loss data, 39
operational loss distribution, 112
operational losses, 39
operational risk, 43, 96
option-pricing theory, 27
ORACLE_HOME, 48
Oracle listener, 49

Oracle R Enterprise (ORE), 5, 48
ORCLPDB, 49
ordinal, 28
ordinary least squares, 62
orphaned tables, 86
orthogonalization, 131
outdated, 63
outliers, 126
out-of-sample testing, 33, 107
out-of-time testing, 107
overwrite, 81

P
package, 54
paradigm, 117
parameters, 141
par rate, 181
PDB, 49
PDBORCL, 49
permutations, 141
plm, 63
pluggable database, 49
plyr, 63
Point In Time (PIT), 93
Poisson–Lognormal Distribution, 112
positive approach, 115
precision, 194
predictions, 142
predictive power, 130
predictors, 93, 129
presentValue, 190
primary data, 12, 93
primary external data, 207
Primary Key (PK), 23, 76
probabilities, 135
Probability of Default (PD), 17,
    106
probability of error, 32
problem-solving, 16
profile, 93, 127
Proof of Concept (POC), 19
Python, 16

Q
quadratic optimization, 108
quantification, 2
quantifying, 107

R
R, 16, 47
random observation, 32
rank order, 29
R Archive, 113
rating migration matrix, 121
rational default, 27
rationale, 156
raw data, 30
rcorr, 130
reageing, 121
real-time, 47
records, 137
recoverable value, 171
recoveries, 175
regulatory capital, 99
regulatory enforcement, 125
regulatory requirements, 71
relative VaR, 103
reliability, 38
repositories, 73
reputational, 7
Request for Proposal (RFP), 17
resources, 199
retail credit, 22
Return on Assets (RoA), 130
Risk-Adjusted Return on Capital
    (RAROC), 106
return on equity, 31
R_HOME, 48
risk-adjusted, 105
risk analytics, 1, 5, 107
risk analytics landscape, 15
risk appetite, 110
risk-based decision-making, 106
risk-bearing, 119
risk budgeting, 105

risk capital, 105
Risk Control and Self-Assessment
  (RCSA), 43
risk events, 43
risk-free, 99, 180
risk-free rate, 88
risk governance, 44
risk grade, 120, 134
risk management, 1
Risk Management Committee, 44
Risk Management Unit, 159
risk modeling, 28
risk professionals, 14
risk quantifications, 25, 41
risk rating, 41, 120
risk solutions, 41
risk-taking, 2, 91
ROE, 31
ROracle, 51
RQADMIN, 49
rqScript, 53
RQUSER, 48
RStudio, 5, 47
run as administrator, 50

S
sample, 123
SAS, 15
scorecard, 133
script, 58
Securities Industry Code (SIC), 83
securities portfolio, 27
securities portfolio optimization, 108
securities returns, 32
segmentation, 136
serially uncorrelated, 173
service providers, 69
severity, 43
silos, 41
simulation, 166
single customer view, 37
single exposure risk, 7

slice and dice, 40
snapshot, 94, 161
social sciences, 115
solutions, 15, 203
spot rate, 180
SPSS, 15
SQL developer, 48
SQL plus, 48
SQL server, 48
stakeholders, 159
standalone solution, 205
standard normal distribution, 102
Standard & Poors, 94
statistical software, 15
storage space, 82
stored procedures, 4, 47
strategic, 169
strategic advantage, 157
stress testing, 8, 113
Structured Query Language (SQL), 47
subprime, 1
substitution, 66
substrings, 87
SYSAUX, 51
system designs, 3
systemic risk, 113
System Integration Test (SIT), 20

T
tactical, 169
target, 93
taxonomy, 10
technical jargons, 19
technical specifications, 15
technology, 7
Terms of Reference (TOR), 17
term structure of interest rates, 88
The British Banker's Association,
  96
theory, 115
Thomson Reuters, 181
thresholds, 136

Through The Cycle (TTC), 94
time-series analysis, 81
tnsnames.ora, 49
train a model, 132
transactions, 37
transact SQL, 4
treasuries, 180
Type I error, 34
Type II error, 34

U
unconditional, 133
unconditional log-odds, 116
unconditional probability, 173
Unexpected Loss (UL), 100
uniroot, 182
universal model, 27
UNIX, 48
unreliable data values, 61
updatable, 87
update, 206
updated, 38, 157
User Acceptance Test (UAT), 21
user department, 73
users, 205

V
validation, 44
valuations, 171
Value at Risk (VaR), 32, 101
VARCHAR, 22
variable, 58
vector autoregression, 101
vector machine, 30
volatility, 108

W
Weight of Evidence (WoE), 28,
    114–115
what-if analysis, 186
wholesale credit, 22
woeBinning, 118
workout process, 175
Worst Case Loss (WCL), 100
worst-case scenario, 161

X
xVA, 177

Y
yield curve, 88, 180